Letter Lessons

Steps to Perfection for Jesus

CORA EVANS

Letter Lessons

Steps to Perfection for Jesus

The Mystical
Humanity
of Christ
Publishing

San Mateo
2018

Letter Lessons
Cora Evans
© 2018 The Mystical Humanity of Christ, Inc.

Imprimatur
Most Reverend Richard J. Garcia, D.D.
Bishop of the Diocese of Monterey, California
March 22, 2017

About the Cover—The cover design is an allusion to Jacob's ladder: "And he dreamed that there was a ladder set up on the earth, and the top of it reached to heaven; and behold, the angels of God were ascending and descending on it" (Gn 28:12).

In the Gospel according to Saint John, we read the words of Jesus: "Truly, truly, I say to you, you will see heaven opened, and the angels of God ascending and descending upon the Son of man" (Jn 1:51). Jesus puts himself in the center of Jacob's vision and the way heaven and earth connect. The cover illustration depicts our gradual ascent to God by means of the Letter Lessons.

Cover design by Claudine Mansour Design, Mission Viejo, California
Interior design by Russell Graphic Design, Pasadena, California

Library of Congress Cataloging-in-Publication Data
Evans, Cora

978-0-9975246-1-1 Quality Paperback
978-0-9975246-2-8 eBook

Printed in the United States of America

PUBLISHER'S STATEMENT

Letter Lessons—Steps to Perfection for Jesus is based in part on the private revelations of Cora Evans.

Public Revelation—Sacred Scripture

The Catholic Church recognizes the clear distinction between public and private revelation. Public revelation, meaning the Old and New Testaments, ended with the death of the last apostle. It is complete; the age of public revelation is closed and there will be no new public revelation.

It is no longer public revelation [Sacred Scripture] that grows, but we grow in our comprehension of it.

Private Revelation—A Possible Means to Growth and Understanding

The purpose of private revelation is to help a particular soul grow in faith and to develop a greater love of God.

For even though public revelation is already complete, it has not been made completely explicit; it remains for the Christian faithful gradually to grasp its full significance over the course of centuries. Throughout the ages, there have been so-called private revelations, some of which have been recognized by the authority of the Church [Saint Bernadette of Lourdes, Saint Catherine of Siena, Saint Margaret Mary, Saint Faustina]. It is not the role of private revelation to improve or complete Christ's definitive Revelation, but to help live more fully by it in a certain period of history.[1]

LED BY OUR LORD

This phrase formally summarizes our journey. It is the motto that expresses the publisher's awareness of God's intervention as the mission entrusted to Cora Evans, to promulgate the Mystical Humanity of Christ throughout the world, unfolds.

---

1 *Catechism of the Catholic Church* (65,66): Second Edition, revised in accordance with the official Latin text promulgated by Pope John Paul II in 1997.

A.M.D.G.

First used by Saint Ignatius of Loyola, the abbreviation for the Latin *Ad maiorem Dei gloriam*, "For the greater glory of God" is the motto of the Society of Jesus (Jesuits). It was Cora Evans' practice to use the abbreviation in the header of every letter to her Jesuit spiritual director, Father Frank Parrish, S.J.

The Numbering of the Psalms

The numbering of the Psalms used in *Letter Lessons* is that of the Hebrew Bible, the Revised Standard Version and the New American Bible. It varies somewhat from the Greek, which is followed by the Latin Vulgate and vernacular versions based on it. The alternative numbering is given in the brackets.

Footnotes

Important reference sources and citations are included in common style footnotes. The original Letter Lessons did not include footnotes.

IHS

The abbreviation IHS appears at the top of each letter in PART TWO —Thoughts from the Heart. In Greek the letters form an abbreviation for the name Jesus. In Latin they translate to *And his name was called Jesus*. The Monogram or Christogram is used throughout the Catholic Church. Saint Ignatius of Loyola adopted IHS as the seal of the Society of Jesus (Jesuits).

Books Referenced by Cora Evans

Some of the books referenced are considered Catholic Classics including: *Confidence in God* (see Sixteenth Letter Lesson footnote), *The Devout Life* by Saint Francis de Sales (see Twenty-Seventh Letter Lesson footnote), and *The Little Flower Prayer Book* (see Part Two, letters dated October 1 and October 3).

Other books referenced may be out of print and available as used books, including *The Paraclete, Explanation of the Gospels, Mariology, The Perfect Prayer Book: My Daily Psalm Book, Carmelite Mysticism, Personality of Christ, Our Forgotten Guest*, and *The Divine Crucible of Purgatory*.

Scrapbook Collection Referenced by Cora Evans

Cora makes references to her personal scrapbook which is not available to the publisher at this time. This limited our ability to identify sources of various poems and prayers contained within.

RECOGNITION

The Mystical Humanity of Christ, Inc.,
Gratefully acknowledges the Extraordinary Generosity
of the
Theresa and Edward O'Toole Foundation
Bert Degheri, Co-Trustee

PUBLISHER'S ACKNOWLEDGEMENTS

The mission entrusted to Cora Evans by our Lord continues, and we wish to express appreciation to Most Reverend Richard Garcia, D.D., Bishop of Monterey, California, for opening the canonical inquiry into her life and heroic virtues and thereby declaring her Servant of God. We appreciate the work of the tribunal, canon lawyers, theologians, and the historical commission. We wish to thank Fr. Joe Grimaldi, J.C.L., Postulator, for his inspiration and insight. Special appreciation to the family members of Cora Evans: Dorothy Evans, daughter, and Bob Spaulding, nephew. Also, Irene and Mark Montgomery, June Haver MacMurray (deceased), and the trustees of the June and Fred MacMurray Foundation, Peter Marlow Jr., Bill O'Connell, Gabrielle Lien, and her late husband, Warren. Special appreciation is expressed to the Jesuits of the California province; Rev. Michael Weiler, S.J., former Provincial; Rev. Vito Perrone, COSJ; and Rev. Gary Thomas for their spiritual support and advice; Michael Huston, advisor, retreat leader, and board member; and Pamela McDevitt, for her encouragement and guidance.

APPRECIATION

We wish to express loving gratitude for the family members who provided Cora Evans with a close circle of friends who supported and encouraged her during her spiritual life and experiences, especially: Mary and Jack McDevitt, Mary Joyce and Dick Huston, and Edna Roletti. We love you, we miss you, and we pray your soul is in Heaven with our Lord and your loved ones.

SAINT ALOYSIUS GONZAGA, S.J. (1568-1591)

Aloysius Gonzaga was a member of a powerful Italian noble family in Mantua, Italy. He received his first Holy Communion from Saint Charles Borromeo. At the age of eighteen, he rejected the family's wealth, announcing his intention to become a Jesuit priest and his desire to become a missionary. During Aloysius's years of formation, Saint Robert Bellarmine was his spiritual director. Known for his way of prayer, Aloysius would offer penitence by mortifying his senses to maintain his focus on his love for God. While caring for victims of the plague in Rome, Aloysius fell ill and died with a crucifix in his hands. He was twenty-three years old.

Aloysius Gonzaga is the patron saint of youth. His feast day is on June 21.

COLLECT

Feast of Saint Aloysius Gonzaga

O God, giver of heavenly gifts, who in Saint Aloysius Gonzaga joined penitence to a wonderful innocence of life, grant, through his merits and intercession, that, though we have failed to follow him in innocence, we may imitate him in penitence. Through our Lord Jesus Christ, your Son, who lives and reigns with you in the unity of the Holy Spirit, one God, for ever and ever.

Contents

Publisher's Statement 5

Acknowledgements 7

Forward 11

Introduction 13

Part One Letter Lessons 17

Part Two Thoughts from the Heart 215

Epilogue

The Remarkable Story of Cora Evans 285

FORWARD

The best way to lead others to the truth

Give new life to every Catholic's faith in Jesus Christ . . . A Church which fervently lives the spiritual and contemplative dimension, and which gives herself generously to the service of charity, will be an ever more eloquent witness to God for men and women searching for meaning in their lives. To this end, it is more necessary than ever for all the faithful to move from a faith of habit, sustained perhaps by social context alone, to a faith which is conscious and personally lived. The renewal of faith will always be the best way to lead others to the Truth that is Christ.

Saint John Paul II, Apostolic Exhortation Ecclesia in America (73)

The Mystical Humanity of Christ—A Path to Holiness

I've always been of the mind that the Mystical Humanity of Christ was the life of the interior Indwelling of God's Holy Spirit. That Christ, the blessed Trinity itself, dwells within us. It's that we become His other humanity, His resurrected life. He died and left the world, true, but He continues to live in His resurrected life through our humanities. To me this is the very heart and apex of our Catholic faith. It is a devotion which is strengthened by the Eucharist—the cornerstone of our faith.

Father Frank Parrish, S.J., Spiritual Director for Cora Evans

Prayer for those who do not confess Christ

Almighty ever-living God, grant to those who do not confess Christ, that, by walking before you with a sincere heart, they may find the truth and that we ourselves, being constant in mutual love and striving to understand more fully the mystery of your life, may be made more perfect witnesses to your love in the world. Through Christ our Lord. Amen.

Let us pray for those who do not believe in God

Almighty ever-living God, who created all people to seek you always by desiring you and, by finding you, come to rest, grant we pray, that, despite every harmful obstacle, all may recognize the signs of your fatherly love and the witness of the good works done by those who believe in you, and so in gladness confess you, the one true God and Father of the human race. Through Christ our Lord. Amen.

INTRODUCTION

A Providential Relationship

In 1978 I was reading the manuscript for this book, *Letter Lessons*. The first assignment in the *Letter Lessons*, written by Cora Evans twenty-four years earlier, ends with a call to action: "Every day for a week write a letter to a sick friend." I was at a loss how to fulfill her request. For the life of me, I could not think of a friend who was sick. Then, the very next day, I received a letter from my mother asking me if I would write to an old family friend's son, who was very ill. His name was Jim Ware. What an unusual coincidence, or so I thought at the time. It was during the process of writing to my new sick friend that I connected the dots. Jim Ware happened to be Cora's godson.

This is how the dots connect: Cora became godmother for Jim in 1953. She wrote the letter lessons over a two-year period beginning in 1954. She passed away in 1957, never knowing that her suggestion of writing to a sick friend would one day benefit her godson.

Some dates are unforgettable. We remember them because throughout our whole life, the events of the day are incomparable. When the events are providential, we realize how blessed we are to experience such a joy. We may even have insight into our own destiny. June 4, 1978 was like that for me: the day I began writing letters to Jim Ware, a person I did not know but would grow to love.

In my first letter to Jim, I asked rhetorical questions:

Was it just some accident that I would happen to pick up Cora's *Letter Lessons*? Was it an accident that her first lesson says, "Write a letter to a sick friend?" Was it an accident that my mom wrote to me about you and was it an accident that you are Cora's godson? Could it be, that for one or more likely both of us, it was no accident at all?

Today, I would answer that the experience illustrates the role we play in responding to Jesus' command—love one another. Every time we act on the impulse to express our love for others, we are sharing the love of Christ and taking baby steps to perfection for Jesus.

Introducing the Letter Lessons of Servant of God Cora Evans

You received a personal invitation from Jesus: "If any man would come after Me, let him deny himself and take up his cross daily, and follow Me" (Lk 9:23). Being a Catholic Christian is a call to action. Our God is not passive or indifferent or lukewarm. He is active, involved, and on fire. And He is vying with the devil for your soul. Following Jesus takes perseverance, self-denial, trust, and total commitment. This is not a book about Jesus; it's about you and how you open yourself to Him in ways you've never even considered.

The Catholic Church has a long tradition of writings designed to draw the faithful into a greater understanding of the interior life. *The Imitation of Christ* and *Practice of the Presence of God* come to mind. Many of the classics were written by mystics, including *The Cloud of Unknowing* (author unknown), *Dark Night of the Soul* by Saint John of the Cross, and *The Interior Castle* by Saint Teresa of Avila.

Servant of God Cora Evans received many insights while in the contemplative state of ecstasy. There may come a time when *Letter Lessons* ranks among the classics for its ability to move the faithful forward in their understanding of the meaning of this life, and as one of the most beautiful way to prepare for eternal life.

Letter Lessons will take you to a level of meditation and contemplation that you may have thought was reserved for the cloistered monks of history. You may already know a great deal about Jesus from Scripture, but the question in our time is, do you know Him? By reading *Letter Lessons* in silence and following the daily guidelines, you will experience a higher level of knowing. You will live each day with a heightened awareness of His indwelling presence. Beyond understanding what Jesus thinks of you, you'll grasp more fully His mission and your role in accomplishing it.

Can a single book change your life? Perhaps the Bible, but beyond that, does a single book stand out for having influenced the choices you make every day? Likely not. Here's my point. *Letter Lessons* is set apart by its very nature. Although presented in book form, the original text was not intended as such, but as personal letters from a mystic to her spiritual director, a renowned Jesuit priest. Cora's purpose in writing the letters was to share the knowledge given to her by Saint Aloysius during ecstasies. She wrote the first series of letters (Part

One), one letter per week for thirty-one weeks, to Father Frank Parrish, S.J. (January 11, 1954 to August 9, 1954). The following year Cora wrote daily letters (September 28, 1955 to October 18, 1955). These are presented in Part Two, subtitled Thoughts from the Heart.

The author was a wife and mother, a convert from Mormonism to the Catholic faith, and a mystic who suffered the stigmata. She was entrusted with the mission to promulgate the Mystical Humanity of Christ, the divine indwelling (see 1 Cor 3:16) throughout the world.

Are you ready to give yourself in utter surrender to God? You are about to experience Jesus' heartfelt desire for a personal relationship with you. Cora writes, "Jesus invited us all to follow Him. He is the Master of all perfection. Then, it is only reasonable that He wants us to become masters of self . . . for the greater glory of God and that that beauty and light might become one with God."

My prayer for you, taken from Cora's writings, "May God bless you with all the desires of the Eternal Father and bless the wishes of your soul."

Michael McDevitt
San Mateo, California
January 2018

PART ONE

Letter Lessons

First Letter Lesson

(PROVERBS 30-33)

January 11, 1954

Dear Father,

I am writing this in answer to your request that I write the mystical steps of knowledge given to me by Saint Aloysius. I must admit that your request leaves me with a feeling of utter helplessness, but from this dark well of my memory, with God's guiding grace, I hope to accomplish the good you intend from this dark well of my memory. To begin such a task is only to lose myself in the mystery of time and pretend that I am a citizen of Jerusalem taking notes from the Master's lips. I am just the reporter and filled with many imperfections. The human mind and memories may be likened to a Christmas tree, covered with glittering tinsel, rain, and the years' collections of beautiful balls. The winding tinsel symbolizes the path to perfection, the rain the monotonies in life, and the bobbling spheres, the rise and fall of our mirrored souls. One day we are gold, another green, sometimes red with circles of gold, and here and there among the boughs we find a day represented by a purple one, and we must not forget the silver and the blue balls—now so beautiful in retrospect.

In the measurement of time in the eyes of God, we are as useless as a path of tinsel and as fragile as a tree ball. A tree is not trimmed for the sake of the tree. Man is not trimmed nor disciplined in body and soul by the monotonies of life for the sake of himself. He is brought into perfection and beauty for the greater glory of God and that that beauty and light might become one with God.

The period of time in which Saint Aloysius taught me was two years. In the artistry of his teachings, he set up rules as daily guides which were intended as daily reminders—as the *scale* of practice. He must smile as I write, for am I not a foreign correspondent? Ecstasy language is not heard—the natural ear at that time is dead; can a dead ear hear? And so it is that I translate a language that is not a language; it is a mere tuning of His will upon (my) spirit—His divine impulses playing upon (me) as if (I) were a violin.

Jesus invited us all to "follow" Him. He is the Master of all perfection. Then, it is only reasonable that He wants us to become masters of self. Let us pretend to pick ourselves up as if we were violins—instruments of tone. The five senses must learn to play upon the body and bring Heaven's grace down from Heaven. That grace, spiritual rain, waters the soul, and in turn the soul gives greater life to spirit, and the path or ladder rungs are formed, and we begin the climb with our cross to God. The spirit leads, the soul follows, and the five senses follow as train-bearers for a bride. Every good done in life is a mystical procession of ourselves—a family, before Heaven's courts.

The word *meditation* is a medium word of power and meaning. It is a heritage of good earth in which the roots must be planted for our spiritual growth in the climb of contemplation. Meditation is usually the formation of simple lip service, fostered by the atmosphere of soul and its longing to visit with spirit. That union of perfect oneness, even before death, is known as *contemplation* and that word is learned, loved, and known when it is understood as *application*.

Saint James caught the spirit of the Master's teachings in His words, "Be ye doers of the word"—doers of the lip service which gives us the title of "Samaritans" (see Jas 1:22–27). With our lips, we have said in meditation prayer that we love—now in contemplation we must love, and that is zeal. Public prayers are seeds sown in the earth (our bodies), but contemplation is the planter, the worker, the tireless plougher and giver to the earth, for seldom is a harvest kept by the farmer. He shares his best fruits with his friends and the poor in spirit. The rain for the tiller of the earth (the body) is the Holy Spirit. And the rain that falls upon our parched earth is the divine impulses of the Son after His glorious Resurrection. The mountain streams for our fields are our own tears of either joys or sorrows. With our house (body) set in order, we should each become pillars and fires for God while we sojourn on earth (see Lk 12:49–50).

There is a time and a place for everything in life and application to every hour—even in the hours of sleep. Are we not then imitators in the tomb? And friends should be selected as carefully as we would select jewels for a queen's crown from a jeweler's collection (see Prv 22:24–25; Eccl 6:6, 14–16). If at any time a person may prove to lead us farther away from God, then it is better that we close the book of his or her life in our lives with the sureness that we would close a useless book on the shelf of a library. We must be gracious, though, in that library and place not dust upon the book, for the book could be a guide, a bookmark for a meditation student.

Charity begins at home. That home referred to in Scripture is our own individual body. We must not lose sight of the truth that we are God's tabernacle as surely as if we were on wheels imitating the arc of the covenant. We must not adorn that tabernacle with crosses God did not intend for us to have by being busybodies about neighbors' business through which we could pick up a cross. Every shoulder is formed for a certain cross which God will give or allow, but it is not fashioned for the neighbors' crosses. We must stay simple, not burdened with many cares, and cross out the cares that enter our minds if they do not belong to our state in life or vocation. We shall then balance the inventory by erasing the unnecessary cares in life.

Father, about the time Saint Aloysius taught me the easy steps for a convert child, I heard the Master say, "Calmness of mind shall be greatly rewarded." Then our saint taught me that calmness is the ability to think carefully and weigh well the subject matter in the balance of justice. It is quite necessary for our formal reading to acquaint us with Scripture, both the Old and New Testaments. Also, *history* should be a part of our diets. These studies are the firm foundations for future contemplation. Contemplation is a form of invisible bilocation into the past, where we may live with Christ and follow Him and become apprentices. An apprentice is an apprentice so that he might become a master. Contemplation is to be alone with Jesus. Contemplatives do not mystically travel in groups. Oneness *with* God is all that matters in the Oneness *of* God.

During visitations with friends and group enjoyments, we should trade our gifts as the Master commanded. Exchange of views stimulates good for the soul. In joy, spirit climbs in its mastery of love when fanned by the understanding of soul, who like a mother disciplines the five senses as if they were tiny children playfully living within the tabernacle, the body.

Calmness is mastered greatly by the gift of *knowing* and *loving* silence (see Is 30:15). Silence has a great wardrobe, and daily we may wear new togas. We must watch carefully that we do not walk in muddy paths—arm in arm with evil friends. Dry cleaning for togas and especially for the rising master is most difficult and expensive. Dry cleaning is the confessional cleaning. To speak of faults and the soil of life is only to let the good confessor know our heights and delights—this is a mortification to both body and senses.

APPLICATION AND SENSE MORTIFICATION

Application is zeal for the love of God. Simple application for the week: First, we shall walk daily around a city block, smiling, and greet even strangers with a cheery "Good Morning" and a smile. Three souls must be greeted on the streets. (A walk to the office, certain buildings or markets may take the place of the city block. The people should be strangers—not the usual gardener, grocer, or bus man.) Every day of the week, write a letter to a sick friend or shut-in. Jesus follows us everywhere—an apprentice follows His "way." One day during the week we must seek Him in three different churches and make a visit without the usual formal or read prayers. Our just talking to Him proves to Him that if we were living in Jerusalem, we would be willing to "follow Him" for even three days without care of rest or food. Also, we must mortify the sense of sight five times a day (no more nor less). We must practice overcoming being a detailist—this is most important when talking with friends. Few words should be our goal. As we kneel alone three times each day and bow deeply before divine justice of God, we shall reverently kiss the floor each time as if we were kissing His garment. And finally, with the counter beads, we shall move up one bead each time we have broken silence willfully prying into the affairs of others; we shall move a bead if we revel in relating all the latest news without being asked. (This could be a curb for idle words.)

Our penance for each bead moved during the day must bring its punishment. Remembering Christ within us, how He hated lack of zeal, and how He said through the Spirit that He would "vomit" the lukewarm out of His mouth (Rv 3:16), we must actually taste of the lukewarm by drinking a cup of warm coffee, or tea, or milk for each bead moved. And forgetting the lukewarm penance until night or even until bedtime does not alter the matter—we must drink all the cups (without a scowl, always).

SCRIPTURE STUDY

During the day, or better at bedtime, we may begin the habit—if we do not already have it—of Scripture reading by daily studying well these quotations of Saint Peter and the ones quoted [below] at least once during the week.

1 Peter 3:13–15

"And who is there to harm you, if you are zealous for what is good? But even if you suffer anything for justice's sake, blessed are you. *So have no* fear *of their fear and do not be* troubled. *But hallow the Lord* Christ in your hearts" *(the indwelling).*

Be ready always with an answer to everyone who asks a reason for the hope that is in you (the reason for more study).

1 Peter 4:1–2

"Since Christ therefore has suffered in the flesh, do you also arm your-selves with the same intent; because he who has suffered in the flesh has ceased from sins; that during the rest of his time in the flesh he may live no longer according to the lusts of man, but according to the will of God."

When suffering to the flesh comes from God, through the fall of Adam, and when mortifications become an application, we are arming ourselves with Christ and putting "off the old man" of the lustful earth for the Christ within us (see Col 3:5–11).

Let us develop into masters for the Master (see Lk 6:40). "Be ye perfected; be he exhorted or paracleted; be ye like-minded; be

ye peaceful; and the God of love and of peace shall be with you"
(Phrases from a book, *The Paraclete*, also, see 2 Cor 13:10–11).

Devotedly in the Sacred Heart of Jesus,
Cora

Second Letter Lesson

January 18, 1954

Dear Father,
The lesson for this week will be the holy thought and question: Are we praying in the right spirit? Is our spirit kind, mild, and honest? Are we honest with self? We are tabernacles—and our thoughts are real; we are also a stage. Suppose each good thought represented itself as a beautiful angel and each bad or unkind thought as an ugly old man—vile and unclean. Would we be horror-stricken if we watched for one day the coming and going of these two images into our bodies—the human tabernacles? Let us keep the old man out. The old man hangs his cards on the tabernacle walls. They read: Vices, Revenge, Hatreds, Pride, and False Pains Leading to False Desires for Sympathy. Let us allow the good angel to take them down. For each fault hated or removed for even an hour, we may each allow ourselves a pleasure such as candy, ice-cream, phone call, theatre, golf, drive, or any other similar privilege.

For each ugly thought or deed returned by the old man, we shall clean a drawer, shelf, plumbing fixture, or perhaps one car window.

A contemplative never prays much with the lips and tries avoiding long-worded prayers. He or she knows that God speaks to a quiet soul. The Master invited us all to knock, but there are many differences in the ways of knocking. Some knocks are "snappy"—symbolizing rudeness, lack of poise, and shallow-minded reasoning. Another knock could be boldly loud. This kind of knock is ill-mannered in its "demand" and "command." Are we praying in these symbolical knocks? The quiet knock speaks of meekness and care for the feelings of others—are we caring for the feelings of God? Our own spirit is often shown in our knock. Shall we each study ourselves as we knock on a friend's door every day for a week just to say a greeting, if our regular work of life does not demand the visits? And can we learn another lesson from the smile of the friend? And still another by keeping the conversation on the interests of the friend in a concentrated effort to avoid "I"? All of these suggestions are to bend with the demands of vocations.

Do we wish to be within the inner courtyard and castle halls in our prayers today? Then let us pretend in mind that we are knocking at the Master's castle door and that we hear His footstep. What are we going to say? Are we going to demand or command or offer a greeting of praise and smile? How did we greet the friend? Were we demanding of her? Did we express our desires as a command? Or did we offer love and praise in our smile? Why should we treat God any differently or without consideration for His feelings when we pray?

The Master opens the door and bids us enter. It is His home, and He shows us gem-encrusted crowns and trophies won for and through Him by His saints. We have our desires anticipated by Him when He shows us pictures of His life, His sufferings, and His cross. He is generous in telling of His hobby, as evidenced by His collections—crutches both mental and physical. Have we the nerve to ask for more? Could we dare complain? Or ask for trivial gifts when He has shown us the eternal? Time is passing—let us just love and praise Him; this is the knock of simplicity, trust, and joy. The Master enjoys such a child. We must not forget that we are His children.

During the day, we should think often of the meaning of the psalm prayer, "Why were you dejected, O my soul, and disturbed within me?" (Ps 43:5). We cannot remember, in His presence, the necessity of asking for even one thing. With Him we have everything. Let us engraft all the earth's happenings into His sufferings and believe that union then becomes His will. Let us ask Him to bless our friends but not as we name them one by one. We must cease, even in this way of prayer, being a detailist. *Cease bossing God; just ask Him to "bless"* should be our own "card" reminder hung in our tabernacled hearts. To do this is to practice childlike trust. "Let him hope in the name of the Lord and lean upon his God" (Is 50:10).

Other reminder cards might well be: silence must never be forgotten;

benediction is silence; His path is silence; His way of love is silence; and He speaks to the quiet soul (see Sir 25:17, 32:9; Is 30:15).

The greatest miracle today is the knowledge that we are loved by God (see Ps 8:5; Mt 17:5; Lk 23:46; Jn 17:20–23, etc.). True love is to desire nothing—that nothingness is love as long as we live in the world. Let us not forget that we have become "Godded" through receiving Him in the Blessed Sacrament. Could we ask for more? In this age of the Holy Eucharist, we have far more than the woman of Jerusalem who reached to touch the hem of His toga and received a cure—we have actually received Him (see Jn 6:57–60).

Joy must be complete lest we show our ingratitude. Joy is the reciprocation for His coming down and taking upon Himself our suffering humanity. He became subject to ridicule, whips, cold nails, the cross, and death. Would we do that much for Him? Let us take first the word "ridicule" as our morning thought. We should watch for ridicule and see how gracefully we receive it—how do you? At noon, we should think about the "whips" He had across His body—our fatigue is its comparison. Did He scold, complain, or cry? Have we? Mid-afternoon we should think about "cold nails." Do we receive icicled glares from friends? Has someone raised an eyebrow at our courage in the fight for God? How did we take the spear plunge? Did we cry out "revenge"? Evening—the cross: life has made us tired, but we rise to help others in their need of relief from suffering or by giving encouragement if they are despairing, overburdened, or grieving. Evening could be a trail of enjoyment with our giving delights and His hope to the cross-bearers in life. Bedtime is the time for us to think about death. Our bed is the tomb. As we take our rest, we may examine ourselves. Are we ready if the dawn does not make for us another day? Is our body, soul, and spirit ready? Are we willing to make detours into Purgatory, which is not our true country? If we rise in the night either from personal sickness, illness of family, or for other reasons, its distaste should remind us of Purgatory.

SCRIPTURE STUDY

When we think of our oneness with Jesus in His Kingship for all eternity, let us sing with David in his excitement of joys, for true love and understanding wanteth nothing.

Psalm 96 [95]:11–13

"Let the heavens rejoice"
Symbolically, the coming of Jesus to us in Holy Communion—our oneness in His Kingship [unity] forever.

"And the earth be glad"
Our body is the earth spoken of here, and we should be glad—there is no other way if we are true contemplatives.

"Let the sea and all that it contains resound"
The sea is a figure for God the Father and His power of justice. All that is Him and in Him is the heritage—the gifts of the saints and the saints themselves; cf. Rv 19:7–9, Rom 8:17.

"Let the fields exalt and all that is in them"
The people who have not had the faith preached to them nor accepted Christ. They help us with life, in a material sense; we must not forget them in our prayers of thanksgiving for benefactors.

"Then shall all the trees of the forest rejoice before the Lord"
The trees spoken of here mean the pillars of faith and strength—priests and other holy souls who strive and live for the "indwelling" of Jesus.

"Again we must rejoice"
Constant prayer of thanksgiving, joy, and praise. (see 1 Thes 5:16–18)

"For He comes, for He comes to rule the earth"
The indwelling—Saint Paul.

"It is now no longer I that live, but Christ lives 'in' me" (Gal 2:20).

"He will rule the world with justice." (see Ps 96:13)
The effects of the contemplative life which stems toward justice more than toward mercy.

Let us "knock" by singing another psalm of praise together with David on Sunday of this week: Psalm 111 [110].

SENSE MORTIFICATION AND APPLICATION

The right spirit in all things in life is gratitude. Application of the right spirit is to visit, talk, or write to one person a day who ordinarily grates upon our nerves (culture and traditional laws). Shall we bring good out of that person, even if it is only a smile?

Sense gratification often comes through hearing. We must mortify the sense of hearing five times a day—no more nor less.

An act of gratitude is to find five "creations" in the world such as a newborn leaf, an insect, or even a cloud that we feel reasonably certain that no one else will see and praise God for their being. These little gratitudes will lead to greater ones. Shall we do this daily?

Let us also pray in the right spirit without demand and command. Quietly, let us rejoice and be thankful for what we have and make the most out of trials, mistakes, and misunderstandings.

Penance for each bead moved on the counter for praying in the spirit of demand or command shall be to eat a slice of bread three times a day with butter on the underside. This must be done even in the presence of company, but we shall try not to make an issue out of it.

Devotedly,
Cora

Third Letter Lesson

XTO REGI[2]

January 25, 1954

Dear Father,

A good king is a ruler within diplomacy. He is a governor not of self alone but rather in selflessness; his needs are those of his household, his subjects, and nations. Christ is our King! He is the good King of the universe. He is our God! We are the children of the *royal household*. We are children of God. He is our Father, who feeds and cares for us with His love and tender care.

As children of our King, the Diplomat among diplomats, the Master-teacher in His household and in the world of human relations, how should we act, speak, and pray as we try to obey His command, "Follow Me"? Can you imagine a child of God not using his will to become a diplomat? A diplomat knows the skill of understanding souls and of lending encouragement. Do we follow our Father? Do we imitate the Son of God? To follow the Master is to become a master (see Lk 6:40). These two little words, "Follow Me," with their depth of meaning, are His challenge to us. Accept? We shall, or have, but the ways and means are various.

Considering that we are of the royal family, not to seek perfection would be gross ingratitude to our fathers who gave us our heritage upon which we build and live. This unsatisfied world is unspeakable in its ingratitude toward Christ the King. Ingratitude is confusion

---

2   i.e., To Christ the King.

and unrest because people refuse to understand *loyalty*, the first of the means we shall consider.

Loyalty is the unique utterances of the Holy Spirit within us. Loyalty is knowing the mission of confirmation. Through confirmation, we have been sceptered and given the royal purple cloak. We must wear it proudly.

Loyalty is to know that God has given us a pattern and code of life. Are we firm in this conviction that a pattern and code is the first understanding, then knowledge, which leads to wisdom and diplomacy? Understanding, knowledge, faith, and wisdom are the hands which reach out to God for more of Himself. They are also the hands which receive gems for the royal crown. Wisdom in action is the full-dress toga or gown worn to royal functions. How many times during the day do we (or you) hear the King's summoning bell? Are you always ready? Are you clean, neat, and above reproach? Do your eyes harbor webs and dust? Are you apologetic about laxness? These are dim gems in the crown. How would you feel before the friendly crowd wearing dusty gems in a crown? How would we all feel?

Royalty is regal and stately at all times. Inner self is the coy old lady who is either humility or awful pride. How do we wear the crown? Since we are children of God—children who know that He wants us to follow Him (which means that we are to be future kings and queens)—are we striving for diplomatic perfection? When we are summoned by a friend to do this favor or another, how do we act? It is wise to remember that we are each a little ambassador. We must study well how an ambassador would act, and how he would talk, smile, and laugh, and how well he would lend his wisdom.

Loyalty is also a fine national culture; kings and queens *smile through broken hearts*, for are they not ambassadors for their subjects? Subjects need to see courage, hope, and love—these we must give to His friends and especially to those who do not wear the royal purple.

And would our King allow His children to be mistreated through severe, unjust corrections by His servants? No, He would call His children to His knee and kindly say, "You must be careful and not nag yourself for your failings. Charity to yourself demands gentleness to self. A reasonable displeasure at your own faults is the correct way, but you must not be fretful, nor even bitter. And don't become angry nor give way to much irritation of self, for this is to become more vexed for having been vexed at all."

"Discontentment with ourselves only fosters pride. It springs from a self-love that is disappointed by its own failure. Be calm, steady, and have a firm displeasure with your own faults. Have pity for yourself—charity begins at home" (body)—Saint Francis de Sales.

Royalty is never without bodyguards. Our guards are our angels and saints. Are they disgusted at our carelessness as a member of the royal family?

SCRIPTURE STUDY

Study well the words of Psalm 21 [20]

"The Lord, the King is glad because of thy strength, and because of thy help he rejoices exceedingly!"

Christ the King is *glad* and *rejoices* at our success and the knowledge that we are of His family.

We shall continue reading the rest of the psalm and study well each word. It contains a fountain of knowledge when read in the light of the royal household.

Saint Peter also gives us the lesson for the "way."

2 Peter 1:3–11

For indeed His Divine Power has granted us all things pertaining to life and piety through the knowledge of Him who has called us by His own glory and power—through which He has granted us the very great and precious promises, so that through them you may become partakers of the divine nature, having escaped from the corruption of that lust which is in the world. Do you accordingly on your part strive diligently to supply your faith with virtue, your virtue with knowledge, your knowledge with self-control, your self-control with patience, your patience with piety, your piety with fraternal love, your fraternal love with charity.

For if you possess these virtues, and they abound in you, they will render you neither inactive nor unfruitful in the knowledge of our

Lord Jesus Christ. For he who lacks them is blind, groping his way, and has forgotten that he was cleansed from his former sins. Therefore, strive even more by good works to make your calling and election sure. For if you do this, you will not fall into sin at any time. Indeed, in this way you will be amply provided for you the entrance into the everlasting Kingdom of our Lord and Savior Jesus Christ.

SENSE MORTIFICATION AND APPLICATION

Let us try three different times a day to read from a good book one sentence for meditation and think about it several times during the day, making some sort of application of its thought. Let us open the book at random. If we neglect to do this, we must move one of the counter beads. At the end of the day for each bead moved, we shall say a rosary of Our Fathers, with the meditation that we were suddenly summoned to the King in an unkempt condition. Can we imagine ourselves without a crown and without the purple cloak? Let us each strive to feel the feelings of neglect about our self where apologies are not allowed.

A gentle reminder for neglect is during the day to drink warm water with a pinch of soda added for bitterness. These impressions are a great discipline to foster recollection and alertness—these, in turn, bring calmness, which shall be greatly rewarded.

Devotedly,
Cora

Fourth Letter Lesson

(SIRACH 11:15)

February 1, 1954

Dear Father,
To know and analyze the word REPROACH for ourselves in the climb for perfection is chosen for this week. It is not uncommon for misled souls to use the word as a means of impressing friends that they are nothing and of little use in the world. To say that we are of no worth is to say that we are slothful and not trying to perfect ourselves for God.

To reproach self in this manner without properly thinking is a means or result of pride (see Sir 21:26). To say *I am nothing* is to seek a compliment, for true friends will come to a defense. We must steel ourselves against this flattery which comes from the above phrases. When two people, who are on common ground of understanding, express their rise and fall of the soul and its ways and means of attaining the goal is not telling about the sin. The confessional is the parlor room for that way of defeat. When reproach, as a means in the spiritual climb, brings smiles and cheerful encouragement to all—then, it is good. It is one of the many devices used by men and women for keeping conversation holy.

Reproach must be treated in general conversation with the caution of truth. Before we say (if we could in conscience), "I am nothing," we must ask ourselves, "Am I of no worth?" In truth, we cannot say we are worthless, for Christ suffered and died for us. To Him we are priceless and worth any price. Dare we say His judgments were wrong? We are each destined to be an everlasting tabernacle. Suppose we could see ourselves as gold and set with gems which depict graces, good deeds, and love of God; in truth, then, could we say, "I am nothing"? No! Souls are masterpieces—our visible life is the canvas upon which we try painting the image of Jesus. An artist who has worked with his canvas in storm, dim light, and morning frosts cannot say it is worthless. His effort alone has made it a pearl without price.

And we must not forget that through receiving the sacrament of baptism and then Jesus in the Blessed Sacrament, He, the artist, for the moment took the brush from our hands and with a stroke of blessing through His priests' administering, gave life to each portrait. In life, our faults and sins may have dimmed the portrait. Now that we know "charity begins at home," we must through understanding better correspond with grace and make use of the confessional; we must attempt, with God's grace, to restore our portrait to its original living beauty. In the restoring process, we shall know that as children of the royal household, we must be *kept* in the state of cleanliness, dignity, peace, and love, framed in the gold-leaf beauty of Mother Church.

Returning to our thoughts of *reproach* after considering our place of election—a prince or princess of God—do we think it pleases God, our King, to hear us, His children, say, "We are nothing?" Any one of His children, by election, is lifted above the world, and his elevated or exemplary "way" cannot be other than one of love and peace. He well knows that the eyes of the orphans are upon him. He is the "spiritual tower to them" that must not fall. Whether they realize it or not, the sufferers outside the "wall" look to the elected through the Blessed Sacrament for courage, guidance, and even pageantry which makes life to them worth living. Gold and jewels of grace are paraded—they are not hidden. Jesus said in parable, "Trade your gifts till I come" (Lk 19:13). Trading the views and facts of spiritual treasures among ourselves is to obey His command and is another means of keeping conversations holy. But we must remember to trade those gifts with *friends* who know the value of pearls. We obediently must not throw our (His) "pearls before swine" (Mt 7:6).

Since we are either a prince or a princess of the royal household, and we now know that we must cultivate the spirit of dignity that is expected of us, we must yet learn that dignity is regal only when it is founded in humility. This shall not be difficult when we realize that we are apprenticed to the Master teacher and personification of humility—Jesus. And we must not forget that great saints in the calendar of the Church wore ermine and glittering crowns as well as poverty's vesture. We must live our state in life and that which is demanded of us—it is the root of progression and wisdom which fosters prudence (see Prv 9:10). We must never cease with personal education (see Wis 6:12–13).

In our analysis of self in regard to *reproach*, we must learn how to draw that thin line of truth so that we do not confuse loss, grief, sorrow, accidents, and death of our closest kin with sin. We should share these sorrows with friends. Now and then it is necessary for emotional release to seek solace from living friends, but care should be used in our selection of friends (see Sir 6:6). We must not make telling our sorrows a habit. We should allow friends to mourn with us. Sorrow in its place (Eccl 3:1) is a source of grace, but even sorrows should be shared with wise friends.

When telling of sorrows, crosses, and ills we must cease being a detailist. It is great wisdom and perfection not to allow our conversations on personal sorrows to exceed nine days. Jesus said that we should, if necessary, mourn nine days. Are we not an apprentice in this, too? A detailist broadcasting sorrows that should be buried and forgotten is fostering pride. And when we make our friends feed upon this poor diet through hearing, we steal from them time, patience, love, and great graces which they could be earning in other ways than listening to the draft of forgotten yesterdays. Are we thieves in the night? We must cease feeding friends carrion which could make them become critical hawkers.

A hawker is a weak soul who has never loved the dart of silence. He is often long-faced and would love showing his penance by wearing the purple in public. He is no better than a tramp dog living in a fools' paradise as a self-styled judge with the neighborhood newspaper. Unless we are ordered to judge by a superior through some power of vows or work relationship, we must decline giving judgment. We may give opinions if we are asked.

SCRIPTURE READING

We shall study Psalm 111 [110] in the thought of friends or circle of friends.

I will thank the Lord with my whole heart, in the circle of the just and in congregation. Great are the works of the Lord, worthy of study for all who love them. The fear of the Lord is the beginning of wisdom; prudent is the conduct of all who practice it; his praise abides forever.

1 Peter 2:1–3

"*Lay aside therefore all* malice *and all* deceit *and* pretense, *and* envy, *and all* slander. Crave, *as* newborn babies, pure spiritual milk, *that by it you may grow to salvation.*"

SENSE MORTIFICATION AND APPLICATION

"Apply thy heart to My doctrine." Prv 22:17

If we discover through former habits that we have reproached our-selves in any way to have received a compliment, we must move a bead on the counter. For each bead moved we shall read aloud a psalm of our own choosing, offering it to God for His greater honor and glory.

The sense of touch must be mortified this week. At Mass we must not allow our arms to rest nor touch the seat back ahead us. Keep-ing our arms above the rest to about a half inch will allow no one to observe our penance if we are careful (see Mt 6:17–18). Also, we shall kneel on one knee at a time if our health permits. When we dust a table, dresser, car, or chair, we must leave a spot undusted as a mortifi-cation. If it is particularly noticed and drawn to our own attention, we must remove the dust and say a rosary of the fifteen mysteries.

Individually, we may pray that we will have the grace to ask permis-sion to not eat meat twice a week for the rest of our life. It is a great means of strength which, when gained, frightens the evil one from our midst. Friday is one day, and we may choose the other.

Devotedly,
Cora

Fifth Letter Lesson

February 8, 1954

Dear Father,

This week let us keep our minds' meditation upon an ocean liner. Our ship, the human body, is all set to sail. We do not know ahead of time the pending storms, squalls, and calm. No doubt at this hour we are delightfully walking the starboard [deck] while we listen to the symphonic poem of the sea waves. The water of the sea is a mystery—it is a symbol of God the First Person. Somehow, it grasps at our sense of awe, and we feel both the pangs of joy and of fear. As a creature, we are each a little giant—for God allows us to see, feel, and smell the sea and even taste of its salt spray and hear the moan and sigh of the tides. Yet, in all of this we do not *know* the sea. We realize that we are another mystery upon that sea—we are a ship with an anchor, and that anchor is Jesus.

Somehow, we are seaworthy because Jesus is our trust and He has placed us in this petition of life and given us the gift of faith. Faith must grow, and as it grows with our corresponding will, we taste of the might of the sea in measures equally given and earned. We are often overcome with the ruthlessness of the sea. However, we soon learn as we gaze across the fighting waves of power and see in its calm the North storm's (devil) frowns that faith teaches us there is always a calm after a storm. To know the sea is to love the sea, and to know the sea is to follow the life of Jesus and apply His life to ours; this is the true "way" of engrafting ourselves into the will of God. For hasn't Jesus said that no one can "go to the Father except through me"? Through this knowledge as seen through the eyes of Jesus, we can then contemplate God the Father in the symbol of the sea.

39

First of all, through study, let us *know* that Jesus *waited* on the shore for His fishermen. (This is to teach us that we must not hurry the delights of new grace.) And Jesus was thoughtful and kind while He waited; He broiled fish for the tired fishermen. He was hospitable. If we love Him, need we ever fear the storm? Should we fear the power of the sea? "No," is our answer if we have followed the pattern of Christ's life. He is the Way. We know as we cross the deep (life) that He is waiting for us with a banquet and a fire of warmth (love). Let us banish fear and trust in His loving care. According to grace earned and retained, He treats all of His friends alike. Let us keep in mind that we are His fishermen.

When Jesus saw the fishermen approaching, He could have walked upon the water to meet and greet them, but He chose to wait on the beach for them to come to Him. This is a symbol of Heaven's laws in regard to the finite knowledge of law and order and culture in all things. Hurrying to Jesus is to *reach* ourselves out to Him. When Peter walked on water did he not *reach* his hand out to Jesus? The word REACH will be the lesson subject for this week. Any ship set afloat (and that is what it is built for) is ever reaching for a destination. For what destination are we reaching? There are three ports: Heaven, Purgatory, and Hell. Let us ever keep in mind that we are reaching for Jesus. *Reaching for Jesus* must be our aim and routine in life lest we become as driftwood without an aim for the greatest harbor.

Let us think about the word *reaching*. It is the firsthand expression of a newborn child. He grasps for something—his anchor of security. Reaching is to stay childlike, ever interested in the knowledge that delights us with God. A newborn child does not question what his attendants are thinking or why they do this or that with his person. He reaches only for security, which brings him an anchorage of peace. This is a child's beginning lesson and one which we should always keep in our thoughts when we walk through the arrangements of life. In life, let us set our goal to reach for the anchor's offering of peace to soul and body. Knowledge through the pattern of reaching is the wisdom of God, and it is a cloak of glory which we will wear for all eternity. We add jewels to its pattern when we deny ourselves the foolishness of the world.

Reaching is also to rise above the fear of being censored by people. We must not make our friends or relatives our "king." Reach for only

One King. Make life with Him a delightful game, even though the North winds tear away a sail, for well we know that we may reach for the confessional and, through the power of the Priesthood, replace or mend the sail.

Father, in the art of this week's lesson on application it is well to have a picture of a ship somewhere near our place of work. It will, during the day, recall to our minds the thought of reaching for the shore of eternity. Several times a day we should meditate upon that picture and think about our progress and how well we have guided our ship. We could ask, "Are the five senses (our invisible sailors) well-disciplined? Does our sailor named "hands" curse when he drops the dust cloth? Is his sigh aggravated when he reaches for it? How do we act in our homes, offices, or places of work when we drop an article?" Is this not a lesson on reaching, which—through discipline—could become a beautiful gesture and meritorious? Instead of scowling and giving a dagger look and heavy sigh, let us bend, reach, and thank God for the school of monotony. When the phone rings, we must reach. Before reaching, let us make the sign of the cross over our lips and silently say, "Jesus." He, the indweller, will answer and talk for us.

Shall we meditate upon how we would like Him to answer the phone? What would His voice sound like? We would want Him to be cheerful; do our voices radiate joy when we reach for the phone? Voice tone is like a smile. Does our own voice smile? No, then we must make it smile through the practice of speaking before a mirror. We shall find it easy when we make monotony a game with God. This discipline is the real beginning step through which we shall learn that nothing is impossible nor even hard to accomplish for God—for is He not the indweller? Our clay shells, our bodies, are only vessels or means of communication (instruments). Time will tell in the teaching of our five sailors (senses) the joys of discipline.

Every time we reach for a dropped article such as clothing, phone, shoes, pencil, towel, or any other object in the collection of life and allow a passing thought of scorn or a cuss word to escape our hearts or lips, let us move a bead on the counter. For each of your own beads moved at the end of the day prostrate yourself upon your back on the floor and repeat the Act of Contrition aloud and with modulated voice.

SENSE MORTIFICATION AND APPLICATION

This week the sense of smell is to be mortified. The following suggestions may prove a help. Jesus wants to be inventors. Much is left to the mother of invention within us.

Instead of the usual flowery fragrance of hand lotions, a few drops of vinegar upon the hands will mortify the sense of smell. Lava soap instead of the usual luxuriously perfumed soaps will serve the same purpose. When we come in contact with bad odors, let us thank God for the purgation.

Are we reaching for the right things in life is another meaning to the thought *are we praying in the right spirit?* If we are not reaching for the right things in life, we could become sneaks, snoopers, and thieves. These titles belong to persons who do not reach for the right things. A snooper is a "peeping Tom." His eyes are ever reaching for scenes that are not becoming in this state of life. We could ask, "Are we Toms who delight in peeping though windows in neighborhoods? Do we like reading about neighborhood scandals, murders, thieves, and accidents?" These public scandals and neighbor troubles do not belong to us. They are bad odors and should be as displeasing; they are individual people's skeletons for which a contemplative does not have a taste nor desire. Are they not also spoiled mind food? Why should we poison ourselves?

In our further questioning ourselves, we could ask, "Do we reach for the magazine *True Confessions* or its counterpart? Do we allow children or those under our direction to feed on foul comics or pictures? Do we reach for the Bible, the *Imitation of Christ*, or Lives of the Saints along with other reading material such as the *Catholic Digest* or a good history book? All of these could be found in the library of God."

SCRIPTURE STUDY

Psalm 56 [55]

"Have mercy on me, O God, for men do trample upon me, they oppress and attack me without ceasing."

In our lives today, we could say that worldly people try to make us reach for trash upon which to live. We could ask ourselves, "Can you imagine reading a book of trash in Heaven? If Jesus walked by and asked what you were reading, would you blush?"

"My foes are forever treading on me, for many fight against me."
The devil and his human workers are ever throwing ideas in our path of life. Many people fight against moral principles and the true culture of God.

"O Most High, in the day when fear comes upon me, I will trust in Thee."
Reach for Him and say, "I will trust in You!"

"In God, whose promise I praise, in God I put my trust, I will not fear, what can man do to me?"
Man can do nothing to us unless we will and consent intellectually. Man might harm the body through accident and war, but we do not will it. Let us reach for His guidance. We must not feed the mind upon verbal nor written books of sin.

"All day long they disparage me, all their thoughts are against me, unto harm."
Let us strive after good friends who are one in mind and purpose of gaining eternal life.

The contemplative life must not cramp our style of cheerful laughing and having innocent joys with funny literature or through hearing a good joke. And we can even laugh heartily at the devil's antics. He is a proud spirit, and he hates ridicule and correction. He abhors being laughed at—he thinks he is a great intellect which he is, according to spirit, but he does not have a body; therefore, he does not understand the bodily actions made possible through hidden intellect.

For further Scripture study, let us read Second Peter with the thought of *reach* and the right goal in life.

2 Peter 2:1

"But there were false prophets also among the people, just as among you there will be lying teachers who will bring in destructive sects."

Lying teachers in the broader sense could be sinful storywriters, photographers, or artists in their manner of printing and painting. Seekers after indecent dress and vulgarity in dancing are reaching for the wrong things in life and are in the same category. Let us not be a promoter to these causes.

SENSE MORTIFICATION AND APPLICATION

During the week if we fail to speak quickly in defense of decency and good books, let us take a taste of salt.

Devotedly,
Cora

Sixth Letter Lesson

February 15, 1954

Dear Father,

Today, within a few hours, will be yesterday—it is a part that is gone. Only in eternity will we see time as a fleeting second, and in the sharing gifts of God we will recapture yesterday at will. How will it look to us? Will we smile and say that the part is but a facet of knowledge? If we have gained wisdom through the discipline of knowledge, then happily we can say that we did not waste time. *Time is precious. It is a gift* not to be misused.

Since we are to become masters of self, we must become a master of time. We have learned that charity begins at home. Now suppose that we look at time in the same light. It, too, begins at home. Our bodies, our homes, and our duties, according to our chosen vocations in life, remind us by their unavoidable presence that we are each, as an individual, a separate and going business concern. Are we not laying up treasures for eternity? As we grow spiritually stronger in grace, the more perfect in God we become. It is only natural, then, that people will come to expect and demand more of us who live for God.

Time is a known condition of life; therefore, the monotonies of life must be governed by rules. To live and to give means work. Is our schedule in perfect condition? Do we try living to hours and keeping time by the clock? Do we know the discipline of stopping in the middle of a simple job because the hour has struck? This is applied discipline, and it is as necessary as the accomplished deed. Let us plan our hours according to these conditions by the hour, half-hour, or even quarter-hour, not forgetting the hours for pleasure and general relaxation.

For the housewife, I should like to suggest these simple rules. Other vocations may follow similar ideals, which may be prompted by the Holy Spirit. Let us give each room in our homes a title according to the days in the week—Monday, Tuesday, Wednesday, etc. Sunday should not be given as a name to a room. In the general way of housework, the usual [routine] must be followed, but in the room [whose title corresponds] to the day of the week, we must do some additional work which is not ordinarily done. If we allow thirty minutes for each room during the week, and if this schedule is rotated for the course of a year, we will discover that no general housecleaning will be necessary at any time.

No doubt, at first, the thirty-minute schedule will test our courage and fortitude, but remember the discipline counts for more than the work in the sight of God. Discipline builds character. Good discipline is a help in keeping people from falling into scrupulosity. We must avoid that disease at all costs. It is a germ that does not feed on trust. At the same time, we must not become perfectionists to such a degree that our families cannot live in comfort. A home is a home to be used rather than to be looked at as we would a picture. If the thirty-minute period elapses before we accomplish the task set for ourselves to do, we must leave the work and finish it another day. If the unwashed window or half-polished table is noticed, we may thank God for the humiliation. We may not offer excuses, for it is in no way a neglect of doing our work.

Suggestions for men (to be done without a frown):

1. Check car's needs: oil, air, etc.
2. Recondition leather luggage
3. Discard old shoes and ties
4. Repair plugs and electrical appliances
5. Clean and rearrange things in garage
6. General work on the house and in the yard

If, during the week, we feel the sting of conscience for having wasted time, we must move a bead on the counter. Shall we do reparation for each bead moved by visiting or writing to a sick or shut-in friend? Or shall we give alms to a poor person—one whom we do not know? Once during the week, as a means for reparation for our past faults, let us take a walk around the block, and as we approach each telephone pole or light pole, pretend that it is our crucifix waiting for our crucifixion. Shall we reflect upon the early Christians walking toward their certain death in the Coliseum? With this in mind, could we do less than to say a fervent act of contrition as we approach each pole?

TIME has also a deeper meaning in the contemplative life. It is a wisdom far above the life of meditation, just thinking or reading. For instance, why did Jesus use the parables? Was it not for the people in two different classes of learning—world knowledge and the wisdom of God? The Master said on several occasions, "He who has ears to hear, let him hear" (Mt 11:15). He was speaking of a greater knowledge known to His contemplative souls. These people are pearls of rare price. His greater knowledge is a pearl understood by the few. "Many are called, but few are chosen" (Mt 20:16) could be another meaning to His words. Let us strive to understand the greater pearls.

SCRIPTURE STUDY

Our scripture study for this week in reference to *time* is to read Matthew 24:29–30 and the same subject matter in Luke 21:25–28. "At that time, (This could mean in almost any generation or at the very end of time.) Jesus said to His disciples, 'And there shall be signs in the sun, and the moon, and in the stars, and upon the earth distress of nations, by *reason* of the confusion of the roaring of the sea and of the waves; men withering away for fear and expectation of what shall come upon the whole world; for the powers of Heaven shall be moved, and they shall see the Son of man coming in a cloud with great power and majesty.'"

(Men may wither or become lukewarm because of *reason* staying at a *starvation level in knowledge of God*. The mystical interpretations to this subject matter are copied from a book entitled, *Explanations of the Gospels*, Imprimatur, Michael Augustine, Archbishop of New York, September 5, 1892. Quotations that follow are from the book:

- What are these signs which will be seen in the sun, moon, and stars?
- Our Lord in Saint Matthew's Gospel tells us that the sun shall be darkened, the moon shall no longer give her light, the stars shall fall from heaven, and the power of heaven shall be moved.
- It will be thus in the natural order, but how can this be understood in the spiritual order?
- In the darkening of the sun we can recognize loss which the Church suffers by the persecutions of Anti-Christ. In the obscuring of the moon, we see the ruin produced in men by the decay of charity.
- Our Lord tells us that if these days are not shortened on account of the elect, none would be saved. The stars falling from heaven represent teachers and preachers of the law and the faith who have fallen away, like the stars dragged down by the dragon described in the Apocalypse. Lastly, in the dissolution of the forces of nature is represented the decay of the Christian virtues, and in the consternation of peoples is seen the disorder caused by the decay of good morals and the triumph of impiety.)

Also for the week, study Psalm 68 [67] in the light that we, who have not tried for the life of discipline and greater love of creatures, may learn that we are a *desert* in the world. And now that we *want* to learn *He* will ride through that desert of our souls scattering His graces as if they were stardust.

Psalm 68 [67]

"God arises."

Have we not asked Him to come because we are trying to follow His command, "Be ye perfect"?

"His foes are scattered, and they who hate him flee from his presence."

Our old slothful habits of sin have fled through routine, discipline, and study. And the old worldly friends who hate discipline flee from us—Christ within us.

"But the just are glad, they rejoice in the sight of God, and they rejoice exceedingly."

Are we not numbered among the just? We should be able to answer, "Yes." Are we not glad that we have awakened ourselves in time in the sight of God within us? We should rejoice and we should be happy.

"Sing to God, sing praises to his name; prepare the way for him who rides through the desert."
Let us not forget that we are the desert. He is making new inroads.

"Whose name is the Lord, and rejoice before Him."
The desert of us has willed for His coming. We send forth His name through our actions, deeds, and prayers. We openly rejoice by saying, "We love."

"The father of orphans and the guardian of widows—God is in His holy dwelling place."
Christ within us is the father of orphans and the guardians of widows. Through us He uses our bodies to accomplish His works of mercy and love. We are His holy dwelling places. Let us strive for greater perfections in the knowledge of the indwelling.

"God provides a home for the abandoned, he leads captives forth to prosperity; only the rebellious dwell in a parched land."
If we are abandoned, He builds new homes for us. Our bodies become living portable tabernacles.

"O God, when thou didst go forth before thy people, when thou didst march through the wilderness, the earth quaked, rain also fell from the heavens before God, Sinai trembled before God, the God of Israel."
The above is a symbol of victim souls suffering for those people living in their deserted deserts and parched lands. God through friends will go to friends and bring the rain of grace. Bad earth [sinners] quake before the presence of good.

SENSE MORTIFICATION AND APPLICATION

This week the sense of taste is to be mortified.

SUGGESTIONS

When we desire salt, pepper, or sugar, we shall not take them. When we desire coffee, we shall take tea or vice versa. We must drink Postum[3] at one regular meal whether we like it or not. We must also refrain from using toothpastes for one week. In their stead, we may use salt or soda.

Devotedly,
Cora

---

3   A wheat-based coffee substitute.

Seventh Letter Lesson

February 22, 1954

Dear Father,
Worldly news, hurried talk, events that awe us, and happenings to our lives often leave us with the knowledge-wisdom that the majority of people are frustrated. Since we as Christians should have already learned the first principles of love, charity, and the warmth of security made possible through the thirst for education and the right use of government, we should readily see the deeper trials hidden in the word FRUSTRATED.

Let us trust that we have lifted ourselves, through the grace of God, into denials and governing of self, above the common frustrations which deal with the animal nature. Frustrations are met in all walks of life and in different degrees in the meditative and contemplative world. This letter lesson will logically try to simplify the word for those people who are trying to rise above meditation as the main diet in love of God. The dark night of the senses is the first fought with when we consider whether or not we are going to school our senses in a routine discipline. That dark night of sense lingers and even, at times, keeps stride with the will, bending first this way and then that as a torment inflicted by the lower-nature *soul*, trying to bring about defeat. After a person has made up his will to climb higher and higher to God for His love alone, meditation becomes tiresome. Worded prayers seem useless, and he thinks faith is lacking, and man often prays not to lose his faith. This is the natural rise of the soul to unite with *spirit*. It is wisdom for a contemplative to bend down to practices of meditation, such as attending a rosary devotion, Stations of the Cross, and others, but he quickly returns to the higher castle room of quiet where his delights are found in praising, adoring, and loving God without any thought of reward in this life or the next. It is a delight of perfect trust. Saint John of the Cross writes, "God established the soul in the dark night of sense, that He may purify, prepare, and subdue its lower nature, and unite it to the spirit, by depriving it of light and causing it to cease from meditation."

In our discipline of the senses, let us learn the meaning of certain words which may help us overcome the desires of the senses which govern the soul. For instance, calmness, which is so necessary in this life, is never fully realized where there is frustration. We must fight for calmness as we would fight for the preservation of peace for a nation. We must find the roots of that evil, *frustration*, and root them out of our lives as we would a bad tooth. Let us keep in mind that calmness of mind shall be greatly rewarded.

First, what is frustration? It is to disappoint. Therefore, if we do not disappoint God, we can feel pretty sure that we are not disappointing our neighbors and friends. In the analysis of any word we must know the word, its sound, how it anchors into our lives, and how we must battle with it according to the law of order.

Let us refrain from ever saying, "He or she is frustrated." Let us not judge. It would be good logic to judge ourselves with that "off-sounding" word. If a person claims he is a lover of God then he cannot be frustrated, for true love of God knows calmness and the laws of right use of reasoning. For a person to excuse himself under the guise of nervous frustration is nothing more than to admit that he cannot face life. If a person cannot face life, then how is he going to face the great gift of acquired contemplation to which, according to many of the great writers, we are all called? A frustrated person seeking sympathy is a deceiver who might as well admit that he has stopped climbing the path to perfection. Is he going to admit that he is a coward? We know that in Christ's army there is no room for cowards who stay down rather than follow Christ, who rose time after time with His cross. It is not a frustration to fall for a while, but it is a cowardly frustration to stay down and seek sympathy beyond a reasonable period of nine days. The common use of excusing self under the guise of nerves which causes one to fly into a rage, is nothing more than ungoverned temper in an immature person. Temper, frustration, nagging, and abusive language are SELF.

If then, there is anything "frustrate-able" about us, let us defeat it now. Let us cease disappointing God. That is the first step. Let us hate deception of any kind. Let us not trick anyone, except at innocent games and parties where all present know the sportsmanship of a game. Let us not deliberately baffle anyone with our knowledge of great learning—that, too, comes under the title SELF. Learn the art of talking to all classes of people, all for the love of God. It is wise if we can prevent any form of balking or be the cause of preventing stubbornness in others. Balking is usually fostered because a condition or case history of a subject is not fully explained nor understood. In difficult conditions which might arise in groups or nations, it is wise to use the minds of arbitrators. *Consolations* are often the justifiers that have used ill will and loss of faith.

Jesus is the Prince of Peace. He is our Arbitrator. And He gives freely His most choice consolations. A compliment is good for the soul. If we must admonish, then twice to the same person we must give praise—this is justice. Our priests are our human instruments for arbitrations in all matters that pertain to faith and morals. Let us follow Jesus by becoming a prince of peace to our neighbors and friends. Peace can be given in the tone of our voices—shall we try it?

For this week, and for every time we, as individuals, have failed to bring joy to a person with whom we are in close association, we must move a bead on the counter. And if we have reacted with "snappy voice" when called upon to work in a church benefit, dance, or any other charitable cause, or if at any time and for any reason, we give anyone an "icicled glare," we must move another bead. Still another bead must come down if we have pouted when we have not been waited upon immediately. During the day if we have lifted our voice above the usual kindness, we shall calmly kneel and recite a rosary in reparation. This practice will help us not to forget that our voice resounds instantly through the Sacred Heart of Jesus.

The discipline for us for such immaturity as thus evidenced in beads moved, is—for each bead—to move a piece of furniture to another place in the house and allow it to stay there for the week.

Jesus is the Way. He is the Prince of Peace and He gave us many ideas for our perfection. One was given in His words of correction to some Sadducees, "You err because you know neither the Scriptures nor the power of God" (Mt 22:29). When Jesus was on earth, the Old Testament was all anyone could read. How well have we read the Bible of old? Because of our ignorance have we stopped a promising convert? Let us study. We must be well versed—it may mean the saving of a soul.

Suppose a non-Catholic asked for a proof either from Holy Scripture or logic that Mary had only one child. How would we answer? The following is a good way and one which seems to satisfy:

John 19:26

"When Jesus therefore, saw his mother and the discipline standing by, whom he loved, he said to his mother, 'Woman, behold thy son.' Then he said to the disciple, 'Behold thy mother.' And from that hour the disciple took her into his home."

A quotation from the book entitled *Mariology* by Pohle-Preuss, page 98, reads in answer to the reason for the above, "To honor one's parents by faithfully providing for them is not only the duty but the right of every child, and Jesus would have violated the rights of His brethren, had He had any, by entrusting His Mother to John."

Study Psalm 26 in the light of courage and confidence so that we may never fall under the fault of frustration.

"The Lord is my light and salvation."
Application today—He, the indweller, removes doubt.

"Whom shall I fear?"
Fear the devil and his human agents who would make us think there is no God and that we are useless and defeated.

Read the rest of the psalm, asking guidance from the Holy Spirit.

SENSE MORTIFICATION AND APPLICATION

This week we are to mortify the eyes. Once a day, at random, we shall

open the dictionary and the first word—regardless of length or short-
ness—whose use we do not understand, we must memorize its spell-
ing and then use it in speaking.

Devotedly,
Cora

Eighth Letter Lesson

March 1, 1954

Dear Father,

Today, in meditation's gift of imagination, let us pretend that each one of us is a ciborium, a cup of gold, in the tabernacle on the altar. We realize that the real ciboria actually hold the light of the world, Jesus in the Blessed Sacrament. Our own golden cup is then a co-ciborium which has held the light of the world, particularly when we have received the Holy Eucharist. We would not consider taking a real ciborium into a place of sin; neither should we consider taking ourselves into places of danger to virtue. However, working requirements may at times alter conditions. Under these circumstances, we should be clothed in prayer and interior mortifications and consider ourselves each a sacramental which could dispel evil. This is actually missionary work for God. He, in His Humanity (body), lived among sinners and influenced them to such an extent that His cheerful goodness was felt by the great majority.

The safety of our body, the living ciborium, is made possible through continual and routine crucifixions of the five senses. It is a must in the higher expressions of the spiritual life to continue His life of the Resurrection in and through us. He has asked us to follow Him—that does not mean that we end with the cross, for we must remember that He lived among men for forty days after His Resurrection. We are to help Him continue that life by giving Him our bodies without restraint. Then when we smile, it is His smile, His handclasp, His prayer through us as He exercises His gentleness, His firmness, and His demand for justice over the evils of life.

The Blessed Sacrament is our badge of honor—Christ is our coat-of-arms! His desire is to remain imprinted upon us forever—let us "put on" Christ joyfully (see Eph 4:22–24). A royal family always has a coat-of-arms, and His gift, the Holy Eucharist, is ours! Let us live for that which is good and holy!

Considering such a holy state in which He has placed us, let us ever be grateful and show our gratitude in and through everything. Now, in the gift of imagination, let us watch a priest and his care over a ciborium. Our watch over self should be kept in a comparable way. The ciborium is costly; it is of gold, highly ornamented, and often set with jewels. Sanctifying grace, the price of His redemption, does that to us. Are we as careful as we should be with our costly ciboria? Does our watchfulness reflect gratitude? The priest preserves a ciborium from dust, corruption, rodents, and thieves. He is the prison-keeper of the Holy Eucharist. Similarly, our own will is the keeper of the keys of self. How well do we watch protectingly over ourselves from dust, corruption, rodents, and thieves?

Dust is the symbol of venial sin. Corruption is mortal sin. Rodents are sinful people with whom we are not too careful in our associations in life, business, and just passing in the street. Thieves are those would-be friends who would take us from God. They would sell a ciborium for a price if it were possible for them to steal from an altar. Let us each firmly resolve to put a guard around our heart—it is our ciborium—a jewel of which only God knows its price. He died for it!

Dust falls on everybody every day—yes, even by the hour, but God has given to each of us a dust cloth which is our will. At will, we wipe away the effects of venial sin through the use of His Holy Name, *Jesus*, or through venerating the cross or through the proper use of holy water. A priest at Mass dries our souls' tears by making the Sign of the Cross over us before he gives us Holy Communion. Just think, by drying our tears he wipes away all venial sins; he is the polisher of our tabernacles!

Now, using the imaginative gifts, let us think about the horrors of such a sight if we should see a rodent creeping all over a ciborium as a priest took the sacred vessel from the tabernacle. How would we react? Would we recoil at such a sight? And if the rodent could shift the lid of the ciborium, he would eat of the food within. Are we allowing a rodent to eat our hearts away in the sight of God? Imaginatively, too, think of how Heaven's citizens would recoil if they could see such a sight. Do they—when they witness our own soul's dimming through sin?

And suppose a thief broke in and took the ciborium from its rightful place—what sorrow! And a thief usually hurries away. A thief is never at peace; he is never calm. Let us suppose he stumbles—that could be the symbol of grace coming into his path—and falls and drops the ciborium. He is afraid of the light (grace), and he runs through the darkness leaving his prize. As he hurries away he curses. Now, let us consider, "What is a curse?" A curse is "to utter a wish or a thought of evil against a person." And this ugly paintbrush's passing over souls can be accomplished through just the power of thinking, as well as with the use of the tongue. Are we guilty? Also, to curse is to ask divine vengeance to come upon a person or thing. Could we curse a ciborium at the Mass when it is exposed? Why, then, a human ciborium? To curse is to give a final judgment. Christ asked us not to judge. Why do we disobey? A curser might as well say, "I will take the merit of the crucifixion away from that person," or "I will make the crucifixion an ill-planned law."

Purgatory may be likened to a huge schoolground with its many buildings, each of which is titled after a sin in life. Can you imagine yourself going to a college in Purgatory to undo the sin of cursing? Man cannot be saved in ignorance; we are taught through the Scriptures (see Prv 5:23, 10:21; Eph 4:18; Eccl 4:17, 7:13, to mention a few), so in Purgatory we learn the undoing of our wrongs here on earth. Let us get the right schooling here and curb ourselves, especially from cursing—even the slightest thing.

Shakespeare says, "The common curse of mankind is folly and ignorance."

We are to follow Jesus. His mannerisms are exquisite. Are ours? Do we answer the telephone gruffly or hurriedly as if we were working for the fire department? Are we polite and kind in cheerful greetings to the Fuller Brush Man or other salesmen? If the grocer inadvertently selects the wrong item for us, do we flare into a rage? Let us weed out any such fault today. It is indeed folly to think we, at times, can act like growling dogs.

A growl is often a polite way to curse. A curse is the devil's way of prayer. How many times do we use his prayer book? And we must not forget that he answers "prayers" immediately. We should offer a prayer, as David often sang, that we might be delivered from the evil tongues of people (meaning the cursing and cunning).

Cursing is also to state a fact in mind as a finality of care or thought. Who are we to state that we are through with a person for life? Regardless of how many people we have met and how many we dislike, we are obligated to them in one way or another. We must daily pray for all of our friends, good and bad. Jesus has taught us that we are our "brother's keeper," and He has told us that we are all brothers and sisters. As brothers and sisters in Christ we all belong to one royal household—Heaven. It is true that personalities often clash, and that in these cases it is far better to separate with smiles and good will than to arrange for future getting together with rancorous dislikes and hatreds in disquieted hearts. We may find it necessary to stay away from certain people for the sake of our interior peace, but every time they come to mind, we are obligated to pray for them as we do for others (see Lk 6:27–29). Cursing has a way of changing the facial expressions; a cursing person often has a curled lip. Let us watch our own smile, for it is the high-relief work on God's tabernacle door. Let us smile, smile, smile, and remind ourselves to be glad, for life is only a breath—to curl not the lip and sour not the heart. A loud voice, cursing, evil jests, and dirty jokes are the earmarks of a low culture. In these matters, it is imperative that we remember we are of the royal household.

Have our tongues and mind-tongues been like flyswatters killing flies on a barn door? How many times have our fire-throwers caught a friend? Do our flyswatter tongues have long handles? Do they reach into the private affairs of neighbors' chambers? Rodents have a way of scampering through even open windows—we may each be one—are you?

SCRIPTURE STUDY

Read Saint Paul's epistle to the Thessalonians concerning charity (4:9–12):

> But concerning brotherly charity there is no need for us to write to you, for you yourselves have learned from God to love one another.

For indeed you practice it towards all the brethren—make even greater progress. Strive to live peacefully, minding your own affairs, working with your own hands, as we charged you, so that you may walk becomingly towards outsiders, and may need nothing.

Father, I think I should explain that the psalms that I have been quoting are taken from a small book entitled, *The Perfect Prayer Book: My Daily Psalm Book* arranged by Father Frey. New English Translation from the New Latin Version, Director of the Confraternity of the Precious Blood.

Father Frey writes, "We must make these psalms the expression of our own *personal prayer-life*. In the enemies of which David speaks so frequently, we can see our own spiritual enemies: Satan, sin, and temptation. The deep love for Jerusalem expressed by the psalmist we can take over and apply to the Church, to Christ Himself. You need not say all the psalms as given for each day. It is well to choose those that fit your present needs and circumstances."

I have read somewhere in Catholic literature that David was a figure of his time for Christ. David could not practice the indwelling, as we have the privilege, because of not having received the Blessed Sacrament. But from time to time he was lifted up out of himself into rapture or ecstasy and there visited in a special way with God the Second Person. In those experiences, David understood the indwelling. His colloquies, better known as psalms, are often expressions of his conversations with God the Second Person as though the Second Person spoke through him.

For example, Psalm 21 [20] reads,

"O Lord, the king is glad because of thy strength, and because of thy help he rejoices exceedingly!"

The word Lord was often used in the old Law in reference to God the Father, the First Person. The "king" spoken of here could mean the Second Person. The king was singing in gratitude for the time when he would live on earth as Jesus. When, in the psalms, we sing with David the songs he sang according to his memory, they apply to all of us in application to self and conditions of life as if Christ, the indweller, in this new dispensation of time were singing through us.

SCRIPTURE STUDY

Psalm 109 [108]

"O God, of my praise, be not silent, for they have opened a wicked and deceitful mouth against me."

When we practice the indwelling we, too, can expect to have reproaches and rebuffs and lies told about us. This was foretold by David in his colloquies.

"They have spoken to me with a lying tongue, and surrounded me with words of hatred, and attacked me without cause."

We are of the blessed age of his gifts and knowledge and may expect bitter hatreds from people who are not of our faith. And we can expect them without cause.

"In return for my love they accused me; but I continued to pray."

Let us follow Him and pray for our enemies.

"And they have repaid me evil for good, and hatred for my love."

When we understand that it is Christ continuing His suffering in and through us, we are given courage to stand the ingratitude given us when we have tried to defend truth in both words and actions.

"Set thou a wicked man over him, and let an accuser stand at his right hand."

No doubt, David was trying to tell us that nations would attempt to set and would set wicked men over and above Christ or in His rightful place of authority. Governors in high places symbolize on the "right hand" [see Mt 22:44, Heb 10:13, Rom 8:34] according to authority. Russia has set itself against the Church by a few men in "high" places.

"When he is tried, let him go forth condemned, and let his plea be in vain."

David is seeing the life of Christ in even us and how he will be condemned, and how his plea in us will be taken in vain. The Russians are suffering this pain. Who other than God knows that we, too, may have to follow this line of persecution?

SENSE MORTIFICATION AND APPLICATION

This week we must curb the sense of hearing. If we hear cursing—even on the street—or overhear an evil joke, we must move a bead on the counter. In reparation for each bead moved during the day, we shall deny ourselves a certain program on radio or television or recording on our record changers. And if we ourselves curse in thought or action, we must move two beads and for every bead moved find an ugly thing, for example a willow about two feet in length, and arrange it in a vase of flowers or alone in a vase on a table. At the end of the week, according to the number of willows, we shall visit the Blessed Sacrament and pray fifteen decades of the rosary. Keeping the willows for a month in our bedrooms and allowing them to remind us of the times we have scourged our Lord with our tongues will provide us with a means for recollection, contrition, and firm resolve to curse no more. If we have been so unfortunate as to find several willows, we may take a month to make the required number of visits. Each time we must pray the fifteen decades (reparations for *one* willow)—the fifteen mysteries each time the fault or sin is committed.

Devotedly,
Cora

Ninth Letter Lesson

(SIRACH 11:15)

March 8, 1954

Dear Father,
Without the knowledge of discipline, life would be a dizzy path of whirls that could astonish the strong and kill the weak. But we must remember that weakness can be made strong with discipline, and that the yoke of calmness can become the fragrance of roses. Crosses do become sweet when we know why, reason and hereafter in the plan of God. Obedience to discipline is to smile at the thought of future expectancy for the flight of eternal life which is God's love. Through discipline, the joy of that trip can be most beautiful to both mind and will. If we find the thought of the eternal trip fearsome, then it is time to question ourselves, "Why?" Through reason, we know that death comes to everybody—no one escapes the process of dust. Death is a must and should be looked upon as something wonderful and joyous for souls who have loved God. Jesus, the good Shepherd, has said, "Fear not!" Why, then, do we not obey?

Fear (see Wis 17:11) is self—the proud old mule who would rather seek the shade of earth and the cool nook rather than the knowledge of reason brightened through the discipline of the five senses. Let us willingly leave the dizzy path of life and its folly for the calmness of God's heart-shade. Heart-shade is the nearness of His hand overshadowing us. We of the royal family cannot escape His cloud unless we shatter the golden chain that binds us to His communion rail. Let us not resist the chain of strength and its discipline of Church laws (see Wis 6:19–20). Through love we can polish the chain and make it stronger with the steels of courage and fortitude.

Even though we are in His cloud of wisdom and shielded with the prized coat-of-arms, we too must feel the wind, rain, and sleet. The royal family feels the cold as well as the orphans outside the wall. But with His grace we should understand the cause, reason, and wisdom of life and fear not the hour when death might come, for what have we to lose?

Severe storms that cripple and mar human hearts can often be erased if we so choose and take the necessary time searching for the answer. We shall seek men of knowledge and wisdom, and they will teach the philosophy of patience, time, prayer, and reward for eternal life. And other storms are often puzzles for even the most learned, but if we follow men of wisdom, as if they were our grandfathers who always give gifts to us children at Christmas, we will be rewarded. In time, there is always a day when broken hearts find Heaven's glue— there is enough for all and for even the smallest fragment.

True, certain hearts will be crushed through evil hands and crushed against the wall, and fragments may be lost for long periods of time, but God will find a way to mend that heart if we choose to listen, study, pray, and foster discipline for the future cause of joy that could come from that storm that wrecked home, culture, future security, and even hope for the day. God, the Weaver, mends His tapestry slowly, but perfectly, and even better than it was in the beginning. Let us help Him with the threads of black which symbolize dismay and discouragement—with the red threads of martyrdom which unwind from the heart of pain and broken love—and with the golden festival threads, gladly given, for gold enhances the black and the red. God will weave over the devil's mar and spear-point tears.

Porcelains are admired for their translucent beauty. A Honan porcelain, the queen of the ancient porcelains, is described as "blue as the sky after rain, when seen between the clouds, as clear as a mirror, as thin as paper, and as resonant as jade." Ancient porcelains are also admired for their weathering, their meticulously mended breaks and cracks by master artisans, and for their heat- and cold-glaze fissures. We, and even our children's children, may continue to admire them because of their lasting or enduring qualities due to "minute particles of weathered granite" in their composition.

Our hearts closely resemble the Honan porcelains in their many qualities. May we each close our eyes and meditate upon our own heart? Is it blue as the sky in the Blessed Mother's beauty? Has is suffered the cleansing of the rain—monotonies of life accepted? Is it seen by others as residing within the cloud of God the Father? Is it as clear with truth and as witnessing of His truth as a mirror? Is it thin as paper in conscience or thick and calloused by imperfections and neglect? Is it resonant as jade in charity or as "sounding brass and a tinkling cymbal" (1 Cor 13:1)? Will it endure and will its beauty live on in the minds of others because of our frequent reception of "minute particles of weathered granite"—our CHRIST THE (tested) ROCK (see Is 28:16). It is well to remember that a heart without a mar in mended chip cannot tell of battles won and victory because of a Samaritan's love in the cloak of "brother's keeper," who gave aid in the saving of the pieces. To escape from clefts or fissures in our hearts is not to know the frost and warmth of spring. And in times of misfortune or of trying, we must remind ourselves that an unmended or broken heart knows not the gift of wisdom nor the Master Artisan.

It is applied wisdom to stay away from a person with a heart so smooth, an unbroken ice which should tell us that its hardness—self—has not given of itself in the slightest degree. This person has won only victories in defense of self. This person has not known the Master after his original glazing. It would be folly to listen to his voice. He is a keyboard of one key. He is an escapist. To escape in any form of life is to become a "hooky" player. A person who reasons with the thought of hooky in any form of his vocation is not a *loyal* person—his crown is dim and insecure—he shares not what little light he may have with his friends. He becomes an ill-managed person who gives not the love of hospitality.

How eagerly we learn the systems of hygiene for the body and the necessity of fighting germs, but are we as careful about the hygiene of our souls? Preservation of health is the most necessary art in life that the soul might live, but are we guarded for the preservation of health for the soul? Is our own soul so weak that it complains at the least little headache, as if searching for a reason to become a hooky player in the bed of sloth for the day? In any vocation, every person has his rules and work to keep. Are we in the march and in step? Let us live life (our vocations), and God's grace will be sufficient if we discipline ourselves to value time, loyalty, care, and calmness. It is progress and life to encourage pursuit of our vocations. All vocations are interesting and of value in the eyes of God. Each is its own field of great hope, possibility, and art. What have we mastered in our vocations?

In the married state, *hospitality* is the middle C on the keyboard of life. Are we hospitable to husband or wife? That is the first lesson, and it is mellowed with kindness, charm, smiles, and loyalty. Are we hospitable to the children whom we have invited to come and live with us until they are grown? They did not ask to be born; man and wife asked them—they are a family of guests who have agreed to come under our house rules. Are we hospitable to friends? How often do we ask Jesus, His Mother, and the saints to visit us in our homes? How often do we give parties in their honor? Hospitality is a means of making someone a king or a queen for a day or for the hour. Have we given such honors to anyone recently? At least once a month, let us share the delightful gifts of hospitality with someone or ones outside the immediate family (see Rom 12:13). Share the needs of the saints, practicing hospitality. Let us pretend that we are honoring Mother Mary and Jesus. Preparations must be done in calmness, for our guests have the discernment gifts. Have we raised our voices at a servant or member of the family because we thought the preparation processes were not moving as they should? Mother Mary and Jesus can see the harm and wound on an injured person's heart even more than they can hear our voices in greeting. Let us be careful, for they are with us all the time. Even a scrubwoman or servant janitor must be regarded as God's child. Who are we, then, to belittle them?

If admonishing is necessary, we must do it quietly and out of hearing of the household. We are all keepers of the "way" of life. A storekeeper is a child of God. A telephone operator is also of the royal household; do we speak to her rudely in voices of demand and command? Do we answer the phone with "hurt intrusion" in our expressions? Hurriedly? Mercilessly? Gruffly? If a street sweeper brushes his broom close to our feet, do we scream? Do we remember that the plumber, butcher, grocer, repairman, and chore girl are all children of God? He can see and feel our scourges on human hearts. He can see the effects of our greeting given in kindness. He can see our admonishing in calm quietness with respect to culture and God's creation, the human soul. Do we blush at the past? Then, let us seek the ivory flush of calm quietness by treating each and every one of God's children with kindness, especially in voice, stemming from an abundance of love in our hearts (see Mt 12:34).

A human hooky player is a red squirrel. He is an escapist. He scampers up trees and frowns upon humanity chattering incessantly; he knows not hospitality. Are we fostering only the animal in us? The animal soul knows only preservation from hunger—not eternal gain. Are we any better than the red squirrel "who mounts his pulpit on the branch of a tree—well out of harm's way and proceeds to scold, chatter, and tell the whole world about it"? If we practice hospitality with Jesus and Mary as honored guests, we will soon come down from our false pulpits and chat among God's friends (or God-given friends) about eternal gain. Conversations about the hoarding of nuts, the nerve of marauders about our properties, and broken limbs whose hollow makes a comfortable nest from winter storms will not be missed.

Do our friends see God in us and in our hospitality? If not, then seek a physician of the soul and one for the body, for illness is near. Saint Thomas writes, "There are men and women who do not know God. *They are made for happiness. Ignorance* commits them to *frustration*; they have eager hearts, pushed to the breaking point by all of nature's demands for happiness, but these hearts have only the wrong places to go" (see Prv 15:17; Sir 30:18, 31, 32; Is 58:10–12).

Are our homes the *right places* when we practice hospitality? Are we showing the path to happiness? If, through us, they seek happiness, do we throw a boulder in their paths? Does an angry tongue cause frustration of any kind? If we are guilty, we are going to suffer a long purgation in Purgatory (see Sir 28:17–26). We are writing our own quarantine. Kindness in the love of reason and love of God does not frustrate anybody.

Jesus was not an escapist. He was not a hooky player. He was earnest. He was real and loyal. Are we? If we are really living the indwelling, can we be otherwise? He IS and is with us! Jesus could have made excuses for the day of the Crucifixion. He could have made it another day. He could have been suffering from a "preventing" severe head-ache. But He lifted His cross and carried it for us without complaint. Do we follow Him? Simon of Cyrene is the symbol of a physician—when we need help, he will be called. Medicine will help us lift our crosses. Jesus went about His vocation to suffer and die for us. Are we following His "way"? Are we allowing Him to continue His steps of loyalty in benediction through us?

SCRIPTURE STUDY

Our Scripture study is in the thoughts of this letter lesson and Matthew 27:34–37.

> And they gave him wine to drink mixed with gall: but when he had tasted it, he would not drink. And after they had crucified him, they divided his garments, casting lots, (to fulfill that which was spoken through the prophets, saying "They divided my garments among them and upon my vesture they cast lots"). And sitting down they kept watch over him. And they put above his head the charge against him, written, "This is Jesus, the King of the Jews."

The wine mixed with gall is the symbol of what our tongue gives to people when we are angry. It is bitter; it could kill. And it could make one drunk with frustration. Are we guilty of offering vinegar and gall or wine and gall? Let us die to self. Let us fulfill our way of life until the end (death), and then if our wealth or possessions happen to be divided among thieves and sinners, or according to that which would not ordinarily be our will, we should ask ourselves: are we any better than Jesus who did not say to whom His robe would be given? Even while He was dying, the sinners were casting lots for it, and yet He knew of what worth it would be to the world in future generations. First, (see Mt 6:25–34) we must seek to build up treasures in Heaven, and then all things will come to us according to that which is good for us in life. It is meant for some people to be poor, others rich, and others to embrace the medium way of life. People in the different degrees of wealth, poverty, health, sickness,

and cares of all kinds build greater knowledge for the future generations. We are all in the plan of God. He taught us not to be solicitous
(see Jer 17:7–8) over that which we wear nor that which we eat—we
must trust to the providence of God—does He not care for the spar-
rows? Yet, at times, they freeze to death and even starve, but who are
we not to say it is in the plan of God? When we see the needy, it is
through us that we must show the abundance of God if we have the
means to help others (see Rom 12:9–21). Through man, God works,
smiles, and blesses. We are our "brother's keeper."

If we are meek, quiet, and kind, our enemies, too, will sit down and
wait. That waiting, to see what we are going to do next, could mean
their conversion if we are patient and cheerful in all kinds of suffering.
People naturally love watching joy in all things; then, let us suffer joy-
ously (see Heb 10:32–39), so much so that anyone watching us could
exclaim, "This must be the way Jesus suffered in patience, that man
may show it in his deeds. This person must be a citizen of the King."

Our life is to be our scriptural study in meditation according to Psalm
145 [144].

"The Lord is gracious *and* merciful, slow to anger, *and* abounding
in kindness."

Are we gracious, hospitable, and are we merciful? Are we slow to
anger? Are we abounding in kindness?

"The Lord is good to all, and merciful toward all his works."

Are we good to all? Are we merciful toward all His works? Do we
appreciate and care for a means of His mercy—the inventions of man?

SENSE MORTIFICATION AND APPLICATION

This week we must mortify the sense of touch. Every time we find
ourselves escaping or playing hooky from a certain duty which is ours,
within our vocations, we must move a bead on the counter. For each
bead moved on the counter, we must take a tub bath without using
soap (we may use soap on hands and face). Also, for a general mortification for having in our past life given scandal to people, we shall

crumple a sheet of tissue paper and insert it between our own bed pillow and its case (a fresh sheet of paper each night). The noise should remind us of one of the many pillows made from dry leaves, which the Master no doubt used in His lifetime during His travels searching for us. Also, once a day, we shall scrub with soap one article in the house or garage such as a tub, basin, comb, brush, stove, white side-walled tire, or anything else that needs a cleaning, and while scrubbing sing a song of praise that we, too, can be cleansed through the confessional (singing may be done in whisper tones). We must not forget the priests' many hours spent in work, prayer, and study that they might, through God, scour our souls.

Devotedly,
Cora

Tenth Letter Lesson

(MATTHEW 6:33)

March 15, 1954

Dear Father,
Are we barbarian invaders of ourselves and others? We know from the writings of Saint Francis de Sales that we should be gentle with ourselves. Doubtless, we are watchful about our bodies, cold, heat, health, and the knowledge of eating proper foods, but are we as careful with our souls? In the laws of the great ascetics, we know they often flogged themselves as penances for themselves and others. We, who are not given to such orders and private laws, are allowed to frown upon those disciplines, but little do we realize the floggings we give our souls with needless and disturbing penances which are not good for the soul.

Actually, we are barbarians with invisible hooks and racks and most unmerciful to our souls with our mind-inflictions. These self-imposed inflictions are undue worry, loving attachments to the scandals of neighborly affairs and those of the press, and the failure to place our lives into patterns of law and order. We cannot work too diligently at replacing the "barbarians" with law and order. The "putting off" of these barbarians who flog us by the hour is the beginning of "seeking first the Kingdom of God," which is an order from God. Can we have peace if we are continually wrestling with a savage? If we fail to whip him now while we have the strength and life, we will meet him face to face at the hour of death. We cannot escape him; he is the devil's tool. He is clever, particularly so, at the hour of death.

It is then that he uses scrupulosity, a tool that is deadly to the soul. We must cast the barbarian from our souls *now* by daily working—a manner of wrestling—by the hour, for the greater glory of God. It is part of the war of life. Every day [our barbarian] will try new tactics, and so we too must be prepared with new vigor and strength (see Mk 9:48–49). We must not wait until we are upon our deathbeds to say, "I haven't the time now to seek the kingdom of God." And let us never make excuses for ourselves if there is a tinge of sloth in our makeup by saying, "I wasn't well enough to do this or that." Or, "I didn't have an education." Some of the greatest saints could not read, but they talked to God. He instructed them in humility, loss, patience, and poverty of soul (see Mk 9:22–23) as well as in poverty in life. He made them great because they did not *shirk responsibility* (see Lk 8:46–47).

Perhaps it would be well if we considered this quotation from a good book: "Very few people have the opportunity to seek the kingdom of God at the end. Christ, knowing that religion was a thing for our life, not merely for our deathbed, has laid this command upon us now: 'Seek *first* the kingdom of God.'"

If we obey this command, we must not escape responsibility (Acts 5:29). Every day together with its trials, joys, and sorrows is another step in the pathway to God. At will, we make our own stairway sway or calm, fold as an accordion, or even become serpentine, but we can never get off the stairs until we reach Heaven or fall into Hell. That stairway, if it becomes serpentine, could bend far into the purgatorial schools. Why should we take a detour? Let us keep our own stairway straight by staying steadfast, with law and order in our mental makeup as well as in the care of the body and its surroundings.

Neighbors are often barbarian invaders, too, of our peace and way of life with God. We must learn the art of gentleness and fortitude if we live with or close to a living barbarian. There are many men and women who, even though they are dressed in a finery of culture, would look more natural in nose rings and straw skirts. Are we barbarians in the wrong dress or men's apparel shop? Are we misfits in the wrong country? Let us redress ourselves into that state of life into which we were born or belong and act as we should. If we are so unfortunate as to live with a nit-wit who wants to stay a barbarian, let us suffer in patience (see Lk 21:19; Sir 2:1–5; 1 Cor 9:12; Heb 10:23–24, 35–39). Even a savage, in time, can be tamed through the touch of gentleness, kindness, love, and understanding. It might be necessary to use baby talk and manners to win a soul. But perhaps we are going to say that we are above that? Did not Christ become a babe for us? To Him, we were barbarians. Christ in His infancy cried as any other child. In His crib He kicked His feet and bumped His nose with His chubby fist. Are we childlike that we may win souls? Are we willing, at times, to become jesters for Him? Are we acting any given hour of life for Him? We must become little, childish, and even stately and diplomatic with the changing hours and moods of people—all for Him!

Private virtues of self soon become green meadows for other people. We can and should become the playground and way for people who have slammed the door of responsibility because of discouragement (see Jer 2:13). Happy is our lot if they seek our park for rest and God's mending inspiration. Happy also is our lot when we find in our park an inspired beginner who was attracted there by the warmth of His sunshine through us. Do we offer them all hospitality, kindness, and love? Christ did!

Responsibility should be a perfected virtue in us. I have often called the virtue of responsibility the good wrestler. He is a fighter. A good fighter is quick on the draw—do we sense the wants of others? He is quickly "on foot" and clever with his hands; he is usually credited with having a good, calm brain.

Now, suppose we should advertise ourselves as the wrestlers to our neighbors by the day. We advertise ourselves to God every day. We are like signboards, and He sees everything about us. Let us suppose that God made a law that we should advertise ourselves by the hour by writing on a bulletin board about our virtues. We would be shocked, humiliated, stunned, and ashamed of ourselves! In particular, should we be ashamed to be the agent of a virtue named *responsibility*? He is part of us. How have we cared for Him? And now suppose the bulletin boards had to be posted upon our front doors for everyone to come and read at their leisure. If this were possible, it would stop gossip; there would be nothing hidden from anyone. Personal shame and the rise to perfection would overtake pride. And superiority would end because we would have nothing of self to brag about.

Shirking responsibility is an educated way of saying, "I am deliberately slothful." Are we double-talkers? Suppose that in our shirking duty in slothfulness, our angels posted our bulletin boards on our doors. Doubtless, we would read something like this:

> This hour—this woman or man has failed in duties and responsibilities.
> She failed in her duties and responsibilities.
> She failed to raise the window shades in her home (body) which would allow the sunlight to creep in. (Morning prayer)
>
> She did not think about the beautiful horizon and the sunrise. (The ciborium—the horizon and the Host rising before us in the priest's hands.)
>
> She did not get up this morning. (She refuses to contemplate the life of Christ. Jerusalem is only a thought away—closer than our nearest neighbor.)
>
> Her house is untidy. (She refused the art of application following Christ's life in this hour of life. She forgot that she was an apprentice.)
>
> She failed to eat breakfast and now suffers from lightheadedness. (She failed to make spiritual communions, and virtue is leaving, causing her to become cross and weak.)
>
> At this hour she is dressed in a sloppy kimono and is trying to be a loud-mouthed magpie. She has gossiped by the hour over the phone and has planned an eleven o'clock coffee with neighbors who assuredly will tell the private affairs of their husbands and family. What a terrible thing—to sniff through soiled linens. What a drippy snooper she has made of herself! Dirty linens are scattered throughout the house. (She has forgotten to make frequent examinations of conscience.)

We sigh and say, "Thank God, the bulletin idea can't ever be true!"

But it is true in the sight of God. Let us hope the bulletin reads, in the usual and good way of having overcome details, "There is a good fight going on in this house." God will understand and not expect us to become detailists.

SENSE MORTIFICATION AND APPLICATION

We each may be our own judge. Every time we have shirked a responsibility, we must move a bead on the counter. The following are a few norms for judging:

- Are we on time (within reason) with our duties?
- Did we raise the window shades?
- Did we watch the Son rise (Holy Mass)?
- Have we been "doers of the Word" in application and thought?

For every bead moved, we must scrub a foot-square space on linoleum, cement, garage floor, bathroom floor, or drain-board surface—one square foot and no more. While we are scrubbing it clean we should think about how small we actually are and how little we have made our world by the restrictions of undone or unfinished duties. Also, for each bead moved, we shall say five Our Father prayers in reparation.

Our general mortification is for us not to file our fingernails for the week. In the event of a snag, we may use scissors. The use of fingernail polish is forbidden to us ladies for the week. If we do not ever use it, we shall use the clear polish and keep it in good condition.

Our sense of smell must be mortified this week by daily bathing in the cheapest bubble-bath fragrance we can purchase or bath-salts of a disliked fragrance. Or, instead of the usual hand lotion, we may use two drops of vanilla flavoring on our hands. If, on the streets or at work or during recreation, a bad odor comes our way, we shall inhale deeply—all the while thanking God with a Glory Be to the Father prayer that we may suffer it instead of Jesus—believing that we, instead of Jesus, are taking it (someone's odious affront) and that by this act of love we are wafting incense heavenward in its stead.

SCRIPTURE READING

Titus 2:11–14, 3:1–9; 2 Peter 1:8–11; James 1:19–27

2 Peter

"For if you *possess* these *virtues* and they *abound in you* they will render you neither inactive nor unfruitful in the knowledge of our Lord Jesus Christ. For he who lacks them is blind, groping his way, and has forgotten that he was cleansed from his former sins. Therefore, brethren, strive even more by good works to make your calling and election sure. For if you do this, you *will not fall into sin at any time*. Indeed, in this way will be amply provided for you the entrance into the everlasting kingdom of our Lord and Savior Jesus Christ."

Saint James (in part)

"Therefore, casting aside all uncleanness and abundance of malice with meekness *receive the ingrafted word*, which is able to save your souls. But *be doers of the word* and not hearers only, deceiving yourselves."

Psalm 131 [130], resignation to the will of God.
"O Lord, my heart is not proud,
nor are my eyes haughty."

We might be dressed in ermine and wear jewels according to our state of life, but only God knows that our heart is not proud in spite of the state of life. In practicing the littleness of self, we must not allow a haughty look to escape our eyes. Does an infant in a crib know how to give an icy glare? Neither do I deal in great affairs nor in things too lofty for me. There is only one affair in life, and that is to attain the love of God. We are all going to be saints, but don't ever let the thought arise in our minds that we are better or loftier than the poorest beggar who might be disguised in rags where we might be wearing jewels. We must not seek either education or awards just for the pride of having the diplomas or honors. We must seek them only if we want to be Samaritans and lend help to those suffering under oppression or as means of fostering better understanding in human relationships and appreciations of culture patterns through knowledge.

"Truly I have climbed and quieted my soul."

Can we truthfully say that we have tried climbing the ladder to perfection? To have done so is to know that we are quieter and calmer than we were a year ago, and that we love the silences of life better than the amusements that once enraptured us.

"As a little child on its mother's lap; as a little child,
so is my soul within me."

Are we good actresses and actors for God? Are we gentle with self? Are we careful with our souls as we are careful with our bodies? Do we stay away from sin and places of sin as we would a sign on a house that reads "smallpox"? Are we well balanced on this scale of truth?

"O Israel, hope in the Lord, both now and forever."

We are the children of Grandfather Israel (Gn 32:28). We have his heritage upon which to draw. All the merits and good works of ancestors are with us as helps. Are we holding torches for those who follow us? Or have we lost the path for someone by not leaving our footprints in the sands of time? Our hope is the hope that all may live for eternity in God's joys and His particular love which we, the children of Israel, have been promised.

Devotedly,
Cora

Eleventh Letter Lesson

(ISAIAH 51:12)

March 22, 1954

Dear Father,
Our little world (the body) may seek and have Heaven's delights on earth if we know and love God as He desires. God has given us many blueprints and maps through the channels of His Church through which we may choose the way or span of happiness, as much as the world may offer, or the path of sorrows. From the earth, our hearts, and leading to Heaven's door are many bridges. Some of these spans are great and majestic while others are as if they were knotted and tied, rough ropes hardly possible for man to tread. Many people travel over these or over spans of cobweb threads with their open dangers and sticky entanglements. Would that they would seek the great and majestic for though they are various, they are the strong, well-lighted paths foundationed on the firm rock (Peter; see Mt 16:18–19). Some are seemingly lowly and unadorned—those chosen by the penitential saints—though in reality they are glorious and emblazoned with jewels; some are exquisite, gossamer in fragility, and yet they are all paths or spans hallowed by the glistening dust from the feet of saints.

Let us in meditation watch the people, like spiders or their victims, clinging to the webs of little grace. If we could read their hearts, we would see two faults in every case: (1) disturbed because of a friend or relative and (2) restless in the pursuit of happiness which they do not seem to ever have. People are disturbed because of troubled hearts over world conditions, faith, and what other people may think of them because of their religious convictions and zeal, state in life, or circumstance. People are also restless because of fear and lack of faith in God, governments, and people, and in even themselves (see Jn 14:27–28). Fear is the cancer of the blood—it strikes upon every member of the body (see Wis 17, 18:1). Fear is usually a reliving of something in the past. Let us cease being old in mind. Does an infant remember the hour of his birth? If we are to remain childlike, we must forgive and forget. Did we (you) ever think that within the meaning of "charity begins at home" is the forgiving of self and the forgetting of the past? We must forgive ourselves for what we may have done in the past that is disturbing and live for today with God's grace. Fear has many fingers which reach into the future—this meddling is a useless thing—for we have no guarantee that in the immediate or remote future we will even be alive on earth. The future belongs to God and His providence—we must stay too little to peer over that bridge which is *time*. And FEAR of pending death is a useless vanity. Can we cheat death? Death is a cloak of ecstasy for all the good and a cloak of misery for the bad. Let us remember that we are of the royal household and each stay as a prince or princess who would rule his or her subjects with calm, and not with fear of what might happen tomorrow or next year. Calmness of mind shall be greatly rewarded! If we fear death and judgment, then we are not thoroughly cleansed from major sin. And we might as well say aloud that we have forgotten God's mercy and the blueprints and laws in the form of maps which He has left us in order to find our ways out of the hedges and across the vast space to Heaven's door. This minute we live; the next we are not sure of. Therefore, we must hope and know we are in the state of grace. If so, what have we to fear (see Is 43:25)?

It is true that there are daily trials from earthly enemies and happenings in life—either social or national. These happenings are for the most part not sinful to us. Righteous indignation is not a sin (see Eccl 1:18). A rebel must be brought to justice—that is not a sin. A mother must correct her children—that is not a sin. A banker must be firm with his tellers—that is not a sin. But people should, if they love God, become justifiers with themselves and others. They should use logic and reason and then firmness for the more perfect way. Jesus did not raise the whip over the money changers without first having used logical reasoning. It is wiser for us to count to ten before acting but wiser still to make use of ten logical reasons why this or that should be done and in what tone of voice and manner of actions before acting.

That action which we logically find ourselves bound to do must not disturb our interior peace. If we find ourselves being scrupulous and without peace of soul, then we are lacking in the balm of knowledge (see Prv 12:1; Sir 21:21). We must study that which we lack, whether it be history, logic, culture, language, voice, music, economics, philosophy, or the government of what is expected of us in our state of life. Peace and fear do not mix. We must follow the Master, and, in His peace, keep them separated.

A good means to eradicate fear is to rejoice at the least of little things. It is something like counting our blessings. So the practice for us for the week must be for every time we have feared or become scrupulous, we must sing aloud—whispers if we must—a thought of rejoicing. Let us rejoice in God's goodness and mercy. How many times have we rejoiced with God that He has made us a member of the royal family? Do we rejoice that we can execute wisdom and love over friends? When we are wounded, do we rejoice that we can engraft its hurt into Christ's wounds and make it His will? Do we rejoice that pain so engrafted is never wasted? Do we rejoice that through the Morning Offering prayer, we do not waste anything unless we fall from grace? Do we rejoice that we can hear children's laughter? Do we rejoice as we listen to the meadowlarks' call or the drone of bees? And do we rejoice that the blue of the sky can be invisibly painted with rose, gray, or pearl? We may certainly rejoice that cleanliness is known and is almost a must in this nation. Do we rejoice that we were born of good and clean parents? Do we rejoice that the sorrowful orphans outside the walls of the City of God can be heard (see Ez 47:22–23) and that the Master Himself leads them in to His banquet—the Mass? We shall learn to rejoice that we can smile and *find God in the little things of life* (see Job 12:7–8).

And the real soldiers of God, mostly the happy ones confirmed through the bishop's hand, find the broad King's highway on the great span of whichever bridge of Heaven's fairway they choose. Proudly they march beneath the great banners hung by the dead of an ancient past. They appreciate the gift that they are torch-bearers of a living faith. Their faith is the contemplative realm, where hourly they soar aloft into the eons where *with God there is no time*. Often, they find themselves to be citizens of Jerusalem, actually pretending that they are speaking to Jesus. The true contemplatives know the symbols of the banners that fly across the bridge in the elevations above them. They are billowing black, gold, white, and red. They love telling about the red as martyrdoms, and the gold as celebrations and banquets at God's table. The black are the happenings of nations and foes that make them thank God for the wisdom and logic and reason preventing their fall into despair and hatred. As proudly they tell that black is beautiful in the depth of trials for by it the red of the sunrise is enhanced, they rejoice that they have seen the black and the red. White, they tell us, is the glistening diamond of purity of body, intention, and soul (see 1 Thes 4:7–8).

Contemplatives tell us that they are the real "doers of the Word" (Jas 1:22). They are Samaritans who keep their pearls (Mt 7:6) hidden from the people along the roadside as they pour freely the wine of smiles, cheerful laughter, and kind words of encouragement to all (see Sir 30:27).

Their goal along the way of life is to find their personal friends. "One-minded" groups and people [gather] at family reunions where conversations on the glory of God and His nearness are told, taught, and believed; believe His words, "Where two or more are gathered together in My Name, there am I in the midst of them." He manifests Himself in many ways (see 1 Cor 12:7–11): in His gifts, in His creations and in Himself (see Jn 14:21). He longs to be with His children (see Prv 8:31), and He often instills quiet peace among groups who love Him. At other times, His peace may be felt through smiles, encouragement, and praise of deeds. He loves to give consolation through His living members. Often He pours forth His fragrances—they are His invisible smiles. The contemplative knows He is near. And often Heaven's dew is seen to be falling like snow or rain, yet never filling a space, and music rings throughout the crystals that rise and fall like slivers of unending caresses. These spiritual friendships must stay together in mind and in prayer—all for the love of God! Disruptions come when bridges jar or cross one another with friends who are of the meditation's world or those who love treading on the cobwebs of little faith. Understanding is a must in this dilemma of confusion, lest the soul become disturbed. Understanding is to know that in the great Church are three worlds: one the contemplative, one the meditative, and the other the slothful. We must become a teacher of wisdom standing before a class and knowing full well who is an A student and who is a B and C member. With this wisdom, there is no chance of throwing pearls before swine and washing them through tears of regret. The knowing of the A, B, and C student in the plan of life is not judging (see 1 Cor 11:17–19)—it is knowing our own in God, knowing our own strength and what we should do. However, this knowledge must be used with great ethical care, lest we scandalize His little ones who are still growing into the "A" stages of life with Him.

A Samaritan with his hidden pearls and flask of "wine" (smiles and laughter) cannot be a "doer of the Word" with wishful thinking. Saint James said, "faith . . . without works is dead" (Jas 2:14–26). Are we dead? Do we quickly rise to the fight for the higher life known as the contemplative life? Have we helped to polish a gem or raise a banner for generations to be born, on the bridge of contemplation? Let us stand guard on that bridge of ours and watch our cheerfulness, carefulness, loudness of voice, cheap culture, and speech with worldly slang about ourselves as if they were mice trying to run through the arch of the bridge. We must stop them or take a reprimand from the Master, for no mice are allowed over the bridge. Every mouse that gets by the guard of our intellects sounds a key as if it were running over a piano keyboard. What a terrible melody! Let us shoo them away lest we awaken the rest of Heaven. For these mice, we need a constant guard who is the priest in the confessional—his is the only trap for such beasts. He has a trap for every size of rat whether it be as large as an elephant or as small as a baby mouse, and its size and ugliness never scandalize a priest.

The room of asceticism must have a key, and that is the confessional. With these [asceticism and penance] together, we are quite free to doze while we stand guard on our bridge. The "rest" is ecstasy and rapture when the Master beckons from His tower. Let us be ready for the divine call when we stand on the bridge of sighs and smiles with its wisdom and knowledge of a grand old past.

Let us consider as we stand watch how Jesus would have acted if we had seen Him in life. Can we imagine Christ having a loud, boisterous voice? Was His walk blustery? Did He freely use slang, especially when He spoke to children? Did He belittle good, holy thoughts and actions? Did He hate the pageantry of color, culture, and national custom? Did He make the mind of man blush with awful jokes? If Christ had exhibited any of these faults, what would we have thought? Would He have been an ideal? If we follow Him and yet engage in such practices, then we are making our own report cards for our conditional stays in one of the classrooms in the Purgatorial Schools where we the "doers" must undo the sloth we have lived.

Knowing that God is a God of order and peace (1 Cor 14:33), we must strive knocking at His door (His Heart) with childlike asceticism and in a methodical manner. The slow, methodical way is the only safe and little span or "way" to God's great arch and door of Heaven. It is sheer folly to begin the ascetical climb with periodical attempts and then lapse for weeks and months with the thought of beginning again. It can be done, but it is dangerous. Asceticism is not a frolic for jitterbugs and scatterbrains, nor is it like a Fourth of July, one-day celebration. It is a steady climb for those who seek not a vacation for self.

Let us keep a rigid adherence to His raised baton, for someday on the downbeat He will summon us to give an accounting of self, discipline, culture, and education that we have learned through living life and vocation and what we have accomplished with its gift. He may ask, "Have you hidden your light beneath a measure?" (Mt 5:15). How would we answer? Would we try saying that we did not realize that it was sloth and that we were just too timid? Would we have to add that our zeal would not allow us to tell of Christ outside of our bedroom doors, lest the neighbors think we were strange?

Perhaps He would answer saying, "I made you a soldier at confirmation. A soldier knows none of the laws which you have spoken, nor would a commander tolerate them. Why have you failed to take the sword of trust and fight until death?" Facing Truth, we would not make excuses such as "we were afraid," for in knowledge we know the Scriptures tell us He said, *"Fear not!"* Why have we not obeyed? We must weed out *fear* from our souls, along with the tumbleweeds of sloth and timidity. Timidity must not be confused with weakness. It is true that the Scriptures also tell us that *fear* is the beginning of wisdom (Sir 1:16). True, we should fear stepping down from our bridges into the cobwebs of worldliness. In case happenings in life, business, or war bring about these effects, we must guard ourselves with prayer, calmness, and the "flask of wine" of cheerfulness and care lest we fall into the snare. Fear is the fullness and the crown of wisdom in that prudence is its fulfillment (Sir 1:18,20), but *fear* is not the completion of wisdom because fear will gradually disappear the less we are obliged to step down into the world. Fear is lessened if we do not scatter our pearls before swine—but there is nothing wrong about our scattering our smiles, cheerful manner, and worldly gifts. We are of the royal household and wear the purple of a King. We are always on our way to a banquet whether it be today, tomorrow, or next year. Let us keep the hems of our garments clean and free from dust. Let us be well groomed for the banquet.

The greater wisdom without the taste of fear may be gained through the virtue of submission and obedience to the Church laws. Submission is the outward sign that we are willing to learn. Do we have the awful courage to say, "I know everything. There is nothing else to learn." We cannot be saved in ignorance. Scripture study should be like a left hand to our mystical body and the willingness to listen to the voice of the Church our right hand. The study of history, too, is of prime importance if we are willing to help unwrap a twisted mind because a grandparent refused to keep his ears close to the voice of the Church.

A thought for the week taken from a good book is: "Have you ever noticed how much of Christ's life was spent in *doing kind* things—in *merely doing kind things*? Run over it with that in view, and you will find that He spent a great proportion of His time simply making people happy, in doing good turns to people."

SCRIPTURE STUDY AND APPLICATION
FOR THE WEEK IS "FEAR NOT!" (IS 41:10)

Fear makes for slothfulness. Are we slothful?
  Fear removes the armor of a soldier. Are we defrocked?
  Are we fearful that God will not be known among men?

What are we doing about it?

Are we afraid of the mortifications? They are the polishing cloths.

Are we (you) afraid of the cross God has fashioned for each of us? We must "try" picking it up—He said the yoke would *become* sweet. "I will give you rest" (Mt 11:28–30).

Are we afraid of suffering? Was Jesus afraid? Was He forced to pick up His cross (Jn 10:18)?

Are we fearful that our zeal will make friends talk? "Blessed are you if you suffer" anything for His sake (Beatitudes).

Are we afraid of going overboard on religion? We can go overboard on religion but not overboard enough for Jesus (scrupulosity). We must not go overboard with "pamphletitis" and "candleitis." We must not go overboard with false piety in long faces and downcast eyes. It is to His greater glory to go overboard on smiling. We must not go overboard with the beads. Rather, let us remember to just talk to Jesus and His Mother.

We shall practice daily saying to everyone we meet, "God bless you."

Study: Psalm 89 [88]

"I will sing of the kindness of the Lord forever; with my mouth I will make known thy faithfulness through all the ages."

Does a fearful heart sing? The above is a pledge of happiness, for happy we must be if we sing forever about His kindness. Let us not forget to sing praises to God for His priests in the confessionals who daily renew the washing of our baptism through absolution. "With my mouth I will make known thy faithfulness through all the ages," is understood that if we are timid and question what people will think of us as going overboard, how are we going to sing His praise? Are we guilty of not making known the Master and His kindness?

"For thou hast said: 'Kindness is set up forever'; in the heavens thou hast established thy faithfulness."

Can we imagine any part of Heaven as not being kind? Kindness is the atmosphere for all eternity. And it is the gentle breath of Heaven on earth when we are kind. "In the heavens thou hast established thy faithfulness" may be understood as the truth of Jesus speaking through Peter and his successors. "What is bound on earth is bound in Heaven"—God is faithful to us; He does not lose patience (2 Thes 3:3–5); His faithfulness is forever.

"I have made a covenant with my elect; I have sworn to David my servant."

The "elect" spoken of here means the successors and priests of all time—since David. He has made this promise with David.

"I will settle thy offspring forever, and I will establish thy throne throughout the ages."

"Settle" means a final order—something not to be subject to change. A priest and his powers are forever [Sir 45:30, Christ's priests Heb 7:17]. The throne of Peter is to be lasting throughout the ages. Shall we meditate about the dreams David's tribe must have had about a throne through them that would last forever and not be subject to change or overthrow?

Verses 15–18

"Justice and right are the foundation of thy throne; grace and faithfulness go before thee."

The everlasting throne of Peter is ruled by justice and right. Justice is the foundation, but grace and faithfulness on the part of God to us has come before the foundation of the throne through the birth of Christ and His death and the coming down of the Holy Spirit [1 Cor 3:11].

"Happy are the people who know how to rejoice; they walk, O Lord, in the light of thy countenance."

The contemplative people are the most happy. They know how to rejoice even though their hearts are weeping because of the happenings of the world. "They walk" could mean see the face of Jesus—He does not stay hidden from those who walk with Him. Walk is an expression of trial, work, and fortitude. The true contemplative knows and believes that "where two or more are gathered together" in His Name, there He will be with many of His divine impulses which may touch any one of our senses. The divine impulses touching upon our senses are a consolation and should make us happy. Having God this close what have we to fear?

"In thy name they rejoice always, and by thy justice they are exalted."

First, David speaks for us in this generation since Christ. He is telling us that we will be strengthened by the practice of the indwelling. Christ is our splendor. When David speaks for his own generation, by the favor of God honoring the lineage of David their might is exalted. How blessed we are in this generation. Are we making the best of this happiness and joy, or are we filled with fear?

Every time we have deliberately stepped down into a lower culture or stooped to uncouth manners, we have exhibited actions unworthy of a member of the royal household. If we have mentally feared what our neighbor or someone might think of us for any circumstance or action, we have had thoughts unworthy of a member of the royal household. For either of these "unworthinesses" and according to the number of times they have occurred, we must move beads on the counter—one for each time. For every bead moved, we shall do reparation by writing a four-line verse using the word "fear" and "dear."

SENSE MORTIFICATION AND APPLICATION

The sense of taste must be mortified this week by our each eating a large, dry, shredded wheat biscuit. With it we may drink a glass of warm water. This is a good practice for overcoming a silly fault of old age, which makes us think we must have a set pattern of whims of likes and dislikes. We shall pretend that we are behind the Iron Curtain, and the biscuit is all we have as food. We must eat it with relish and not with the usual groans and frowns. We shall not forget to offer the mortification to our Lord for the starving people in the world that they might find food.

Rejoicing even drives fear of old age away.
Old age with us does not hold sway.
With Christ we have gone away.
We smile knowing of a better place and a day.

Old age move away.
Asceticism is a new name—it is grace—

Old age of set ways move away.
Fear is nothing but old ragged lace.

Devotedly,
Cora

Twelfth Letter Lesson

(MATTHEW 6)

March 29, 1954

Dear Father,
May it please God that every word I write become the cement of restoration, rebuilding, and making anew that which destruction and illness brought to souls through heresy and complacency. That invisible monster swings his axe and hammer at our gates (hearts; see Ps 74 [73]:5), and heresy fire-throwers set the sanctuary on fire, and that which should be a holy dwelling place has been profaned (see Ps 74 [73]:7).

How easy it is to take our gifts of imagination back to the time of King David, but are we traveling with that ease in the short span of today, and what today will teach, are we willing to learn? Let us pretend that we are in a plane at an elevation of sixteen thousand feet. The contrasts of security are so different than when we are on earth. Temporalities, such as bank accounts, diamonds, furs, and whether or not someone is wearing a crown account for nothing in security while we are in the air. It is a lesson to be far above security, especially if we have placed our trust in earthly means. Air travel has a way with the hearts of men—they turn to God, and happy are those people who do not fear death and can look out over and enjoy the immensities of God. In the "immensities," all can share with David his flights into ecstasy and understand his reasoning and why he called upon all things to give praise to God. David knew he had dominion over the things of the earth. Do we realize that in our will we, too, share in that command?

David could not be tied to the earth and its simple numbers when he thought of God. So it was that in his colloquies he called upon the immensities, knowing that his invisible command was answered through *will*, for well he knew that God had said to Adam that he had dominion over the earth. It is the most perfect way not to waste time and to attain *purity of intention*.

The highest expressions of adoration to God are praise, love, joy, and thanksgiving. These expressions belong to the higher form of prayer known as contemplation. Where there is true love and when one is completely absorbed in God, is there anything lacking? Let us rise above the animal nature and, in the calmness of His way of love, live life to the best of our ability and according to our vocations in life. Today is today and upon which our eternity could depend; why do we, as individuals, persist in staying the wrestler who buffets yesterday and tomorrow, which do not exist?

We are suddenly awed by the magnificent patchwork design of fields and the panorama of color blending beneath us in our speeding plane. The earth, in its design like an old-fashioned quilt, fascinates us, and we find ourselves wondering to whom each square belongs and thinking how much fun it would be to actually know. Why should we wrestle with curiosity? It belongs to God. All things on earth He has only loaned to us that through them we may love Him more and use them as charity, gifts, and needs for ourselves. Since He has loaned us everything, should we not strive to properly care for and appreciate the gifts of earth? Do we deliberately mar our friend's fence, car, chair, table, or garden? They are God's gifts to us, too, and He will ask us at death about their care. How are we going to answer?

And from the plane window we see a blue lake nestling in a twist of brown rugged earth—we smile in wonderment at the littleness of earth, for does not the lake remind us of a robin's blue egg in a nest? And the myriad droplets of silent white foam on the ocean breakers are the frost-touched aspen leaves broken loose from the trees of the forest?

What a shock is it to us to realize suddenly that the earth has grown so small because we are so high. These flights are not lasting—and so with the plane we, too, must come down to the meditative world, grow strong, refuel with grace, and ready ourselves for another flight where we see only God and not the ugly and sordid actions of man and devil-ploughed earth from earthquakes and floods; where we hear only God and not the cries of friends and the roar of cannons. Even a blizzard and its hazards when we are in "flight" would appear as a beautiful, billowing curtain at a friend's window. To see God only in all things in the moments of contemplative prayer is *purity of intention*. Only in that peace as above the earth in a plane may the truer love and praise expressions be given from human heart to God. We must, for moments a day, rise above "self," things, and needs of creatures and just love Him in the delights of being absorbed in Him. We must remember in these moments that *true love wanteth nothing*.

The plane ride offered us new horizons—the earth was smaller, yet we watched it in a broader sense of delight, and like fledglings resting in the shrubbery, we dream again of flight, and we strive for the greater purity of intention which will lead us there. In the arts of contemplation, we learn that the expressions we once gave in petition are now "listen" (see Sir 32:9), for well we know the wisdom of old that "God speaks quietly to a quiet soul." Can we be quiet in soul if we are filled with petitions? Are not petitions the effects of squalls? Did not the Master say and command the storm (that storm could be within us), "Peace, be still!" (Mk 4:39)? Calm comes when there is peace. It is true that in the meditative world of prayer there is a certain type of peace and calm, but not in comparison with the contemplative life of prayer. Shall we sit or kneel alone quietly for at least five minutes a day and close the pages of life that need a particular care of petition and rest—bask in God and His quiet, and praise Him if we wish with a Psalm of David?

Psalm 148:1

David understood at will the power of his command over the things of the world and in their numbers, unknown to him; he is ordering them to praise God for him.

"Praise the Lord from the heavens, praise him in the heights."
David is in his heaven—contemplation. From these heights he will praise the Lord.

"Praise him, all his angels, praise him all his hosts.
Praise him, sun and moon, praise him all you twinkling stars.

Praise him highest heavens, and waters that are above the heavens.
Let them praise the name of the Lord, for he commanded and they were
    created.
Praise the Lord from the earth, sea monsters and all depths of the sea.
Fire, hail, snow and fog, stormy winds, that do his bidding.
Mountains and all hills, fruit trees and all cedars.
Wild beasts and all cattle, reptiles, and winged birds.
Kings of the earth and all peoples, princes and all judges of the earth.
Young men and virgins, too, old men together with children;
Let them praise the name of the Lord, for his name alone is sublime.
His glory is above heaven and earth, and he has given great strength to
    his people.
A theme of praise for all his faithful, the children of Israel, a people near
    unto him."

Let us be the people who stay near to Him with praise, love, and thanksgiving.

The two languages in our lives are meditation and contemplation. They are different and beautiful, and both are needful for our well-balanced growth. A pendulum of a clock swings evenly in order to keep the perfect hour. Let us balance our hours with the care the jeweler uses in the perfect regulating of a clock. In our meditative world of prayer, we practiced childlikeness that life is a petition, and it is a good habit to pretend that we are the little Christ Child asking His Mother for this or for that. And oftentimes she caresses and consoles, as any good mother would, her child. But in the contemplative world, we are grown and practice the indwelling, saying with Saint Paul, "It is now no longer I that live, but Christ lives in me" (Gal 2:20). It is now that we practice the life of Christ and become totally absorbed in God the Father. He said to His Mother, the symbol of the meditative world, "I must be about my Father's business" (Lk 2:49).

In the meditative world and when we offer a rosary for one or five intentions, that is good and charitable, but during the day we should offer a rosary to God for Him to do with as He wills. That is purity of intention—that we do all for the love of God without telling Him how to spend the gift we are offering.

SENSE MORTIFICATION AND APPLICATION

Let us strive to offer more perfect gifts, but knowing our weaknesses, it is necessary to restrict the senses and where they would take us. Sight is the sense to be restricted this week. Every time we would ordinarily pick up a newspaper or a magazine to read, let us reach for our Bibles and read Psalm 1. We shall then meditate upon each word in an effort to find the deeper meanings.

Happy the man who follows not the counsel of the wicked,
Nor enters upon the path of sinners, nor sits in the assembly of the
  insolent;
But his delight is in the law of the Lord, and he meditates on his law
  day and night.
And he is like a tree planted beside streams of water,
That yields fruit in due season, whose leaves do not wither, and what-
  ever he does prospers.
Not so the wicked, not so, but they are like chaff which the wind scatters.
Therefore, the wicked shall not stand firm in the judgment, nor sin-
  ners in the gathering of the just.
For the Lord takes care of the way of the just, but the course of the
  wicked shall end in ruin.

Our failure to read the above is to move a bead on our counters. For each bead moved at the end of the day, we shall read ten words in the dictionary with their meanings aloud and offer all these penalties in reparation for the sins committed through bad reading.

Devotedly,
Cora

Thirteenth Letter Lesson

(PSALM 22)

April 5, 1954

Dear Father,

It is a good daily practice to pause and ask ourselves, "Do we believe God cannot be outdone in GENEROSITY?" We must have a mental yardstick applied to truths before we can truthfully answer. Tradition has built the ruler and guide for us, but what conclusions can we truthfully draw for ourselves by saying that we know He cannot be outdone in *generosity*?

First, let us think about His title "The Good Shepherd." Can we imagine a good shepherd build stringy [being stingy] and selfish and acting without prudence? None of these apply to the Jesus whom we love. Could He have been more generous than to institute the Holy Sacrifice of the Mass—to perpetuate the Last Supper in its gift of anticipation that we, too, may share in the gifts of supernatural wonders even in this twentieth century?

And because we are such little children, we could naturally look to a good shepherd as one giving gifts. Could anyone be considered good and not give gifts? People win for themselves the title "good" because they give generous gifts of worldly treasures which they may have gained, or through hospitality and even the humble smile and chuckle. To think of Christ as the Good Shepherd, we naturally "see" Him in contemplation walking in green pastures beside a crystal stream of water in the dusk of evening, where the bleat of the lamb tells that all is well. The sparrow flutters madly in his dust bath of warm earth, the sun tinsels the leaves and bark of trees, and a kitten claws and stretches on the green pasture grass. These languages please the Master. They are not complaints. Their actions are the enjoyments of God's providence. Let us suppose we could run to His side as He sits beside a boulder for a back rest and lays His staff across His knees. Would we dare intrude upon His solitude and peace with our noise of complaints? If we are thoughtful people, we would simply thank Him for His *generosity* and ask Him to teach us the gifts of kindness, hospitality, and how to be generous as He would want us to be as children of the royal family. Notice, we are asking to be taught! These gifts cannot be mastered in a day or in a year. They are like the five senses which must be constantly worked on for perfection.

The Good Shepherd is the "way" of life, the Master of all perfections for the teacher and the mystic. He blends all His teachings for all. Often, He shows the way to the contemplative life by suggestion and then He expects people to become thinkers, inventors who dare spread their thoughts beyond the horizon that their mortal eye can see.

Let us sit beside Him and enjoy the green pastures where there is no fear. The caw of the crow scolds in her way of unknown language—no doubt, she is still scolding Adam for taking away her peace. The wise-looking owl shows his humiliation for the earth in such a way that he comes out at night, and his call is *who* has brought this misery to our land of peace? When little creations suffer and do not have the reason to think conditions out for themselves, why should we complain, when we know the reason for suffering (see Heb 13:12–13)?

Let us be still and listen to His breathings upon our soul. Let us know that God speaks quietly to the quiet soul. In our minds let us keep the thought in contemplation that we are with Him in the quiet green pasture. The language through which He will teach is known as the joys of the Orient on High (see Lk 1:78; Zec 6:12), where words are not necessary nor are they used; it is His generous caress upon the senses which causes us to speak in colloquy and learn from the feelings of joy that please us. To many, God gives the distinguishing gift, and they make the Orient joys a discernible language of earth.

Watch—Jesus is watching and listening to a hummingbird near a flowering shrub. Ah, the mind staggers at such knowledge. Here is a lesson for a day. And let us watch the avenues of mind and where it takes us because of the shrub, little jet wings, and a something we know as a little bird with a long, thin needlelike bill through which it sips the nectar of the flower. God put life (soul) into the seed of the shrub. The breeze planted it. The rain and sun and dust storms were the implements in the Gardener's hands, and the seed grew into the shrub. God planned the color and shape of the flower. It is something like a trumpet—no doubt, God was thinking about calling His followers through the tones of horns, and so He formed the trumpet flower. And the grown shrub is shade for beast and man and refuge for the birds at night. The hummingbird comes to gather the honey of the land which has found its way into the throat of the flower. All this is the providence of God's *generosity*. The deep roots of the shrub embrace the earth and tie it into a bond of security, and the mountain stays in place in spite of the rains and the snow. Because of the shrub, man is safe to walk in the ravines—is this not the generosity of God in His providence? How often do we thank Him for the little things in life that mean so much to our existence?

Every day this week we shall mentally find five things which we either see or use and think about their history and how the providence of God created each for us. What have we done for God in return? The tongue can say that we are thankful, but the greater way is to act and show appreciation by protecting the property of the community, homes, and gifts about us and even our pets, for they are all God's masterpieces, ruined through Adam. We, by our care, are privileged to restore them to some degree of perfection. Training a rose climber is the same as mending the Master's torn toga. Let us renew and make anew everything in our power and all for the greater glory of God. He was born to restore us (Heb 9:26). Let us, through willingness and with helpful hands, restore something in our homes or about ourselves each day—that is, restore something to a better condition than it was in yesterday. Suggestions:

1. Replace old shoe laces with new
2. Mend a piece of clothing or plant a flower
3. Repair an electric lamp or iron
4. Retouch, with paint, a marred surface

God does not waste a thing. He puts everything to use; do we? Are we hoarders—what about the attics and cellars? Is there anything there the poor could use or make anew?

The Good Shepherd teaches many mysteries through the little things of life, and if He wants us to appreciate them with His loving care, then how much greater should our regard be for human beings? Are they not God's masterpieces of infinite worth? Perhaps He will show us a little of the mystery of man at prayer on the many rungs of the ladder in his climb for perfection. The human race is His flower garden; evil has changed some of the flowers into weeds, but through grafting and care they could be made beautiful again. Are we helping the Gardener to graft souls who have never heard of Him into the strong vine of the Church? If not, is it because we have not listened carefully to His words in Scripture and His way of life in prayer and overcome the wild animal nature within us? First, we must conquer "self" before we dare venture into the convert war for souls.

Let us watch with Him a rambling rose climber. Its blossoms are deep pink and the fragrance is sublime—what is its meaning? The long vine sheets travel far, and there are many; some even climb to the house eaves and peep over the roof. There are others that find a dark cellar window. The vine growth seems to be without restraint. But wherever we find the blossom, it is beautiful and brings smiles to even the scrub woman who might be working in the cellar or to the sick child on the second story as the rose finds the window of his room. Other roses might find their beauty shared by nothing other than a cobweb with minute baby spiders. The rose petals, as soft as velvet, might become the tiny spiders' lush carpet. God loves the spiders, too. He allows a bit of Heaven on earth to even the smallest creatures. Why shouldn't they take their first steps on velvet?

And the Good Shepherd could answer that in the providence of His will, He allowed that rose to grow near the cobweb for another purpose unknown to man. In that cobweb clings a speck of dust—it is the real dust of a saint and to him and in honor of the effects of the good the speck of dust has done in benediction to the earth and people, God gave the rose this hour as tribute. Let us try ceasing our questions, and instead of asking "why," let us just thank God. Now the mystery of the rambler rose is that it symbolizes the contemplative soul. It dares to climb. True, its gifts are many times misused and neglected, but God, the Gardener, takes care of that. The rose must return to dust and then again it can begin a missionary work through blessing. Our Gardener is generous! He never wastes a minute nor even a speck of dust. In His *generosity*, all is meant for man.

And in that great garden there are hundreds of common rose bushes. They are exquisite, too, and they give great joy, but they are known as meditatives who have not dared to climb and crawl that a little sick child may see the peeping rose at her window, or that the soldier wounded in the Field of Flanders might forget his pain and reach for a rose, bringing memories that might ease his bitterness.

And the lilies in the great field, white, starched rounded cuffs with golden fingers pointing upward, are symbols of little children. Little bluebells in the dell are, in symbol, sad people who are sorry for themselves and who do not seem to be conscious of the rose and its power. They are each like the Irish tinker, so busy with his own little bell's noise which seems to annoy people; they give no thought to others and to the tones that may sooth. The bluebell people, like the tinker, never seem to find the joy of that which they claim was lost just because they have never learned to face life. Their restlessness with "self" and conditions into which they were born allow them no time to meditate nor contemplate. And look at the sunflower out in the field of weeds. He is the laughing apostate. He is neither flower nor weed. His face is always turned to worship the earthly sun of something of a bright light. He is not consistent with either beauty or fragrance. And at night he is stingy; he covers his sticky face with sticky golden fingers. What a beautiful flower he could become if he were engrafted into the true vine of God.

Now that we have seen the mystical flower garden of God and know that He is a Gardener and a Good Shepherd, reason tells us that He must weed and prune His garden. That which He is going to prune [He does] according to seasons, knowing a time and a place for everything in us. We are a part of that garden. If we are climbers, then we may expect the greatest pruning. Sister meditation does not suffer the loss of her gown and the delights of her creeping here and there—she has not known the delights. But the climbers have known the delights; they have traveled far, and so they must stand the shock of having a favorite stem cut away. They must trust the Master and that He knows where to cut, for well He knows the care for the roots, unseen by them.

To graciously accept the pruning is the beginning art and culture of submission. The roots penetrate more and more deeply into the earth after each pruning and there thrive more and more adequately upon heritage and the taste of the Rock of Peter.

SCRIPTURE STUDY FOR THE WEEK

John 10:9–10

The Scriptures are heritage food.

"I am the door. If anyone enters by me he shall be safe, and shall go in and out and shall find pastures. The thief comes only to steal, and slay, and destroy. I come that they may have life, and have it more abundantly."

"He shall go in and out" is the contemplative growth in souls. It is the more abundant life in the green pastures with God.

Saint Paul to the Philippians 3:13–16

"But one thing I do: *Forgetting what is behind, I strain forward to what is before,* I press on towards the goal, to the prize of God's heavenly call in Christ Jesus. Let us then, as many *as are perfect, be on this mind*; and if in any point you are minded otherwise, this also God will reveal to you. Still, in what we have attained let us be of the same mind, and let us also continue in this same rule."

In our meditations let us find the two lives, meditation and contemplation, to which Saint Paul refers in the above.

Psalm 119 [118]:50

"This is my consolation in my affliction, that thy word revives me."

The contemplative knows he will hear God in the quiet chambers of his heart when afflictions come upon him.

Psalm 119 [118]:51

"The proud are most insulting to me; but I depart not from thy law."

Ridicule comes to those who would fly to God—we must not turn back.

Psalm 119 [118]:54

"Thy statutes are the theme of my song—in the place of my pilgrimage."
Our theme is the desire of everlasting life, even while we live on earth.

Psalm 119 [118]:55

"In the night I remember thy name, O Lord, and I will keep thy law."
Are we willing to awaken during the night and think about His name? Shall we try it as an act of love and adoration rather than of penance? To do this we could arise from bed and sit in a chair and just visit with Him about the power of His name.

Psalm 119 [118]:56

"This happened to me, because I observed thy precepts."
David was rewarded with God's nearness because of discipline. We may share in the same delights.

Psalm 119 [118]:62

"I rise at midnight to praise thee for thy just ordinances."
Let us arise at midnight to thank Him for an hour during this week.

Psalm 119 [118]:64

"The earth, O Lord, is full of thy loving kindness; teach me thy laws."
Let us continue seeking Him and the plan of providence in all the little things of earth. It is a necessity in the art of appreciation.

SENSE MORTIFICATION AND APPLICATION

Considering that we must grow into the art of appreciation, let us think about *hearing*, which should be mortified this week. Let us mortify the sense of hearing in such a way that we would better appreciate the afflicted who are hard of hearing. Each day, especially when we want to hear music on the radio or hear some comedy or drama, we may turn the radio on at such a low volume that we cannot hear it, and tolerate it for half an hour. Or we may turn the television on and watch the performance or movie without benefit of the sound. Then, with greater compunction, let us thank God for the sense of hearing. (If other people are in the room listening to their programs we must not interfere, but without being noticed we may place cotton in our ears.)

As an additional mortification, we shall move a bead on the counter each time we hear the Lord's name used in cursing or in an ill-mannered way, whether it be at home or on the street. In reparation for the lack of respect, we may listen to a beautiful song or to just music and offer all for the love of Jesus.

Devotedly,
Cora

Fourteenth Letter Lesson

April 12, 1954

Dear Father,
During the lessons which will be written and also in thought of those we have read, it is well to keep in mind that the prescribed mortifications in the letters are not acts of foolishness. Weighing any subject in its logic is to know both sides of a subject; therefore, let us meditate upon sin and its foolishness when we compare discipline and mortification as a necessity in life.

In the eyes of God, sin is man's foolishness. Sin is to raise the flag of defeat over ourselves. Sin is not only foolish, but it is ridiculous and unnecessary, because that which we do in sin we must undo through the confessional, penance, mortifications, and reparation, as well as live with a sick conscience. If these lessons suggest acts for reparation that seem foolish to the normal way of life and thinking, it is well to consider what clowns we are on the stage of life and of what little worth we are. Penance suggestions and acts of mortification are definite impressions on the senses which make for our lives patterns for better or worse. Does not a silly-acting clown make impressions on a child even more than a trained mouse? Impressions on our souls from application in the *spirit of penance* are the brakes against future occasions of sin. Actual mortifications are necessary in the ascetical life to stem the tide of "self" for contemplation. Let us become as impressed as a child who watches a clown fall face down, bend backward, kiss the floor, and try drinking from a glass bottom-side up. If these strange, unnecessary acts can be accepted in the light of pleasure, then let us reverse them as means of penance and mortification. These impressions received in childlike interests are soldier guards placed round about us.

The more sin is impressed upon us as ridiculous through sorrow and mortifications, the more our souls are repulsed at sin. Let us become attuned through childish penances to know the ridiculousness of sin. The lack of KINDNESS, such as a child can give, is often the cause of sin. Let us view the subject of kindness in a greater light according to the laws of the contemplative.

Charity begins at home (the body), and this is also true of the virtue of kindness. The more we are kind to self, the less sin we experience in life. Saint Francis de Sales admonishes us to be gentle with self; also we could say that we must be *kind* with self; these are the inroads to perfection. When we consider the word *kindness* we find ourselves tipping the evenly balanced scale of life toward the thought of sentimentalism, which also has its place, time, and reason for its use in life. Sentimentalism does not mean for us to be gushy or loud. *Kindness* is often shown with outward gestures and expressions that are classified as *kindly* sentiments.

The first ideal is gentleness and *kindness* to self. Let us remember that charity begins at home and that home, as we have learned, means the body. Our body is our real home on earth. *Kindness* must become the movable tapestry in our home.

Let us ask ourselves a few questions as guides for the higher rule toward perfection.

- Have we classed intellect as a person known to Mother Superior who is in charge of five postulants, the senses?
- Has Mother Superior regarded the five senses as willing souls wanting perfection?
- Has Mother Superior been kind and gentle?
- Has she allowed, without any corrections, any one of the five postulants to over-indulge in food, drink, unnecessary pleasures, work, or sleep? And are they stingy with prayer, the atmosphere of their true country where they may inhale the eons' culture of silence, love, and peace?
- Have the five little sister postulants chosen good companions?

- Does any one of the senses think it has been endowed with the overflowing of zeal, with which it may reform everyone to its way of thinking and living?
- Does the postulant *hearing* deliberately listen to gossip, thinking she may win a confidence? Is it worth it to undermine her own strength?
- Do they applaud exaggerations?
- Are the postulants kind to self in dress?
  - Are they modest?
  - Are they clean?
  - Are they checked daily for poise?
    - How do they sit, stand, eat, and drink?
    - Are their manners qualified to be a diplomat?
    - Are their actions dignified to become singular in their state of life?
    - Are they inclined to become singular in their state of life?
    - How is the "sound box" of *voice*? Is it harsh, raspy, and hard to listen to because of static, which has not been ruled out because of carelessness?
    - Is voice moderate in tone and speed?
    - Does voice have a north-wind whine? If it does, lower the tone and speak gently in imitation of the breeze of the south.
    - Are the sentences murdered? Does the tongue chop them in two? Are sentences ended with a musical tone which indicates indecision rather than with a period? (This annoyance could cause people interior anger.)
    - Does the will want to use good English? We shall ask a member of the family to correct our English three times during the day as a general mortification.
    - When answering the door or phone, are the postulants on guard? Are manners and voice courteous? The person to whom we speak could be Jesus in disguise.

Let us strive to be favorable in all the listings above. To be favorable is to be assisting, and the art of assisting is to make people happy and that is *kindness*. Every day, let us hope to make someone happy through the kindness of our talents, gifts, culture, smiles, and cheerful chuckles.

It is wisdom to think kindly of all God's creations and children. The worst storm will always bring something good. And in the worst of sinners there is something good and kind within their natures.

But with people it is wisdom to know the diets of each and how much of the richer desserts can be served. As an instance, let us say that when a contemplative is in the company of meditative people or those of a worldly nature, silence, in regard to the richer desserts, is the better food. It would be foolish pride to expound asceticism and the rise of the soul to meditative people, for they do not know the deeper meaning of the parables, and we could be the means of their indignation and contributing cause of a whirlpool in their little minds, which could lead to gossip and ridicule. It is better that silent self stand ridicule, rather than throw pearls before swine who know not their value.

It is far more advantageous with certain classes of people to discuss the events of the day and national current events. Also the "cuteness" of children and their talents is a good, holy subject which does not expose the pearls. This is a charity that is kind to both self and friend, and both will fully appreciate and realize the kindness and watch over tongue on the day of judgment, for both will have less to answer for in the mind of God.

Become a kind diplomat for God and His gifts as well as a disciple in His guise as a Samaritan. Acting upon these laws of wise conduct, we have a right to be a convictionist. A kind convictionist has the good manners to listen to the other person's story in a kind, attentive manner. We must not become whifflers. A WHIFFLER is ever eager to wave his flag with rudeness in the middle of a sentence or conversation. A diplomat listens in equal measure that he speaks. A whiffler is a person who frequently changes his opinions and even his course in life.

- A whiffler is always on the side that is winning.
- A whiffler is not loyal to self nor friend.
- A whiffler is sort of a tramp by habit—never satisfied.
- A whiffler is a chronic worrier—he tackles the job of worrying by the hour rather than having that item in its place and hour.

Worry makes us slaves to self, and too much self brings on the illness of selfishness.

Whifflers are a terrible annoyance to self and community, and their effect may often be felt across a nation. We must learn to be *kind* to God and His friends.

SCRIPTURE STUDY

Use its application to self in following Christ.

Colossians 3:12–17

"Put on therefore, as God's chosen ones, holy and beloved, a heart of mercy, kindness, humility, meekness, patience. Bear with one another and forgive one another, if anyone has a grievance against any other; even as the Lord has forgiven you, so also do you forgive. But above all these things have charity which is the bond of perfection." (Bond means guarantee.) "And may the *Peace* of *Christ resign in your hearts*" (indwelling); "unto that peace, indeed, you were called in one body."

(Friends—as one together in mind and purpose.) "Show yourself thankful. Let the word of Christ dwell in you abundantly; in all wisdom teach and admonish one another by psalms, hymns, and spiritual songs, singing in your hearts to God by His grace. Whatever you do in *word* or in *work, do all in the name of the Lord Jesus,* giving thanks to God the Father through Him." (All this should remind us of the importance of the Morning Offering.)

Let us strive to become good imitators of the Good Shepherd. Any expression that is good is also kind.

Psalm 23 [22]

"The Lord is my shepherd: I want for nothing; He makes me rest in green pastures."

We are proclaiming with David that the Lord is our Shepherd. To do so is to believe that we must remain loyal to His voice, the Church. To digress from this rule is to be eaten by the wolves. The kind Shepherd makes His lambs rest. He knows there is a time and place for everything in life. He knows lambs are weak—He understands our weakness with flesh and blood. Can we imagine a simple lamb being a whiffler? "Green pastures" signifies His will for us in all good. He wills that we rest in green pastures. Green is the symbol of hope—the disposition of our will living close to Jesus. If we are well disciplined, we will have hope, and that virtue will allow us to have a foretaste of Heaven while we yet live on earth. This rest in green pastures is the symbol also of resting for the greater run: the contemplative life which is over the hills and high upon the mountain.

"He leads me to waters where I may rest; He revives my spirit."

Clear waters are the eons above the earth or anything earthly. They are another symbol of interior peace from where contemplatives drink the knowledge of God. That delightful repose is the "rest" David speaks about in the psalm. Is it not reward for being kind to self through the knowledge of discipline that spirit is revived?

"He guides me along the right paths for His name's sake."

Christ is the Shepherd. He is the Guide and Teacher. He guides us along the right paths of life. His nooks of shade are prayer, and the crystal streams in the pastures are the symbols of the Blessed Sacrament upon which we may drink our fill. All is done through His name.

"Even though I walk in a dark valley, I will fear no evil, for Thou art with me."

A contemplative may work and travel among evil men, which the dark valley of life symbolizes. But if we practice the indwelling we should have no fear, for can Christ fear? Can anyone make Jesus sin? Remember, He is the indweller! He is our strength. At will, we can turn evil into good by the simple method of willing all trials and sufferings to become engrafted into the sufferings of Jesus when He lived on earth. That which would ordinarily be wasted suddenly grows into something beautiful and meritorious. How true, He permits evil to roam the earth—it is a battlefield filled with terrors. It is a testing field for us to show through our fighting whose flag we'll stand beside. He did not promise this world to become a bed of roses nor something to be desired for all eternity—this world is not our true country. If we are rising in the right spirit, we should feel homesickness and pilgrim loss in this world even though we have the natural gifts of ermine and gold.

Christ was a pilgrim, and He knew loss and He knew poverty. The Son of God did not have as much as a pillow upon which to lay His Head. On the cross He heard cursing and blasphemies, and today it is the same as then when we allow Him the indwelling within us. Through us He hears cursing and through us He sees horrible sins, and all He expects of this clay shell which we have loaned Him is a silent tongue except when it is used as the songbird of prayer in praise, gratitude, and thanksgiving. Let us follow Him. He did not repeat one word of cursing that He heard when He hung on the cross. Let us become "dead ends" when we hear or see sin—this is another way of being kind.

"Thy rod and Thy staff; these comfort me."
The rod is the symbol of the Church and its authority. And the staff is the symbol of laws given us, through which we may govern self. Self-discipline comes under the shadow of the staff. The shadow of the staff is also God's hand outstretched over us in blessing: Isaiah 49:2.

"Thou settest a table for me in the sight of my enemies."
Since life for us is to mix even with enemies and yet not be overcome, it is well in those troubled hours of anxiety to remember that He the Good Shepherd is preparing the table and banquet for us. He has already given us the invitation, through His Church, to come to Him. And if we are polite people, we will delight with the hope of that hour to meet at His table. Just think, we are going to a banquet table soon, maybe tomorrow, next week or within the year, but always we carry the invitation. We are always welcome.

"Thou anointest my head with oil; my cup overflows."
Our priest, another Christ, is waiting for us. He is our Host. He is serving the banquet. The priest is one of the anointed ones, and when we follow him closely in life through the sacraments and obediences, we become co-workers with him and may even say we are co-anointed ones at the banquet. The cup overflowing spoken of here could mean that David is using the term "cup" as a symbol for our body. How true: at the banquet we are filled with goodness and His kindness to a state of overflowing. He is never outdone in generosity.

SENSE MORTIFICATION AND APPLICATION

For every time we think we could have practiced kindness and then failed to do so, we must move a bead on the counter. At the end of each day, we shall mark on a calendar the numbers that must be remembered on the last day of the week, when we may try to do a penance of reparation.

The sense to be mortified is touch. For each number of beads moved on the counter during the week, we shall touch that many tombstones in a graveyard as we take our walk alone, praying for the dead. As we touch each tombstone belonging to someone whom we do not know, we may think that perhaps their death was sad because they had not practiced kindness. We could reflect that we, too, will become dust. Will someone remember us because of our kindness?

Devotedly,
Cora

Fifteenth Letter Lesson

(ROMANS 12:13)

"Share the needs of the saints, practicing hospitality."

April 17, 1954

Dear Father,
The subject word for our consideration this week will be HOSPITAL-ITY. It will prove to have a strong relationship with the subject of kindness in the previous letter lesson, except for a little difference in tone and individual thought according to the different races of people, their customs, and their heritage.

Kindness in its general term of knowledge can be practiced by all people, from the savage to the king of any land. But hospitality draws a line of sharpness in view of tradition, customs, and tribes of people when and on what stand it must be executed. Generally, hospitality is not as easily used in spontaneity of action as the expression and acts of kindness.

In the reflection that we are to follow Christ, and that He is our model in all things, we must look to Him for guidance. Anyone who is a true maker of laws in His way of life as shepherd or master leaves His followers a plan or blueprint, drawn by His associate's hand, for them to follow. The Scriptures are our visible blueprints. Let us consider, in view of hospitality, the Paschal dinner. Jesus was at the head of the table. He must have been a wonderful and ideal host. Little do we realize, aside from the birth of the Holy Eucharist which would follow that dinner, that He the host was giving us a lesson on the charms of hospitality.

When the feast was over, He wanted to do more for His guests. He wanted to give them something more than the usual dinner. He gave them Himself! Giving more than is expected is the greater hospitality! How often do we follow the lesson He taught? Hospitality and its many cloaks of kindness live for centuries; are we leaving our footprints in the sands of time? One step motivated by a generous heart, hospitality could mean invention and progress or the giving of children who may carry on the torch of good deeds. Are we in any way stopping the assembly line of cheerfulness, joy, understanding, hope, and love of neighbor and God? If we fail in these items, then we are guilty of not raising the flag of hospitality.

And, let us see how far the effects of hospitality stay with us; do we ruin a good work? Can we imagine after the long, trying evening at the Paschal dinner and after the guests had departed that Jesus would sigh and say, "Thank God that is over"? Or could we imagine He would say, "Never again—that was too tiring"? And do we think a good host in His guise of hospitality would say in ridicule to one other member, "Don't you think John could have worn a better toga? He was certainly poorly dressed for our group." These are the petty remarks and long noses that would govern even our neighbor's wardrobe. Let us keep to our own business. It is well and good to say that someone looked lovely and the color was bright and cheery—we must not overlook the good in anything. Hospitality should last long after the party. Even to complain of tiredness and the hope that it would never happen again is to ruin the good effects of hospitality.

Mystically, the upper room to us has grown into a palace with many rooms. Let us think of every room as a banquet room. And every room is furnished with an altar, a throne, where Jesus receives us as visitor or child. Let us think about His joys when we visit Him; could we imagine His sorrow if we spurned His love? Could we as children of the royal household spurn His invitation to stay for the banquet—The Mass? And let us notice, even though He has asked us through the voice of the Church, He is not overbearing nor demanding. Neither does He coax us to stay and eat; He allows us to use our own free will. He quietly invites us to come and we accept or decline. As children of the royal household, we must be ready at all times to extend the welcome He would expect us to give as ambassadors.

The Church is our mother, the tutor. Does not a little prince of any natural kingdom practice through years of discipline, culture, and the arts in order to become a diplomat? Then why should we resist learning the fundamentals of the higher culture? There are such things as proper poise, proper voice, and a kindly way of giving little attentions that make His friends feel welcome. Whether we are of the cloister, in the married state, or in the world of the single groups, the arts, poise, and culture must be practiced, for all are His ambassadors and co-workers with His priests. Whether we live in a tent, hovel, house, apartment, or palace, we must remember that we are His chosen ones, and we must live and act the part by following Him. Any breach of manners is not even expected from a prince. How do we act? The following suggestions are means through which quiet, kingly manners and quiet peace form the body.

- We shall each examine our voices. Are they raspy, shrill, or loud? We must perfect them.
- Are we butterflies flitting here and there without general purpose? (Meddlers or flying insects just showing off our colors?)
- Are we doing our work in an even tempo of movement? We gain nothing by haste or hurrying. A quiet, effectual, and measured pace is a better way for the preservation of interior peace.
- We must school ourselves to avoid asking pointed questions concerning details of health, earnings, inheritance, prominence, or [lowliness] of ancestry, etc., either by blunt questioning or allusion to ourselves.
- A prince knows the value of privacy. Do we delight in showing the family tree in pictures from albums? Do we not realize that change or personal looks and national styles embarrass the person or persons whom we are exposing? It is wisdom not to show or display a picture, except for very rare reasons, of any person—expect Christ and the canonized saints—that is over five years of age since it was taken or painted (if the person is living).

A great degree of hospitality is an extension beyond the ordinary member of the family (see Heb 13:1–3). How often are the poor sheltered or given a smile of welcome within the confines of the home?

Are we hostile at intrusions that might disturb our rest, peace, and plans for the week or month? Jesus could not find peace in the world— even when He sought it in a boat crossing the lake, people followed Him. He did not scold them nor say, "I haven't time."

But for the grace of God, we could have been Simon the leper. How would we have acted if we had been Simon who was entertaining Jesus when suddenly a woman entered and poured out her perfumes from an alabaster jar over the Master's head in blessing of love? Would we have raised an eyebrow? Would we have ordered her out? Would we have said, "This is a breach of manners"?

Let us suppose that at a bridge game or party, someone started talking about the life of Christ. Would we raise an eyebrow thinking it an inappropriate subject? Would we mentally push that person from our group and label him or her as a fanatic? Would we say, "This is a breach of manners"? Are we not willing to listen to scandal, divorce, murders, and many other items about the events of the day, even though we are in a card game? Scripture says, "Woe to the man who will not listen to Holy Scripture." Gospel means "good news." Let us be willing to listen to the best news regardless of who, rich or poor, beggar or leper (symbol of sinner) pours out the words of perfume.

SCRIPTURE STUDY AND APPLICATION

Mark 14:3–9

Why was Simon the leper not a good host?

Hospitality can also be given in alms, smiles, visits, and prayers as well as having guests in the home. Also, we can extend our hospitality to the souls in Purgatory through prayers.

Practice mental hospitality for the souls in Purgatory or for the sick whom we cannot visit because of distance or other reasons. Let us suppose that a cousin came to the door at this very hour; how would we act? We could, of course, stop the work we were doing and visit for a few minutes and then, after the greetings and after having made our guest welcome, we would resume our work. Mentally, let us practice hospitality during the week as well as actually in any condition that may arise.

SUGGESTIONS

- While doing the dishes, Purgatory's citizen phones. Let us dry our hands and (as if they were actually present) sit with them in our living room and talk to them by saying a rosary.
- Suggestions for these intrusions from unexpected mental guests:
  - Pray the rosary while doing the family washing or ironing.
  - While [shopping], we may rest on the city corner bench and pray a rosary.
  - When we awaken during the night (it could have been the unseen knock), we shall get up and partly dress just as if we were to answer the door. We would want to appear presentable. Then, we shall sit down and pray a rosary. (This is the amount of time we would ordinarily spend in visiting with an unexpected guest.)
  - While taking a drive in a car, we may pull up to the curb and pray a rosary pretending that we were called by a friend from the curb. We shall spend as much time as we would spend with that friend in praying the rosary.

During the week, we shall study Psalm 41 [40], reading it in view of hospitality, which is also "being considerate."

"Happy *is he who is* considerate *of the needy and the poor; the Lord will rescue him in the day of trouble.*"
Do unto others as we would have them do unto us—good and bad deeds return to us in life a hundredfold. How are the trade winds going to retreat to us? How true: we reap what we sow [see Mt 7:12; Eccl 11:1–5; Mk 4:20, 24].

"*The* Lord *will* preserve *him and keep him* alive, *and make him* happy upon earth *and will not deliver him to the will of his enemies.*"
What is a promise from the Master? The word "preserve" means keep alive his faith—which returns us happiness if we do not fall into scrupulosity, and even then if we should be so unfortunate, we should trust and start all over again with our resolutions, and He will not deliver us to His enemies.

"The Lord will support him on his bed of pain; and in his sickness remove all his weakness."

In understanding the means of merit and uniting our sufferings to His Passion, we know we are greatly blessed—that is, the support and gift which we will see after death. Saint Paul teaches that in our weaknesses we are strong. Accepting afflictions in union with His is to remove all spiritual weakness, and that great strength is often felt in the body and could be the means of cures. Because of the promise that He will remove all weakness, we also understand that there is no room in life for an escapist. Life is real, and we get out of it what we give.

Good lives and prayers continually rise to God as incense before His throne, but when we sin, the fragrance changes to something most repulsive—it is only reasonable that we consider opposites. Could it be possible that bad deeds and poor prayers mixed with sloth resemble the odor of onions and garlic? Let us pretend that the scene is real. What an incense or breath offense to God! Every hour, our angel is refilling the incense boat. We should wonder about the substance used in symbols of our actions, deeds, and prayers. For this very reason, it is well for us to make an examination of conscience at least three times a day.

This week, the sense of smell is to be mortified. Every time we come in contact with the offensive odor of either onions or garlic at home, office, church, or on the street, let us move a bead on the counter. We may accept the beads moved as a general reminder that Jesus is asking for penance or as a gentle reminder that our censers have garlic cloves burning in them. For each bead moved, we may profitably open the Scriptures to Matthew 5:3–12 and read aloud the Beatitudes, asking for each word to rise as new incense.

The general mortification and *fight against set ways* is for us to bathe in our tubs (every time during the week) with our bodies reclining or facing in the opposite direction to which we are accustomed. (Our backs to the faucets.)

Devotedly,
Cora

Sixteenth Letter Lesson

April 26, 1954

Dear Father,
Let us pretend in meditation to be watching a smooth, mirrored lake. Upon its surface glides a beautiful swan. Notice, there is nothing blustery nor hurried about her paddling webbed feet. She is majestic in her poise. And it would spoil the picture for us to imagine that she would deliberately invite any disturbance. Awed, we look upon such beauty and wonder why it is not promised life eternal, and why—with such harmony and poise—could not that creature have both soul and spirit? What do God, His Mother, and the saints think when they see us without the royal household poise, grace, and manners in regard to other people to whom He extended the promise of eternal life? We should abhor any disturbance to self and others, for it takes away the mirrored beauty of our spirit upon which all Heaven gazes.

Mystically, let us take a key from the Master's key ring and for this week's study choose one labeled ACCEPTANCE. That word is something with which we must learn to wrestle. The punches it will give will no doubt floor us as we feel the twist at meanings of the word. Since we are all actors and actresses upon the stage of life, all waiting for the final curtain to fall, let us realize that these lessons and the highlighted words are our script. How well we are going to learn the moods, words, and actions depends upon us and our willingness to correspond with God's grace. His baton is raised; let us rise and begin our act of knowing greater wisdom.

As we walk on to the stage with Heaven's citizens as our invisible audience, do we stumble? Do we frown? Do we hurry and lack poise?

Can we imagine the swan with any one of these faults? God often allows us to watch the perfection in mere animals and birds that we may learn; how well have we watched?

Has not the scene of the lake, the swan, and the forest coolness caused us to forget earth's trials for a moment? Have we not lifted our hearts to God and thought of His goodness in creating this living majesty for us? Hourly, human hearts are lifted to God in praise and admiration because of a beautiful scene, perfection in someone, mastery of art, or defense of the poor and a helping hand to the sick. What stage set are we working on today?

A suggestion for the week would be to slightly bow the head or the body upon entering a room—is it not a new setting in the play? Our manners will be governed according to the depth of our knowledge as actors and actresses. A mother and father must correct, and at times severely, the children in their care. Bow before entering the room—all is an act in the eyes of God. Correct in calmness—not in anger. An actor who must play the part of a cross disciplinarian is not angry in his heart. Social justice, injustices, and all problems of life should be treated with respect for the heritage our ancestors culminated for us. We should in this age be men and women of wisdom and act accordingly. It is impossible for us in our culture to revert back to the animal brute kingdom. Why then do we try? To do so is to become a moron who does not appreciate the beautiful things on earth; he stands and throws rocks at the beautiful swan and ruffles the still, mirrored lake.

One of the little steps of *acceptance* is to play the game of life well by the hour, day, and week. *Accept* the monotony of life as our duty to earn eternity and not as a trial. Does an actor approach the stage without knowing his script? To know his script is an act of having accepted his duty, his call, and his life's work.

In meditation let us return to the lakeside and watch the swan. Hundreds of other people are watching its poise and marveling at the setting God made. What a moron and brute we would be to mar that lake and frighten the swan. Would not the eyes of scorn be upon us? Let us learn to love silence and then, in turn, appreciation which branches into the root of *acceptance* and love of the script which is given us in life. The shoreline is overcast with stones. Suppose we forget the love of His masterpieces, His lesson on silence He is teaching through the swan and the lake. We feel the ties of diplomacy and culture holding us tight to their laws of obedience—we long to set ourselves free—we pick up a stone—we are going to spoil the calm lake. Suppose we notice the rock painted with the word "Revenge." It would be dropped quickly, and we would become analytical and admit that we were filled with revenge. Our pride hurt, we would choose another rock with which to mar the calmness of the lake, and it would be painted with the word "Calumny." Quickly we would drop that rock, for upon whomever it may fall we would not only [cast] slander but could slaughter the person or scene. Shuddering and yet with wounded pride, we would no doubt pick another rock, but the grace of God has painted upon its surface the word "Spite." Yes, we are filled with ill-will, and we want to injure someone. Let us cast the rock away. The next rock is labeled "Envy." Could it be that we envy the Master's art? Could it be that we are envious of the creature who has not a spirit? Could we be envious of people's joy watching the swan? Was everything made exclusively for us? Everything we touch, hear, and see is for everyone else. Upon God's gifts we have no claim, but in the spiritual love of God and knowing we are His children, we possess and enjoy everything. Slowly, we choose another rock; it is painted with the ugly word "Jealousy." Are we jealous that the swan does not find the necessity of learning script? And that he is not an actor for God? As actors we must remember that creatures are His living mechanical toys. The last stone we would venture picking from the shore before our mean character bent in shame would be "Hate." It is possible to hate anything that has not done us harm? Has a mere swan harmed us? Has the beauty of the lake? Hate is usually fostered by two motives: one is jealousy, and the other is fear. We shall each analyze these two words to the best of our ability and apply them to self in our life and our vocation.

Let us remember that none of the rocks we have picked up from the shore are possessions of the royal household. Never must any one of these stones be found in the hands of people who are climbing the path to perfection in the laws of meditation and contemplation, for well they should know the laws of *acceptance*.

Let us use these thoughts as considerations when we look upon the still beauty of the swan and the silence of the lake. Do we think that once that swan was an ugly mess inside an egg? No, a person without the disease of hate and jealousy would never think about the cause, formation, and birthday—breaking though the shell—which is the symbol of breaking through habits.

Nor would they think of the ugly-duckling stage of life that produced the masterpiece—they see the perfection and even a greater perfection through their meditation. We must *accept* today as today; yesterday is buried. The lake of us mirrors what we are today. The existence of yesterday and today will never cross. Crossroads were not meant for such conflict of what we could have done—what we should have said—how we should have acted—how poor or well we knew our script. Today is today, and we are what we are today. If we *accept* these facts about monotony, life, actors, and actresses, it is then that we will have the knowledge of life through the key of *acceptance*.

When we awaken in the morning, let us pretend that we are reaching out to God for our script for the day. Let us allow the happenings of the day through our wills to become engrafted into the will of Jesus, and then all becomes the will of God. We must remember the will of Jesus was always in accord with the will of His Father, and since we are the children of Christ's royal household, we, too, should use the means of engrafting and making, at will, all that happens to us to gain merit because it is blossoming through the operation of grafting into Christ and the suffering of His Passion. His open wounds are the holes into which we could engraft all our torn-out roots of sorrow, pain, loss, and joys with the monotonies of life.

This engrafting of our wills into Jesus is perfect trust and allows the good fortune of tasting the crystal fountains in the Good Shepherd's pastures (contemplation). The mystical waters are the fountains of knowledge that help the spirit thrive into perfections. This food is ever making the spirit young—spirit cannot grow old. Old age is not in Heaven. Even though the body bends with age and its cares, the mind and will must stay youthful, for only in youth does one grow and there is no stopping along the way on the ladder of perfection; therefore, spiritual growth is a necessity.

Acceptance of the twofold life, the body showing signs of age and the youthful spirit within us, is the true holy life. We must stay free of heart as well as pure of heart. Can we imagine a swan attached? Are we lessening or forming inordinate attachments? The Beatitudes proclaim that the pure of heart shall see God. What does pure of heart mean? According to a Scripture commentary it means "Those free from sin and single-hearted."

"Single-hearted" means are we loyal? Do we defend truth regardless of what our neighbors think? Are any of us a Pontius Pilate, thinking of a greater political gain rather than justice for one man? Do we apply an atomic bomb to our heritage of two thousand years? Let us strive to be single-hearted in all things.

Suggestions against attachments that are hurtful to single-heartedness:

- If we find a fault in a friend, immediately express aloud two virtues.
- Do we delight in rattling skeletons that belong to neighbors and close friends, and especially the dry old bones that could send terror into hearts if certain truths were known in the age in which we live?
- Do we shed tears in greater abundance over our closely related dead than over the cross at Calvary?
- Do we berate and cause ridicule to our late dead by showing the family album which tells of style, more than facial features which change with age? (It is wisdom not to show pictures of our dead or the living when the picture was taken five or more years ago.) Both the dead and the living have changed.
- Of those who are dead, we should hang their pictures in our homes for one day a year and then in accordance with their birthday. Pictures of Christ, His Mother, and the canonized saints should be our gallery of art.

SCRIPTURE READING AND APPLICATION

Scripture readings in the light of *acceptance*: we shall read Titus 3:1–7.

Psalm 27 [26]:2, 11

"Teach me thy way, O Lord, and lead me along a safe path because of my enemies."

His way is the indwelling. He in us will find the safe path. Our enemies are the rocks we would have thrown at the swan.

"Deliver me not to the desires of my foes, for false witnesses have risen up against me, and men who breathe violence."

This was no doubt a prayer of Jesus in the garden Gethsemani. He, in us, is no doubt praying the same today for our weaknesses which He carries as His cross.

"I believe that I shall behold the goodness of the Lord in the land of the living."

David believes he shall behold the goodness of the Lord in the land of the living. David no doubt practiced singleness of heart, and through anticipated knowledge given in ecstasy, he must have known the Beatitudes—the pure of heart shall see God. Many people, while living, see God.

"Wait for the Lord, be strong, *and let thy heart take* courage, *and* wait *for the Lord."*

We must not rush the gifts of God. Wait patiently with courage. Waiting for consolations in this life is often like waiting a lifetime to see and hear an opera. It is worth waiting for because we have gained, in the meantime, appreciation, culture, and wisdom.

Just in case we might have thoughts and questions on the engrafting of our happenings in life to that of Christ which makes [suffering] God's will, allow me to quote from a book entitled *Confidence in God*[4] an arrangement by Rev. F.C. Devas, S.J.

It is a common error—that God sends us trials for their own sake. Looking on pain and trouble as good things is not a sound view. It does us harm by making us think God takes pleasure in seeing us suffer. The greatest possible happiness to be got out of life is in the service of God. God doesn't like to see us cry, even though it is good for us. It pains God for me to suffer pain—that is a lovable and TRUE view of God. To think of the Passion as God heaping torments on His Son is *Jansenist*.[5]

---

4   Considine, Daniel. *Confidence in God: Words of Encouragement Taken from the Notes, Instructions and Letters.* Arranged and edited by F.C. Devas. London: Catholic Truth Society, 1950s.
5   The doctrines of Jansenism were condemned as heresy by Pope Innocent X in 1653.

Taking our lives as they are and being *happy* in them is a true way to perfection. Very few crosses are DIRECTLY sent by God. God permits them, but they come from someone, or something else, or from ourselves—being disappointed in something we had aimed at. We should cut down our estimate of what God really sends us very considerably.

TRIAL FOR THE WEEK

Every time we do not accept what comes our way in life we experience rebellion. Any acceptance in life is the law of monotony. It is a must that we cook, wash dishes, make beds, wash mirrors, sweep, and dust; all these are the tones of monotony. According to our vocation and when we rebel, even in mind, we must move a bead on the counter. At the end of the day and for each bead moved we shall eat a teaspoonful of ice cream and then one of pure honey. Ice-cream is to remind us of the choice food—monotony—we would waste, and the honey is to remind us that we are stuck with the issue until death.

Devotedly,
Cora

Seventeenth Letter Lesson

(MARK 8:35)

May 3, 1954

Dear Father,

Today commemorates the finding of the true cross. In meditation's gift, let us live for a moment in that age when it was found. Truthfully, would we answer self that we would have been as courageous as those people who joined the ranks to restore a lost relic to the Church? They risked facing death; would we? They faced ridicule, failure, and financial loss—would we do that for the Church today? Married men left their wives; children were left to the providence of God; sweethearts bid farewell for life, and as the *crusaders* marched away, no doubt they knew they would never again see the green hills and cool meadows streaked with crystal streams.

Today, in our way of reasoning, we might say all that sacrifice and adventure was quite unnecessary and the Church would have progressed just the same, but reason tells us today that our faith is stronger because we can actually touch and venerate a fragment of the *true cross*. The wood of the cross is indeed a deposit of faith in the visible treasury of the Church. The great number of converts never ceases marveling at the relics gathered from every age, which not only dazzle but make anew the gift of faith and gratitude. To venerate the cross is actually to touch something on earth that Christ touched. Faith is touched and gratitude grows, which brings about in our souls a living flame that brightens the earth. Jesus taught that we must not hide this light beneath a bushel (measure)—gratitude, love, and wisdom must be shared (see Mt 5:14–16).

The *crusaders* of any good cause have given us a firmer belief in the cross. Saint Helen and her followers were *crusaders* for the cause of the cross, and across the ages they have reached the cross to us. Are we returning to them any form of gratitude? Have we paused to thank them? What are we doing for the cause of the cross? Are people or nations two thousand years from now going to thank us for what we are doing? What kind of treasures are we adding to the treasury of Rome? Let us not forget the story of the widow's mite—a tiny, well-said prayer is a jewel for Rome (see Mk 12:44).

Now let us think about another cross—our own body. Looking at our shadow as we extend our arms from our sides—are we not a cross? We are *crusaders* when we strive with our cross (our body) to subdue its faults and sins. To subdue self is to restore the imperfect to perfection—it is a crusader's war hoping to restore something to its rightful place and true order. To restore our cross to God and brighten the dust collected through steady falls into sin means sacrifice and a crusader's war upon the five senses. *Crusaders* follow Christ and His words. Jesus said, "Take up your cross (the body) and follow Me" (Mk 8:35). How often have we started the march with the *crusaders* and cried, "It is too far—I did not bargain for this steep climb; I'm tired, let someone else take up the march"? Let us ask ourselves whether or not Jesus, the real CRUSADER, cried in defeat and laid aside the cross? Life is short; let us be *crusaders* for Christ and not *crusaders* for the world.

Converts are as a general rule great *crusaders*—they have fought a terrific battle and won through the grace of God. Invisibly they wear martyrs' crowns, and their togas are crimson and gold, for have they not slain a musty will steeped in heresy or paganism to the will of the Church? They have brought back a cross (their body) that was lost in the mire of sins.

Now let us consider that when we have found the cross (self) and begin our climb to Calvary, we must seek to lose it—that is asceticism in the contemplative climb, which will foster perfection in all the virtues. The *crusaders* in the tenth century had nothing to show for their trials and war except the battle scars that the memory could retain. Personally they did not possess anything, yet they had the satisfaction of having fought a just cause. They knew God would reward them for any apparent loss (see Mt 16:25–26).

This self which has been found and now must be completely lost in Christ [requires that we] take our wills, the invisible shadow of self, up the hill of Calvary. The closer we approach the silhouetted crosses against the sky (the crucifixion scene), the more we notice that the center cross casts its long, shadowed beam down to greet us as if it were a beckoning hand. And when we reach its edge, have we not added our shadow to the length of the real cross? Are we not making the real cross reach farther over the earth? Our shadow (self) added to the cross is the same as adding another band to the chain of Peter's key ring—we are making the chain longer, and in this way Peter can reach more people. A link in the shadow—cross—is history, which we are making. The life of *crusaders* never dies.

Crusaders have rules and songs. Often they honor their captain by singing or chanting their rules as prayers lest they forget the reason of their life when in the darkness they lose sight of the shadow of the cross. Dark clouds symbolize tears. Starless nights—despair. Adding our shadow to the cross is another expression of the indwelling or the engrafting of our wills to His. The cross is the reason of life. Crosses which must become infused into the oneness of the shadow cross are the monotonies and happenings of life. Let us heed His invitation to become perfect as His Father, and in that invitation, we will find the easiest way, for has He not said that His yoke would become sweet? Christ would not give us anything impossible to accomplish—He is not a double-talker who would extend the invitation for perfection and then say it was impossible. Let us choose one perfection which He had and see how far-reaching it is into our lives. He appreciated beauty; therefore, we must appreciate the beautiful and find the symbol of Jesus in everything. This willing action is the great step of wisdom. Since appreciation is based on knowledge, let us strive to become apprentices who must love monotony and the happenings which could and do come to us from other souls.

Since Jesus was all perfection, He must have fully loved life's monotonies. Can we imagine that He did not like watching the pink dawn spill itself over the grey clouds of night? Did not His mind race along the sky-rim saucer which we call our horizon? He was capable of enjoying all joy, yet He called His Mother to watch with Him. Perfect love is to share all our gifts—they are the beautiful happenings in life. Are we watchers of the beautiful with Him? Do our awes teach the already spellbound that there is still something more to see? On that sky-rimmed saucer edge, we watched Jesus marvel at the ball of fire—the sun rising as though it were caught in a spider's net of long, tapering beacons of light. The quivering pink and grays are as ribs swaying in a Mandarin's fan as East meets the West. Let us perfect this one virtue of watching beauty and seeing Christ in everything, and in perfection, become willing apprentices.

A real *crusader* knows monotony brings joy. The Church teaches us in its calendar of Lent that during that time we must have one Sunday celebrated in that language of joy. On that day, the vestments are not penitential in color: they are rose, the symbol of joy.

Laetare Sunday lifts us in the penitential race, and we see the morning rise of rose-colored clouds and the bursting of the rose in the garden. And lest we forget, we attend a banquet every morning, the Mass; what joys in the penitential season! And so, too, with a *crusader*—he sings his chanting song while he marches on to war. A *crusader* has a rule, which is a formal contract that he will be of one mind with his soldier friends. Have we a contract? Yes: it is the Ten Commandments. Since sight must be mortified this week, let us each write the Ten Commandments and actually sign our contract with God. Then to do battle with ourselves, we must sing a chanting prayer, and no doubt the echo of the Commandments will linger in our hearts. If so, let us sing this song.

The Ten Commandments

I am the Lord—and thou shalt serve
No other Gods but Me;
Religion true thou shalt observe,
Faith, hope, and charity.

Thou shalt not take God's name in vain,
Nor swear unlawfully;
Things holy thou shalt not profane,
Nor curse irreverently.

Remember that thou sanctify
Sunday and holy days;

Work not without necessity
Hear Holy Mass, and pray.

Parents, honor, serve, and love
And cheerfully obey;
And servants must obedient prove,
When without sin they may.

Thou shalt not kill—nor vengeance take,
Nor hate thy enemy;
Forgive and love for Jesus' sake,
All that have injured thee.

The same commandment does beside
Forbid all drunkenness;
Self-injury and suicide,
And eating to excess.

Do not commit impurity,
In thoughts, words, deeds, or looks;
Beware of evil company,
And read not dangerous books.

False witness thou shalt never bear,
Nor tell a willful lie;
Detraction, if thou canst, repair;
As well as calumny.

Thou shalt not harbor impure thoughts,
No look with lustful eye;
Thou shalt not covet neighbor's goods,
Nor eye them enviously.

All this Thou dost command, O Lord!
We cheerfully obey;
And look to Heaven for reward,
Through all eternity.

Since we have touched upon the subject of joy during crosses or life's Lent and of the season itself, let us read the following rather than Scripture this week in the thought of gaining knowledge. This item is taken from an editorial in *Our Sunday Visitor*, March 28, 1954.

Heaven is sometimes represented by a garden of golden roses. Could this, then, be the reason that, from very early times, popes have been accustomed to bless a Golden Rose on *Laetare* Sunday? The Introit of the day is, "Rejoice, O Jerusalem; and come together all you that love her; rejoice with joy, you that have been in sorrow . . ."

This rejoicing Sunday is also known as Rose Sunday. Rose-colored vestments are used at Rome for the blessing of the Golden Rose of Laetare Sunday. Rose color, less penitential than violet, is used on this occasion because the day is one of joy in the midst of the penitential season of Lent. Mother Church on this day sings of our deliverance by Christ from the bondage of sin.

The Introit, Communion, and Tract for *Laetare* Sunday speaks with hope and joy, of "Jerusalem." The Jerusalem referred to is symbolic of the true Jerusalem, the Church, figure of Heaven. Through His victorious death on the cross at Jerusalem, Our Savior opened to us the gates of the heavenly Jerusalem.

The Golden Rose, actually a cluster of roses and buds on one stem, all of gold, inset with previous gems, usually sapphires and rubies, is a work of art wrought by skillful papal artisans. The ornament is formed of a central flower and a number of small roses. In the heart of the principal rose is a small covered cup in which musk and balsam are placed at the time of the solemn blessing of the Rose of *Laetare* Sunday.

The blessing refers to the Rose as a sign of spiritual joy and asks that the Church bring forth fruit of good work and "The perfume of the ointment of the Flower sprung from the root of Jesse,"—our Divine Lord.

In emphasizing the profound significance of the Golden Rose, Pope Pius XII in 1953 said to the Archbishop of Goa and Demoa, that the flower itself, and in the gleam of the gold, are symbolized the Lord Jesus and all His regal majesty; in the fragrance of the flower is recognized the divine perfume of Christ, which is diffused sweetly far and wide, by the faithful as they observe His precepts.

Psalm 119 [118]:11

No doubt, this is David's colloquy when he feels grace has been withdrawn and he must reach out to the gifts of reason which he has learned through the Ten Commandments.

"Princes persecute me without cause, but my heart stands in awe of thy words."

People in high places persecuted David, but even though he may have wept in sorrow, he stood awed with the knowledge of the Commandments and the good they had done in the rise of civilization.

"I rejoice in thy words, as one who finds rich spoil."

When we feel rejected, sad, and that we are losing a battle, it is wisdom to seek solitude and often to sing aloud the Commandments and reflect upon the good they have done along with the coursing streams of hope through history. We, too, will drink from the rich waters of hope.

"Falsehood I hate and abhor; thy law I love."

The reason David was persecuted was because people lied about him and admonished him with their hate—he realized that if they knew the Commandments in a better light, his suffering would have been less. His sorrow was great because of former ecstasies in which he learned that the Messiah would suffer because of the same ignorance.

"Seven times a day I praise thee—because of thy just judgments."

Mystically, David knew the anticipated knowledge of the seven gifts of the Holy Spirit, and in that gift and knowing the art of reparation, he praised God seven times a day regardless of how low he was crushed to the earth. He trusted in the judgments of the Commandments. They were not decisions that made one a slave but the severed chain that gave freedom to the people who lived them. How many times a day do we praise God?

"Great peace have they who love thy law, and for them there is no stumbling block."

Without the Commandments and their lasting effect upon nations who have built their laws of justice upon them, we would not enjoy the peace of sleep for fear the unruly hand of a neighbor might slay us. The Commandments have tamed the savage and given peace and rest—how we should praise God!

"I hope for thy deliverance, O Lord, and I keep thy commandments."
In our dismay and discouragement and joy we should always long for the hour of our death, and we have nothing to fear as long as we have kept the Commandments.

Verse 172

"Let my tongue chant thy word, for all thy commandments are just."
Let us often, in union with David, chant the Commandments and find the art of justice and history though study.

SENSE MORTIFICATION AND APPLICATION

This week the eyesight must be mortified. One of the suggestions may be chosen as a daily task to be performed at night with the light of a candle or a flashlight.

1. Wash dishes or car
2. Make beds—change bed linens and dust room
3. Read book or write letters

This task should take at least thirty minutes an evening. While performing the task, we shall consider the interest and care we should offer people who are losing their eyesight and ask God to bless us with patience if we should become so afflicted. Also, we shall reflect upon the dimness of our own souls in the eyes of God when we do not keep the Commandments. This mortification of dim lights is also good in overcoming set ways, especially when we are so spoiled with the freedom of light though electricity.

Devotedly,
Cora

Eighteenth Letter Lesson

(2 CORINTHIANS 2:14-17)

May 10, 1954

Dear Father,
It is well to recall to our minds from time to time that asceticism is a *way* of guiding our steps of life along the narrow mountain ledge which leads to the heights of contemplation and from there, if God chooses, into the unknown cloud of mysticism. Contemplation in its greatest heights can be self-acquired through cooperation with grace, but the unknown cloud of mysticism is a free gift of God known to a few on earth. To a few on earth He did promise a foretaste of Heaven, and that is the delights known to us as spiritual favors in the hidden depths of mysticism. We must always be ready in the spiritual climb of contemplation in case Jesus needs a living pillar (person) for special missionary duty. That duty—Jesus coming down and taking us through the dense cloud—could be for one minute or something to last for a lifetime that would, in turn, cast its effects from that person upon nations and conditions of life. Saint Bernadette is an example of a long mission life through the higher call into mysticism.

Our WAY or climb is cooperating with grace in daily living close to Jesus and striving for the knowledge of the indwelling which Saint Paul taught. Christ within us is to know that our five senses have been crucified and have died, that we are as nothing but a cocoon emptied of self. And the life put into that cocoon is Jesus Himself, Who in turn continues reliving His life of the Resurrection through us. Through our eyes, He sees, through our ears He listens, and through our footsteps He travels and blesses. We are His portable tabernacles! What a mission in life!

The *way*, then, must be the life of constant cooperation with monotony. The tabernacle (we) must become polished, for is it not destined for eternal life? What is our condition of self now? Are we gold? If so, we are pliable. Gold does not have set ways. Are we brass? Brass is loud and never poised, for it has an alloy with which it must contend and that alloy is stubbornness. Are we lead that is ugly and easily melted into any whim of man's mind rather than the mind of God? And are we made up of silver? It is beautiful for a while, but weather (conditions in life) tarnishes it and it becomes darker and uglier than lead. Everlasting life demands the gold, and the gold of us must be refined and given high luster. The buffer for gold is the right use of creatures and things, and we might add the simpler word, monotony. Thinking of mysticism as the full bloom of our flowering self reminds me of a quotation taken from the book, *Carmelite Mysticism*.

Great Teresa writes, it is enough for those on Carmel to live in God's presence, in *loving humility, content* with what the good God may send. Time and place are of little importance. *Sometimes* on *earth* the flower blooms and in all its glory in the garden of God but most often comes only to bud. But in Heaven all God's flowers will open in the glory of the "Sun." If the good God, like a good gardener, brings some to perfection here, others hereafter, *that is His own mysterious choice.* So again let us insist that the school of Carmel *demand preparation.* The exercise of the greatest virtue. Our lives must be ordered, oriented in the direction of the Order's aim.

Let us in our way of life follow the Great Teresa and demand from ourselves a well-ordered life according to the vocation which we have chosen. It is well at least once a month to take an inventory of self, for it is possible that God's will is that we are to be the full blossom on earth. No doubt the world is in the terrible condition that it is because of the lack of souls willing to rise to the contemplative state. Perhaps God longs for blossoms which He can open for the good of the world, for where their fragrances fall, evil leaves—evil cannot stand on blessed ground.

Asceticism is no guarantee of receiving the mystical life, but it is a way, a preparation if God chooses; therefore, it is necessary in life to live the *way* for the greater glory of God. Asceticism is like classical music; one must learn how to appreciate it and its history. Then one must learn the art of listening, for classical music cannot be appreciated by a noisy soul. God, too, speaks to a quiet soul, and He gives only as much as one can stand. Asceticism, like music, has many tonalities and each strikes upon human souls as a means of polish for the brightening of intellect and appreciation. Appreciation in a soul is attained through heritage, tradition, education, and national culture. These are gifts from God for our use, and we could title these facets GRACE. If it were possible to measure appreciation in any one person, we would find the depth of grace in each which would tell of the willingness to do good for the glory of God. An infant at baptism is graced because of the parents' intellect, will, and appreciation of truth. But the grace, or new light, cast upon the infant cannot become brighter until the babe begins to use reason, which is attained through length of life, heritage, tradition, education, and culture.

Personal polish and poise, kindly manners, and love of neighbor are grace. Are we filled with grace? Has the light of grace in us reached out like a rootlet of a rose plant and engrafted itself to the greater Light— God—which makes us unified with Him and makes our will His will? Grace and steady engraftings into His Divine Nature are necessary for salvation. Let us become tabernacle polishers of our gold and cease being just an apple polisher—an apple, regardless of its high polish, soon rots. Our actions and will must be for the eternal.

Asceticism is a daily reminder that we are not living this life forever. Today is our day in which we may become saints. Putting sainthood off until tomorrow or until death is sloth. Are we guilty? How well have we practiced the scale of the piano keyboard known to us as monotony? Is it not the polishing cloth that conditions the soul? Is it not the brightening of grace?

"Saint Teresa in her own masterly way describes how the *life of grace is built on natural foundations.*"

Are these natural foundations not the monotonies of life?

Saint Teresa continues, "The *life of grace* even in its highest degree is engrafted into the natural, and under its impulse the whole human personality grows to its fullest maturity." She shows how human nature is created by God with a "susceptibility" for these exalted states of grace, but on the other [hand] the practice of the virtues and the active contemplation must recede, accompany, and follow the mystical experience. She further states,

> The Carmelite life has a twofold end. We obtain the first by our toil and virtuous efforts, aided by divine grace. It consists in offering to God a holy heart free from actual stain of sin—the other is communicated to us by a free gift of God, *ex mero dei dono*, not only after death but even in this life, and consists in testing in some way in the heart and experiencing in the mind the strength of the divine presence and the sweetness of the glory from on high.

Also in the light of education and its knowledge, let us read from our Scripture reading, 2 Corinthians 2:14–17.

> But thanks be to God who always leads us in triumph in Christ Jesus, *manifesting through us the odor of his knowledge in every place.* For we are the fragrance of Christ for God, alike as regards those who are saved and those who are lost; to these an odor that leads to death, but to those an odor that leads to life. And for such offices, who is sufficient? We at least, are not, as many others, adulterating the word of God; *but with sincerity, as coming from God, we preach in Christ in God's presence.*

In the light of education and asceticism, let us study a poem written by Tennyson. Even though he was not a Catholic, he had the vision of tolerance and so he wrote a poem about Saint Simeon Stylites. The poem tells of our ancient asceticisms and the good wrought through them. When we become discouraged with the monotonies of trials, let us reflect upon the words of the poem. Also, read "The Poet's Mind" written by Tennyson as a means of appreciation and manners for those artists who are poets and ascetics.

Psalm 84 [83]:4–7

"Happy are they who dwell in thy house, O Lord, they praise thee without ceasing."

140

True happiness in the wisdom of contemplation; it is there, in those delights of a soul colloquy, that praise never ceases. Let us strive more and more to dwell in that house where only praise is known.

"Happy the man whose help is from thee, when his mind is set on pilgrimage."
There is no greater happiness than when a contemplative secretly receives a consolation from God. This hope and delight of consolation spurs one on for the climb of perfection, better known as pilgrimages.

"Passing through the arid valley, they make it a region of springs, and the early rain clothes it with blessings."
Curbing the five senses is passing through the arid valley, and to do so is to become a region of beautiful springs where many friends may come to quench their thirst for the knowledge of God. [Springs of contemplation can never go dry except through mortal sin.] A blessed soul then becomes a valley of rest and peace for those who would listen but for one minute from the voice of the contemplative, which is the fountain. And that region of springs for the contemplative is beautifully clothed from the early rain which symbolizes the directness of God to the soul.

"They become stronger as they go; they will see the God of gods in Zion."
The rise of the contemplative will become stronger as they climb the mountain of perfection. They will see the God of gods in Zion. In God's generosity He will, no doubt, manifest Himself in some way to those who climb high into the shades of the clouds.

SENSE MORTIFICATION AND APPLICATION

Our mortification against set ways and to grow old in body and yet keep young in spirit is to sleep this week with our heads to the foot of our beds.

The sense of hearing is to be mortified this week. If, during Mass, we are disturbed by the unusual noises of thoughtless people, we shall move a bead on the counter. Unusual noises could be: a noisy-sounding purse as it is being opened, sneezing, coughing, giggling, and foot-tapping on the floor, or the sound of rosary beads on the pew. Each time a bead is moved, we should resolve not to become a nuisance. And if we should hear a whisperer—one who whispers her prayers loud enough for those close around to hear, we shall move two beads. At the end of the week and for each bead moved, we shall listen to a record of classical music in kindly reparation to Jesus Who has been annoyed by our carelessness.

Devotedly,
Cora

Nineteenth Letter Lesson

(JOHN 10:26–30)

May 17, 1954

Dear Father,
In the previous letter lesson we have had thoughts on kindness, generosity, and responsibility but, in view of all these facts, have we truthfully considered the implement through which most of these virtues are given to the world? The thought for this week will be HANDS.

Let us mentally think about our hands as ten artist's brushes—His brushes through which He achieves the final touch to masterpieces. His touch has come to us in many ways and, since He is showing us the "Way," we must be watchful apprentices and perfect imitators. We touch with our hands—Christ within us in the indwelling, hourly touching for the first time or retouching dimmed masterpieces—human souls. How will our work in the art galleries of Heaven impress the saints and angels? It is possible within the realm of imagination for them to say, "He could have highlighted this scene with a little care." Are we neglectful with our painting on human souls?

The artist's brushes have three main pots of paint, titled: "Leaders," "Guiders," and "Helpers." This week we must strive, at least three times a day, to guide someone closer to God; through knowledge we shall lead the way with voice or pen. Also, at least three times a day, we must lead through example by *actually helping* someone who is in pain or is overly burdened with cares or sorrows. Our failing to do any of these mentioned (there is the possibility of six beads being moved each day) requires our moving of a bead on the counter. We shall keep a count of the beads moved for a general mortification at the end of the week.

The general mortification for us is for each bead moved, to read the following poem carefully:

The Touch of the Master's Hand

'Twas battered and scarred and the auctioneer
Thought it scarcely worth his while
To waste much time on the old violin,
But he held it up with a smile.

"What am I bidden, good folks?" he cried
"Who'll start the bidding for me?
A dollar—a dollar—now, two, only two,
Two dollars, and who'll make it three?

Three dollars, once; three dollars, twice,
Going for three"—but No!
From the room, far back, a grey-haired man
Came forward and picked up the bow;

Then, wiping the dust from the old violin,
And tightening up all of the strings,
He played a melody pure and sweet—
As sweet as an angel sings.

The music ceased, and the auctioneer
With a voice that was quiet and low
Said, "What am I bid for the old violin?"
And held it up with the bow.

"A thousand dollars—and who'll make it two?
Two thousand—and who'll make it three?
Three thousand once, three thousand twice—

And going, and gone," said he.

The people cheered, but some of them said,
"We do not understand—
What changed its worth?" The man replied:
"THE TOUCH OF THE MASTER'S HAND!"

And many a person with life out of tune
And battered and torn with sin,
Is auctioned cheap to a thoughtless crowd,
Much like the old violin.

A mess of pottage, a glass of wine,
A game—and they travel on,
They're going once, and going twice,
They're going—and almost gone!

But the Master comes, and the foolish crowd
Never can quite understand,
The worth of a Soul, and the change that's wrought
By THE TOUCH OF THE MASTER'S HAND!
  Myra Brooks Welch

SENSE MORTIFICATION AND APPLICATION

This week's asceticism practice is to be exercised in gratitude for
our sense of touch and more especially for our hands. We shall try
turning all the lights in the house or place of work on and off with
the left hand or right hand in case of left-handedness. (When the
lights are either needed or not needed.) This mortification is also
to be thought of in respect to those people who do not have a right
hand and how we would adjust ourselves if either of our hands were
suddenly taken from us.

Our fight against set ways is for us to use paper towels for the body
after bathing or showering. While we are using them we may thank
God for our civilization and its culture and gifts such as towels.

SCRIPTURE STUDY

Acts 2:4 to 4:31

That we may be better attuned to truths, it is well to realize that Saint Peter was not an ignorant man. Does an ignorant man quote poetry and Scripture at a moment's notice for any occasion? We must read the above and see for ourselves. (A commentary on 4:13 reads, "Uneducated and ordinary; not trained in the rabbinical traditions and having no authority to teach.")

Psalm 140 [139]

"*Keep me, O Lord, from the hands of the wicked, from the violent man preserve me.*"

Ten fingers are channels of grace for friends when we touch them, for is not God, the indweller, good? The ten fingers of evil men are channels of evil. If we choose good companions, we will have no fear of the violent man.

Devotedly,
Cora

A.M.D.G.

Twentieth Letter Lesson

(PSALM 103:30)

May 24, 1954

Dear Father,
During our meditations in this week's pilgrimage of life, let us pretend that we are little children in a city park awaiting our turn for a swing. Let us reflect upon symbols for a moment—the swing is the contemplative mind. The earth beneath our feet has offered us knowledge, tradition, and faith because we have lived. Taking our turn in the swing, we suddenly become a symbol of a fleeting breath lifted above the natural plane. As a huge pendulum to an invisible clock held in God's hand, we swing into the future and retreat into the past. Life with its natural monotony and delights in prayer is like a child at play on a lawn—he may race to the pool, play in the sand, or find his delight in a swing. All of these are beautiful symbols with great meaning, but this week we will play in the swing.

The swing is ours! We are poised on tiptoe—we are ready for the pinnacling heights. Heights and the distance forward can only be measured and enjoyed according to the distance we have retreated into the past. Perfect swinging is perfect balance in life, living and prayer. Does not a pendulum have an even swing? Are we perfectly balanced? If not, let us retreat into ourselves and ask the Holy Spirit to tell us about our defeats, and then go to the physicians (our priests).

Ah, in this retreat of the "super-natural," we find new delights through the governing power of knowledge and observation. The earth is ours—it is picturesque in its haze of purple, gold, blue, and green. And we are as still as a cloud, a breath, swinging into the patterns of the King's masterpiece, the earth. As we swing high over a bed of red and yellow tulips, would we mar it? The swan and the lake are at peace—would we cast a stone? Would we break the tree limbs where rest the sparrow's young (see Ps 84 [83]:3–4)? Would we kill their voices that tell of life? These are only little steps and thoughts on how God, the Prince of Peace, loves peace and wants the world to restore it in all things (see Mt 17:9–13; Acts 1:6). Man is truly a mischief-maker who walks carelessly as an animal through flowers, lakes, and homes—destroying all in his path. Let us resolve in the swing of life to *restore* all things through Christ as He would have them by better living the indwelling and learning of His gentleness (see Ps 84 [83]:5–7).

In the "prayer-pendulum" swing of prayer, let us better understand the impulses of gratitude, devotion, and faith in our fellow creatures who must suffer in any and all the cultures into which they are born. All people are God's children, and we must want them all to have perfection through the shower of graces born to them through some person's prayer of charity that they may be restored to the love and knowledge of God. Adam's fall stripped them into the "pain poverty" of life, culture, knowledge, and faith.

We are gaining momentum—the higher we rise, the farther the rise and fall, and then we realize our observation must be quickened and we pray to the Holy Spirit—is He not often depicted as wings?

The flight gives us the impulse that we would like to fly—and then we ask, is this not the fringe of the Garden of Eden which rightfully belongs to us? Before the fall of Adam, he could, at will, travel anywhere—he did not feel the weight of human flesh. Then flight tells us that the complete universe, even that which we cannot see, is our garden—the green pastures into which God often takes the chosen—for did He not say many are called, but few are chosen (see Mt 22:14)? In these quiet eons, He often speaks to the quiet soul, for is not the soul far away from self and where he could not do mischief to the flower beds, the lake, and the friends? Often let us swing into the delights of being alone with Him—His smile will be our grace of delights heretofore unknown to us.

The swing swishes into retreat; let us pretend that we are in the city of Rome. Suddenly we are walking through great halls; they are those in the Eternal City's library. It is our library—how often do we use the duplicates here in our books? Let us look at the shelf of documents written by the popes. We turn many pages, and to our surprise the theme of each one is the call and invitation, "THE RESTORATION OF ALL THINGS IN CHRIST."

Reason, then, teaches us that we must strive to become saints, for only saints can fulfill the desire of Christ—"renew the face of the earth." And here before us is a document written by Archbishop Cushing[6] of our America. He is addressing the faithful with these words, "Then we, too, shall be saints and the power of God shall be manifest IN us and THROUGH us and we, if we be saints and follow the ways of the saints, shall renew the face of the earth."

We further read in the document,

We Catholics are too prone to quote the words of the popes as if these words, merely as words, possessed some magic power to change the face of the earth. We are able to cite impressive passages from the encyclicals and the other pronouncements of the Chief Shepherds of Christendom, and we do so with an air of finality as if our mere quotations should suffice to set the world right. Just as the author of the *Imitation of Christ*[7] could say that the Church needs Catholics willing to IMITATE the Vicars of Jesus Christ more than she needs Catholics able to expound their teachings.

And the document continues in part, "Pope Pius X, and in this all our modern popes have joined with him in spirit and in deed, did not merely PREACH in classroom fashion the sovereignty of God's law, the supreme importance of God's purposes, he personally SUBORDINATED himself to all these. Pope Pius X constantly said: "Remember, I am a poor man and Jesus Christ is all!""

To restore all things through Christ we must die to self, better that Christ, the indweller, may continue His life of the Resurrection in and through us. This was the way and the life of the saints—they do renew the face of the earth.

---

6   Richard Cardinal Cushing, Archbishop of Boston (1944–1970).

7   Thomas a Kempis. *The Imitation of Christ*. Various publishers, first issued in 1418. It is one of the most widely read and influential devotional books in Catholic Christianity. The author, Thomas a Kempis (1380-1471), ordained a priest in 1413, was a German canon regular of the Monastery of Mount St. Agnes.

We are leaving Rome. We are descending and with our toes; we scrape a ridge in the dust beneath the swing. Earth is reality. Life is real and we must act upon the broad stage. Are we not the stars (saints) that keep watch over the world? In this reality—quiet with God we find ourselves bilocated into the far Orient. The people about us are strange, and they are strained in their poverty and want. Let us walk down the narrow street. The horrible smells tell us about the lack of education, invention, knowledge, discipline, management, and government. These poor people are as little orphans outside the city's wall where the golden graces fall as rain. Then we are startled with the fact, as we look across the earth, that the peoples of Christendom have advanced in all the cultures—Christ has lifted them up—He has drawn all things to Him, and in Him lies all wisdom, knowledge, invention, and the laws of right use of creatures and things. How mothered we are in the shelter of Christendom (see Jn 12:32)!

This affords us with all the more reason why we should project ourselves into the living of the Resurrection, that these people may come to the porch of shelter and find rest for mind and soul. True, God could have lifted them up, but we must realize that there is an unwritten law which faith seems to teach that *Christ does nothing for the world except through prayer.* Prayer in the right spirit is an avalanche of Heaven's light when we as Christians pray in unison under the guiding hand of the Holy Father and his intentions. Many of the gifts of plenty in Christendom are wrought through the prayers and sacrifices of ember days when we, as one, ask God to bless the fields, orchards, and earth's needs. Let us resolve to become worthy citizens of God that we may bring the poor and oppressed into the rain of gold and *restore* peace and plenty to those outside the fold of the Good Shepherd.

Before us in our bilocation trip, we see a tiny, motherless child huddled in a cold doorway. He is hungry and sick, cold and wet, yet we do not hear him cry. Why? Reason tells us that seldom do people cry unless they have someone to whom they can cry. A cry is a plea for sympathy which could say aloud, "I need care." In this country, there are no governmental agencies. Civil complaint is of little use. Let us thank God that we are mothered in the embrace of Christendom where peace and charity are taught and lived.

And lest we question about war zones and suffering in Christian countries, we must not forget that reparation in life is a must either by individuals or by nations. We often overlook national sins that must be repaired and atoned for in life (see Is 1:24–28). How true the sins of the fathers often fall upon the children (see Ex 20:5; Ez 18:2).

Now our swing, as an equally balanced pendulum, swings forward and we peer for a moment into the future. As in vision, we see Jesus walking beside a blue stream of water. The background is filled with towering mountains, and nestled in their valley looms a huge ocean whose color is the same as the stream which trickles through a rocky ravine to the feet of Jesus. His stride is slow; His look is pensive and then He speaks, "This stream is all I have to work with; it is no wonder the world is in such a chaos." The child of us in the swing speaks in answer, "Jesus, why don't you use the water in the ocean yonder?" He answers with a smile, "Little child, in that sea there is plenty of water, and each drop symbolizes a prayer from My friends, but every drop of water has a tag attached which tells me how to use it and for what purpose. This little stream represents the prayers from my most loved ones who do not boss me—they give me everything in their moments of prayer to do with as I will. Most people of the world do not follow law and order, and therefore perfect balance is not understood. The day should be set into hours which would represent praise, thanksgiving, adoration, petition, and purity of intention, which is prayer with all indulgences, acts, and deeds offered to Me to do with as I have need. The greater majority of prayers are petition, which is not a perfect balance, and as soon as I receive prayers listed under purity of intention I will see that peace, love, and harmony reign in the world. When man is off-balance then the world follows the same course."

Let us as saints resolve to seek less of petition and of telling God what to do. As true Man, He does not want to be bossed. A little philosophy in regard to God as well as man will teach us to use less bossing and give more praise, love, and adoration or admiration.

SCRIPTURAL MEDITATION AND PRAISE FOR THE WEEK

Acts 20:35

He that would be happy, let him remember that there is but one way— "It is more blessed to give than to receive."

Psalm 100 [99]:1–4

Through our praise, in being mothered in the circle of Christendom, let us sing the psalm with David which reads:

"Acclaim the Lord, all the earth; serve the Lord with gladness—Enter his gates with praise, his courts with a hymn; give thanks to him, bless his name."

SENSE MORTIFICATION AND APPLICATION

This week the sense of smell is to be mortified. We shall refrain from using perfumes, lotions, and having house flowers. In the garden or parks, we must also restrain ourselves from inhaling the fragrance of flowers; to do so is to move a bead on the counter. If, at the end of the week, we have ten or more beads moved we must take a trip to the city park and actually swing in a swing. While we are swinging, we shall meditate upon thoughts in this letter lesson.

Devotedly,
Cora

Twenty-First Letter Lesson

"The only things we ever keep are what we give away."

May 31, 1954

Dear Father,
If we could look into our interior selves, would we smile with delight at the progress we have made during the last few weeks? Let us hope that we are worthy of smiling. And now for a moment let us recall the thoughts of letter lesson six, in which we were reminded that we are each like unto a desert through which, if we are willing and if we correspond with grace, God will travel and scatter seeds in order to make our desert blossom.

The child of each of us in our desert last week pretended that we were in a park swing, taking on the delights of a pendulum's perfect balance. We are tired of the swing, and so we hurry to the sandbox. This play gift also holds a great mystery, as we quickly allow our ten wiggly fingers to hide in the sand. We could ask ourselves, "Are we that imbedded in the foundations of Rome?" or, "Are we allowing Rome's gifts to sift like sand through our fingers?" Let us reflect on the thought that Rome is a firm foundation with a root system that will never be uprooted (see Mt 16:18–19). The Church of Rome is like a huge castle continuing to be built by the popes. Peter was the first builder after Christ laid the cornerstone, for Jesus is that stone. We of the twentieth century are delightfully spoiled with the castle rooms through which we may fly at will as little fledglings. True, there is much to learn and much to see, but we must not forget to search for the tower room, which all castles have, for the broader view. A fledgling's flight out into the eons as he leaves the castle balcony is determined by its growth and strength gained through the searching of the rooms in God's castle on earth. These beautiful flights from the balcony are known as contemplation; then, we come home at night and find rest in the meditation of what we have learned.

Let us, through the knowledge of tradition, study of the Scriptures, and obedience to the voice of the Church, outgrow the cloak of the sparrow and rise into the strength of the eagle (see Is 40:31). A sparrow's morning flight is to the ground searching for food. The eagle rises into the eons before he eats and soars into the brightness of the rising sun. Often he rises above the clouds and then returns only when the atmosphere is too thin for survival. Do we follow the eagle (see Ps 103:1–5ff)? Upon rising, do our souls rise for moments to the limits of our strength to the SON? To do so is to build a firm foundation of faith.

Slowly we sift the sand through our fingers. And the little mind of wisdom questions whether we are retaining knowledge any better than the sieve could hold dust? The child of us presses a sand-ball firmly between his hands, but the mass does not hold its shape—it falls apart. Why? Because it lacks something which we will mystically call grace. We are as fragile as the sand-ball unless we continually renew ourselves with grace, the mystical water of the soul, which is love of tradition, Scripture, and obedience to the Holy Fathers.

It is wisdom and conducive to a happier death to houseclean not only our souls but our homes as well, and rid ourselves of everything we do not use every thirty days. This is a special type of poverty which is most pleasing to God. Let us give what we do not use to the poor that they might enjoy the fruits of time and invention and the means of rising to a higher standard of living. (This is not a command for anyone to perfectly follow, but it is the higher expression of selflessness, spirit of poverty, and the delightful sharing with each other which brings spiritual freedom. There are exceptions of this rule, of course, such as Yule-time decorations, coats for seasons, etc. But all else can be done away with for the good of self and man.)

Through charity and the wisdom of grace, it is a joy to believe that "the only things we ever keep are what we give away." Let us not linger too long in the sand lest we become too narrow and off-balance, for it is a plaything that lacks the something which we call grace. We, of ourselves, without the knowledge of God, truly resemble a desert. He wants it to blossom; therefore, we must rise above the sand with our streamlet of water lest we lose ourselves and purpose in the wasteland (see Is 43:19). We must each become a broad river—so broad and rushing that the desert cannot swallow it nor its purpose. That river is the symbol of seeing through the eyes of God (the indwelling). The streamlet, in man's narrowness, sees only his family trouble. But through the eyes of God, he sees a thousand or more family troubles equal to his. They are all God's children, and He loves them all alike and with God there is no respect of persons (see Rom 2:11; Sir 35:13–15; Is 42:2, and others). Detachment, then, is to pray not particularly for self and troubles, but for all the people suffering from the same condition during the hour when the river feels remorse, sorrow, trial, despair, dismay, and lack of faith. Quickly that broad river must course on and on, sweeping all things before it and by so doing, we pray for all the suffering who are chilled with the same cause. This broad charity will not be outdone in God's generosity.

How narrow are we? Are we losing ourselves and purpose in the sand? When our own child is ill, do we forget all the other children who may be ill? Many of these do not have mothers and fathers of faith to pray for them. Your prayer will be heard, for God will not be outdone in generosity (Sir 35:11). Let us become generous with ourselves and with others.

In the broadening of our river, which in a sense is also to find a greater detachment for ourselves, we may find that we are the "saviors" of many people whom we do not know or have the privilege of seeing. Our Scripture reading for this week should be upon the thoughts of prayer and our obligations to God's children across the world and upon whom our rivers of prayer might touch.

SCRIPTURE READING

James 5:19–20 (see Sirach 35)

"My brethren, if any one of you strays from the truth and someone brings him back, he ought to know that he who causes a sinner to be

brought back from his misguided way, will save his soul from death, and will cover a multitude of sins."

Psalm 127 [126]

"Unless the Lord build the house, they labor in vain who build it."

When our Lord builds anything through us, He is a teacher of wisdom, which is won through mortification to the animal nature, our five senses. He, the builder, builds with gold bricks and none are mixed with straw (see Sir 51:23–30).

Meditation Taken from My Scrapbook

"Truth in the *Bible* is a fountain. It is a diffused nutriment, so diffused that no one can put himself off with the form. It is reached, not by thinking, but by doing. It is seen, discerned, not demonstrated. It cannot be bolted whole, but must be slowly absorbed into the system. Its vagueness to the mere intellect, its refusal to be packed into partible phrases, its satisfying unsatisfyingness, its vast atmosphere, its finding of us, its mystical hold of us—these are the tokens of its infinity."

Also taken from my scrapbook:
"One must not be too narrow. Yet a stream
That brings refreshing to a waiting land
Must keep itself within its channel jealously,
Or lose its purpose and itself in sand."

SENSE MORTIFICATION AND APPLICATION

This week the sense of taste must be mortified. For breakfast we shall eat ice-cream if it is at all possible, and after retiring at night we shall eat three soda crackers without water. Failure to do so is to move a bead on the counter and to keep count of them until the end of the week. At that time, for each bead moved, we shall put a cupful of sand in a paper sack and take a walk scattering the dust and reflecting upon "ourselves" as a narrow stream, afraid of sense mortifications. We shall remember, too, that our Lord is the builder, and He uses gold. We must cast away the sand.

We may continue in our fight against set ways by sleeping for one week between blankets instead of between sheets. Appreciation is sharpened and set ways are weakened. Let us offer a rosary sometime during the week in thanksgiving for linens.

Devotedly,
Cora

Twenty-Second Letter Lesson

(MATTHEW 10:14; JOB 20:11)

June 7, 1954

Dear Father,
From time to time during this letter lesson, let us recall the theme of the last two letter lessons in which the little child of us played in the symbol mysteries of a swing and a sandbox.

Now, let us pretend that we are again that child in the sand, and that we are smiling because we have learned a lesson that all else in life in regard to possessions is as lasting as sand. It crumbles and its formation does not hold its shape. In that spirit of joy, we skip away from the sand toward the pool which we seemingly glided across in our swing. And as we skip, we all chant from within our hearts this poem taken from my scrapbook.

"Love that is hoarded molds at last
Until we know someday
The only thing we ever have
Is what we give away.

And kindness that is never used
But hidden all alone
Will harden till it is
As hard as any stone.

It is the things we always hold
That we will lose some day,
The only things we ever keep
Are what we give away."

Poem from Father Vaughn,[8] 1936.

Individually, we stand at the blue-grey liquid pool. It is beautiful! It is small, yet, it is immense, for does it not reflect the vastness of the sky, with its uncharted depths that rise to the stars unseen and the white moon smiling with its crescent lip? Ah! But what is at the depths of the pool? White sand lies there, mixed with many other colors all glistening in the shimmering, sun-beamed water. The scene is too pretty to ruffle with our step or a splash of our hand. We stand in awe to admire the beauty of God the Creator. The pool's stilled silence reminds us of something sacred—we stand to meditate—we will not wade today. Instead, we will just think about the washed sand.

Let us think about it as a symbol of the saints. And many grains of sand could be the dust of saints, because they are everywhere on the earth. Time, in its mother-kindness of destruction, lifts all bodies as dust from their tombs. Each particle of dust is a missionary; it has a mission to do, and that mission lasts until the end of time (see Jb 19:25–27). Time may use earthquakes, floods, building of nations, and help of insects, etc. to scatter the dust of saints across the earth. This action is but a command of God. Did He not order us to renew the face of the earth? The good people of the royal household can better accomplish this extraordinary mission work through dust because they have become as diamond dust through the touch of the Master, for has He not dwelt with us? Have we not given our bodies that He may continue His life of the Resurrection in and through us? Our clay shells acted, during life, as magnets and grew powerful. That power in the dust of the saints gives and continues giving for the good of the earth and people until time is no more. We must not forget that our active missionary life just begins when, in perpetual ecstasy, we sleep

8   Father William Vaughn (deceased) instructed Cora Evans in the Catholic Faith and officiated at her baptism, March 30, 1935, Saint Joseph Church, Ogden, Utah.

in God (see Dn 12:2). Let us reflect upon the active missionary work of the Little Flower since her death. While she lived, having once entered the cloister she was not outside the convent walls, but her mind traveled everywhere with God. How true: what we sow, we reap!

Our turn at death will come—none escape that penalty inflicted upon us through Adam. Are we prepared as missionaries disguised in dust to renew the face of the earth? Do we realize that *Jesus is the WAY* and that we must follow Him all the way (see Jn 14:6)? Does He not hide Himself today beneath the sacramental dust? We are not going to be exempt from following His life in the pattern of dust.

Every person at death is a great or a lesser saint—with the exceptions of those who are lost (see Lk 20:36–38). Our own power after death depends upon our life here and how we love God and show it through our action, deeds, and obedience to grace. Just think, in time, perhaps within a hundred years, the dust of us could be in the pool mingling with the many-colored bits of sand. Let us ask ourselves whether or not we think we are good enough in our power to silently bless a child who might be peering into the pool of tomorrow? We should have that power—let us do something about it now if we feel our love is not absorbed in God to the zenith of our abilities (see Col 1:9–14). Every saint is to be a channel of grace according to his own wealth (spiritual) when he dies (see Eccl 11:3). Let us each strive to become a great channel of grace for God. Let us be good saints while we yet live in the pattern of Christ's active life, for surely we will follow His life in the hiddenness of dust.

In death, the spirit of us hidden in God will find delights in the keeping of an inventory of our million or so specks of dust as they are moved here and there over the face of the earth as silent missionaries. Every saint knows when his or her relic is being venerated, or, in the providence of God, being used for an immediate cause in the fight against the plans of Lucifer. Just think, a speck of us could fly on the wings of a breeze to Europe, Asia, or the jungles of the great south. Another speck of us could find itself mixed into the plaster of a home—there to bless and chase away evil as long as the house stands. We will have the power of eradication if we have lived good, holy lives. The devil cannot bear the saints. Or, we could be the dust that feeds a rose petal that might give joy at a banquet or a wedding. And joy of joys, our dust could feed a stalk of wheat that might be chosen to be crushed, pulverized, and made into altar bread. Life really begins when we are continuing our life in the sacramental silences after death.

Watch, the child is looking into the pool; he is marveling at the many colors of sand particles as they glisten in the sun as a mosaic. We could now ask, what color will our dust appear to the eyes of man? God forbid that we should resemble coal dust, when it is our duty to become glistening, blue-white diamonds.

Listen, a dark blue grain of sand is mystically speaking to a child. It is saying, "Little child of God, become a diamond at any cost. The light of the diamond cannot be hidden at night like mine. I am dark blue and of little use. I died in a lukewarm state of soul—until time ends, I may just add variety by color contrast or blend with neighboring dust or the beautiful diamond who now rests beside me. I am not powerful, and I am not gifted to perform miracles like my sister friend. When night comes, I am constantly tormented by the evils that the diamond may be scooped away for more important purposes, leaving me alone in the dark of night. The devils remind me of my uselessness (see Job 20:11) and lack of power—they cannot harm me for I am with Christ and I have nothing to fear, but intellect makes me wish that I had lived a better life while I lived on earth that I could now better renew the face of the earth.

"Little child, I am grateful for this most unusual and mystical opportunity for usefulness. Beg my friends among the living to live holy lives for they must 'renew the face of the earth.' That missionary life to come has joys that are unknown in life. The Master has said, 'Blessed are the peacemakers' (Mt 5:9), and the greatest peacemakers are the saints in their lives of dust who have the power to eradicate evil. If dust could actually speak, you would hear lamentations to this effect: 'Why didn't I lay up treasures in the kingdom of God's heart?' (see Lk 12:33–34; Mt 6:19–21; Job 22:21–24, etc.). 'Why did I think only of earthly possessions and mind-esteem?' 'Why, why didn't I live a better life?'"

Applying the following poem meditation to the thought of our dust, we, too, could say:

"I am the dust
That was the rust
That was the nail

That pierced the pale
Hand of Christ.

I felt the surge
Of pain emerge
In spurts of blood
Hallowing the mud
At Christ's feet.

I now am naught,
But the truth taught
Goes on and on
Though all be gone,
In Christ's name."
  (From my scrapbook)

SCRIPTURE READING

1 Corinthians 10:1–5; Psalm 80 [79]

Read this in meditation on the theme of dust.

When I am feeling better, I will elaborate more on the mystical depths of the Psalms. Let us keep in mind in the reading of them that David was a figure of Christ.

SENSE MORTIFICATION AND APPLICATION

The sense of sight is to be mortified this week. It is a good practice to wear dark glasses every time we venture out-of-doors (except when driving a car). Our failure to perform this mortification is for us to move a bead on the counter beads, and for each bead moved, we must turn a book on a well-kept shelf, or in book ends, in the wrong direction which would ordinarily tell of neatness and order. We must leave the book or books in this condition for a week. Or, we may rearrange ornaments on mantels, desks, tables, or buffets in such a way that they would be displeasing to the eye. Men could wear the wrong color of tie for their suit each day, or, if they dislike white socks, they could wear them.

Suggestions for mortifications to overcome set ways and keep us pliable (if we are not pliable to the will of man, then certainly we are not pliable to the will of the Church and of God):

- If we are accustomed to wearing our watches on our left arm, we may wear them on our right arms for the week.
- If we like wearing jewelry, we may leave it off for a week—except our watches if they are necessary.
- We could easily use kitchen silverware in the dining room or area.
- When we black- or dark-polish our shoes, we may polish just the toes.
- When we clean our white shoes, we may whiten just the toes.
- If we ordinarily use cigarette holders, then we could not use them or vice versa.
- We could try drinking water for a week from a cracked cup instead of a glass. Office workers may carry with them or keep in a drawer a folded Dixie cup to use over and over again until it has to be replaced.

Devotedly,
Cora

Twenty-Third Letter Lesson

June 14, 1954

Dear Father,

With God there is no time. Believing this great mystery, let us return to the swing in the park. It is fun skimming over the neat flower-beds, the bright patches of color and the clumps of shrubs. In the swing-freedom above the world, we are a "breath"; could a breath hurt the flowers? Would we mar anything that was lovely and beautiful to God? To restore all things through Christ and in Christ is to mend the mar to anything and restore it to a super-plane of beauty to which it belonged before the fall of Adam. Through faith and in the spirit of mildness, let us restore and not destroy the mystical flower-bed represented to us as God's people over the face of the earth.

There are many kinds of flower-beds in this mystical garden; they represent the nations and their cultures from the savage to the heights of a poet's mind. What philosophers (gardeners) we could become if we chose, in any walk of life, to study and analyze persons and conditions with the gift of calm and tolerance for the tulip, violet, rose, or lilac.

The constant migration-travel into philosophy is to become the broad river which we have considered in a previous letter. The river, representing SELF, must be mighty with prayer in its surging torrents to push forward—yet, so mild on the sloping banks that baby-tears-grass would not be uprooted. Are we that prayerful? Are we that mild? Remember, the mystical flowerbeds are people—the masterpieces of God who were stolen, bruised, and broken by Lucifer. Are we helping him with his destruction? Let us not forget we are gardeners at work as we wear the royal crest. The royal family must work together and cease with hypocrisy. Let not the royal family boast of a Herculean who displays his physical strength by destroying the shrubs and flowers. In the eyes of God, a Herculean is a boaster and bluffer whom the devil may choose quickly as his tool—a buffer.

Mystically, let us watch the flowers we have mentioned above. Look, the tulip is beautiful but its edges are burned—could it be that someone's foul breath of anger stinted its unfolding growth as it opened for God? Why does a flower open? Is it not because it knows no other law than obedience: to grow, blossom, and give to the world its thanksgiving in fragrance—just to remind us that our prayers are like incense rising to God? And the red rose, the most favorite flower of all, is bent low with an earthly weight of creeping aphids. They are the symbol of bad friends—buffers for the devil. And the violet—it has been crushed by someone's domineering and unholy authority. And look at the lilac tree! It is needing water in the dry, hard earth. Its thousand or so little open trumpets are limp—they cannot greet the sun—for someone is irresponsible through sloth. The lilac tree and the thousands of limp trumpets could symbolize the victims of war. The philosophy of analysis over these flowers is first to consider that a mischief-maker has not been curbed. How often do we pray for social justice in our nation and others? Are we too shy to voice opinions in governmental selections of men and laws? Let us not confuse mildness with shyness. Mildness is a fragrance of wisdom, and shyness is something false and cowardly, with its silences often a scandal.

CONSIDERATION

It has never been known that a flower hurt itself. Are we not of greater worth? A flower's life is short. In the thought of eternity, we are a mere breath; our life is short—and life is but to win a battle and wave the banner when the swing slows into death. That banner will be either white or black. Whose side are we on? For whom are we fighting? It is no wonder the Little Flower of Jesus was titled the "little flower." She was the expression of mildness and yet filled with the desire of accomplishment to restore all things in Christ.

Let us strive—and it cannot be accomplished in a day or in even a year, for we are born savages with a wild nature—to become less and less a mischief-maker. A mischief-maker does not intend to kill a flower, but he hurts and mars many though the sins of anger, unjust governing, slothfulness in the study of humans, and laxity in faith and prayers. The life of a mischief-maker is a serious venial sin and, unless curbed through discipline, could lead to the door of hell.

If our eyes were X-ray machines, we would see the great majority of mischief-makers sick with a terrible malady. We would see a grown-up body with a tiny child hidden within. Naturally, the coordination of the two do not offer perfect balance. How is our pendulum swinging in the hand of God? The stubborn child in the grown-up body, of his own free will, decided not to grow up. Somehow he liked the rattle and the romper age, and he failed to realize how ridiculous his actions and whims, without reason, strike upon the mature person. Let us not forget in our reflections upon Scripture that Saint Paul often spoke about the infant growing up and becoming man. And he brought that man under discipline and then Christ came in the mystery of the indwelling, which Paul clearly writes about in his letters.

Now let us consider persons who are unduly worried, sad, oppressed, and in anguish. We would find that in the majority of these cases a mischief-maker, with spiked shoes, had walked through the flower garden of God. The worried who might question God, or the sad who may grieve over too long a period of time, or the oppressed who cling to the ledge of despair, and those in anguish over past sins, war, or grave illnesses are not in these conditions because of self, for never does one sin alone—there is always an accomplice. Perhaps someone was not honest, and perhaps the sad suffer from the loss of rightful pride of a good name. And maybe the oppressed were cheated out of money and position, or they were not heard as a citizen in the laws of justice. And those souls in anguish may not have been schooled in hope, and that courage was needed even by Christ. When He fell beneath the cross, He rose and began again His walk to Calvary.

Philosophy, wisdom, and peace are gifts we should desire having, but they must be earned. They are something money cannot purchase. All are mastered through the desire, accomplishment, and love of silence. Even the deaf and the mute suffer from noise of mind. Silence comes through the following suggestions as a means of taking inventory of self and a "way" of bettering conditions for the love of God.

- Are we, like a violin, tuned too high?
- Are we at trigger tension?
- Have we mastered the art of repose and quiet?
- Are we easily angered? (The Master said we must "be slow to anger.")
- Are we a tank of alligator tears to be used at will?
- Is our mouth a cave wherein lives a snake?
- Are we a parrot with a snappy tongue?
- Do we need melting from our icicled glare?
- Are we a book of foul jokes and too much laughter?
- Do we suffer from pamphletitis? (It is like being overdressed.)
- Do we talk to Jesus and His Mother, or are we just readers?
- Do we believe in sanitation? What about the confessional?

If, during the week, we find ourselves answering, "Yes" to any of the above questions, let us move a bead on the counter. For every bead moved, say a Hail Mary prayer with a loud motor running (such as a vacuum cleaner). The noise is to remind us of a troublemaker and how he mars the peace of mind as we say our prayers. The loud motor's noise of running is also the mortification of the sense of hearing that is to be disciplined this week.

SCRIPTURE READING

Ephesians 3:14–21

Psalm 119 [118]:66

"*Thou hast dealt kindly with thy servant, O Lord, according to thy word.* Teach me judgment and knowledge, *for* I trust *in thy commands.*"

Overcome set ways by using a sponge or damp cloth for stamps instead of the tongue. Failure to follow this procedure for the week is to say seven Glory Be to the Father prayers, asking the Holy Spirit for the grace of discipline.

Devotedly,
Cora

Twenty-Fourth Letter Lesson

(MATTHEW 12:31–33)

June 21, 1954
Feast of Saint Aloysius Gonzaga

Dear Father,
It is well to keep in mind that much of the knowledge given to me by Saint Aloysius (whose feast day is today) was needful information, because I was a convert and—through the grace of God—brought many souls into the Faith. And many other people already in the Faith from different "isms" avalanched me with their problems and those of their close relatives, which they would not take to a priest.

Of all the questions asked me by those in the Faith and out of the Faith, these two problems head the lists. First, asked most by those in the Faith (by the greater number converts): "What is the unforgiveable sin? Are we guilty of it, and what is the nature of the sin? How can we define whether or not we are among the unforgiven?"

Since it is our Holy Father's wish that lay people acquaint themselves with knowledge and with people outside the fold, I will answer through these letters how I was guided to answer this problem in few words. It is well to avoid arguments, for we of the Faith have no need to argue; it is greater prudence to state the case and allow God's grace in that person to formulate the acceptance or defeat. I will quote the answer to the question above which seemed to satisfy the converts more than any other explanation that could be given in greater detail. It is taken from a book written by a Father Vincent.

Our Lord said, "And whosoever shall speak a word against the Son of man, it shall be forgiven him, but he that shall speak against the Holy Spirit, it shall not be forgiven him in this world, not in the world to come." It isn't that the mercy of God does not extend to such sins, for He is infinitely merciful. The sins against the Holy Spirit are sins against *faith* and *hope*. *God cannot forgive us against* our will. If we no longer believe in God, we won't ask for His forgiveness, and if we no longer hope in His mercy, we won't turn to Him, either. Consequently, *these sins tie His hands since He cannot forgive us against our will.*

The above answer should leave no doubt in our minds as practicing Catholics whether or not we are in the state of grace. We know we have faith or we would not believe in God. And we have hope, or we would not obey Him and seek forgiveness. Charity, too, could be added here as a thought and question: how charitable are we to God? By acting upon the graces of faith and hope, we are kind to God—is that not also a form of charity?

The second question was asked by inquirers who could have been possible converts to the Faith had they not been scandalized. The second question is, "If the Eucharist is God and people receive Him every day, why are they not saints?"

Let us ask ourselves who receive Him frequently, are we saints? If not, why not? Jesus said for us to be *"perfect"* as His Father in Heaven (see Mt 5:48). Sainthood is to be attained in life unless we are expecting to take the detour through Purgatory.

Jesus said we could not be saved in ignorance—so—we must strive for knowledge, understanding, and wisdom, which is the pearl of great price and could be known as the contemplative life.

We must overcome the animal nature. We are born a savage, and we have much to unlearn in regard to temper, gluttony, avarice, untruths, troublemakers of unrest, and all other "must not" conditions in life. If a daily communicant is receiving our Lord daily because of wanting His love, then one by one these faults should leave, for light and darkness cannot mix. If we attend daily Mass and receive our Lord because it is one way to appear smart, or as a means of obtaining attention to [gain] a P.T.A. or other vote, we are causing scandal. Let us not scandalize His little ones—"little" because they lack knowledge, hope, and faith. Let us prove to the Protestant and the atheistic worlds that the effects of the Blessed Sacrament in us are a way to sainthood. Let us be saints, for we are saints with a little letter "s" unless we admit that we belong to the devil because we have so willed. Let us keep the little "s" growing, and at death see the everlasting crown with the capital "S." Or are we going to be so unfortunate as to hear the Master say, "Your small 's' refused to blossom. You told me in your words, deeds, and actions that you liked the life of a savage. Heaven does not harbor savages, but since you died with contrition, I shall allow you to take the detour, and be schooled in the Purgatorial schools." Let us imagine that Purgatory is like a college campus—filled with buildings bearing a title for our faults, which we have come to undo. Ignorance is savagery, and so we appear on the campus. We could be wearing bones in our hair which would symbolize "We never got over the fault of picking trouble." We could be wearing lion's-tooth necklaces symbolizing that we were worse than a lion to live with. We could appear dressed in straw skirts symbolizing untidiness and immodesty. We could have war-clubs in our hands with many notches telling of our cruelty and how many souls we killed, particularly through our giving scandal by uncouth actions. And it is possible that we might find a house of beauty bearing the title, ICE GLARE MELTED HERE.

And let us reflect further—every schoolroom must have a teacher. They could be our priests, who in their unbound charity as ambassadors do not have to stay in Purgatory, but stay for us as "angels of consolation." How would we feel if we appeared—dressed in the fashion of savages—before our teacher, a priest whom we knew on earth, and who thinks that we are little saints? Let us pray to God that this measure of punishment never happens. Let us give the Blessed Sacrament a chance to work through us and make us Christ-like.

Regardless of how far up the ladder we have climbed in the contemplative world and "cloud of unknowingness," let us take an inventory of self by answering the following questions (the tiny things and happenings that are often overlooked):

- Have we teased someone until he or she lost patience?
- Do we show our distrust and stinginess by being a *cross-questioner*?

Do we cross-question friends, children, and relatives until they are fatigued? This type of procedure has its rightful place in a court-room when character or life is in the balance. Or are we cross-questioners trying to show our esteem of self and that we could be a good lawyer or judge?

- Does gossip come from our lips as if we were practicing for grand opera, where it is necessary for all to hear our voices?
- Are we yankers? Do we yank things from people's hands—things such as towels, books, chalk, or clothing? Do we yank thoughts from people's lips? From children's? We must remember that *everyone* has a right to express his opinions—especially in this nation. Do we yank a person's thoughts away from him in the middle of a sentence?
- Do we show disappointment and anger by slamming doors, loudly banging dishes, or closing books and dresser drawers with a bang?
- Do the neighbors know the time of day by the loud impatience of our voices? Are we the cocks of the neighborhood whose shrill voices announce that it is dawn, time to eat, go to school, and time for lunch and dinner?
- Mother Mary prepared the last supper. Do we think that she screeched at the helpers and servants? Let us not forget that she was a mother, wife, house-keeper, laundress, dishwasher, buyer, cook, teacher of prayer, and all the other little things required of a mother. Often, she was hostess for her friends. She did all things with mildness.

If we are failing in any one of the above faults, let us move a bead on the counter for each one every day. For every bead moved, we shall say a Hail Mary prayer asking for patience, mildness, love, and kindness by saying "O sacrament most holy, O sacrament divine. All praise and all thanksgiving be every moment Thine."

SENSE MORTIFICATION AND APPLICATION

The sense of touch must be mortified this week. Once during the week, we shall walk slowly down the aisle of the Church and actually touch the pews as we count them. The number of pews is the count of which we must pray Hail Mary prayers for souls to become enlightened upon the subject of unforgivable sin. Many souls would be in a state of peace if they were not worried about the consequences of the question.

Our practice this week for overcoming set ways shall be to eat stale bread—three days or older—when we could have the fresh along with other members of the family. We must check ourselves—have we laughed at least five times today? We must cultivate smiles and laughter. This does not cost anything but the use of good sense.

SCRIPTURE READING FOR THE WEEK

Romans 8:14–25; Psalm 32 [31]

Devotedly,
Cora

Twenty-Fifth Letter Lesson

IHS

June 28, 1954

Dear Father,
Let us not forget we are the little children of the ROYAL HOUSE-HOLD! Playfully, in the mystical life of mind-extension, let us make believe that we are on our way to our classroom. This is our beginning class of a higher art, and we are awed and a little frightened, but the grace of reward for our willingness and love of discipline unites us with love instead of fear. We are ready, at any cost, to untie the devil's spider webs he weaves across our paths in life. We refuse and resolve not to be his slaves. We want freedom!

We stand at attention at the great door wherein we will learn the love of greater wisdom. The great sign printed with gold letters upon black reads, "THIS IS WHERE YOU WILL LEARN OF THE PER-SONALITY OF CHRIST." The door is slowly opened; we enter and take our seats. Looking at the teacher at the desk, we are pleasantly shocked, for it is none other than Mother Mary. She is beautiful! Her smile, calm, and poise electrify us, and we just gaze into a quietness that is above any expression on earth. Her voice! She is speaking—it is mild—and without a trace of command, she is saying, "I shall teach you from the minds of your own generation of people about the personality of Jesus. I shall read from a book entitled *Personality of*

Christ[9] by Dorothy J. Willmann (Imprimatur: Joannes J. Glennon)."

Mother Mary opens the book and begins, "Some persons think that they can, by imitating someone else, make their personalities the same as the one who is admired. This is not only difficult; it is a practical impossibility because each individual's personality is totally different from everyone else's.

"Personality is not a mere matter of one quality or another; it is (not to become too technical) the sum total of the characteristics, tendencies, abilities, background, culture—in fact, of everything that makes up or constitutes an individual—and the way these things and the composite of these qualities impress other people.

"If it were possible to find a perfect personality, then it would be not only desirable but sensible and intelligent to try to acquire the characteristics of that person.

"There has been one Personality Who throughout two thousand years has been found perfect."

Mother Mary pauses, bows her head, and allows us time for meditation upon what she has read. My thoughts were that without guidance we are useless canvases without an artist. He is the artist; we are the apprentices who must try capturing His technique of perfection in *charity,* love, kindness, understanding, and the desire to become one with the Father.

Then I recalled to mind a beautiful thought which reads, "Christ never said much in mere words about the Christian graces. He lived them; He was them. Yet we do not merely copy Him. We learn His art by living with Him, like the apprentices of old with their master." (Taken from my scrapbook collection.)

Mother Mary begins to read, "Ideas of charity are often confused. Too frequently they are limited to notions of almsgiving. CHARITY is a supernatural virtue that causes us to *love God above all things for His own sake* and to *love our neighbor for God's sake.* To exercise charity or to love perfectly, one must have a *knowledge* of the object loved. If we are to love God perfectly, we must know Him. If we are to exercise charity towards our neighbor, we must know him, know and *appreciate* that he is one of God's children.

9   Publisher note: Out of print.

"Christ knew what charity is, understood its full implications, and exercised this virtue. *He loved God above all things.* He united His mind to God by frequent thought of Him and by prayer to Him; repeatedly, we learn from the Gospels, Christ *sought quietude* in which to speak to His heavenly Father."

It is time again for interior thought. Just in looking at Mother Mary, knowledge was made easy, and reason taught me that *seeking quietude* was a part of charity. How well have we lived that facet of charity? We must not forget that charity begins at home, and our first letter lesson stressed the view that "home" was the expression of our individual body. How true are the words of Thomas a Kempis, "In *silence* and in *solitude* the devout soul maketh progress."

Let us resolve to cultivate this virtue of quietness and being alone with God if it is for only five minutes a day. It is not necessary to kneel. Saint Ignatius Loyola found the art of praying was to repose in a reclining chair—his body at ease proved not a distraction from thought and prayer. Let us try it for five minutes a day. Let us pretend that Jesus is near and that He is quietly speaking to us as a kind confessor from behind the curtain. Perhaps He is saying, "I am your God . . . And I stand close by you . . . Is this not enough? I am your God . . . And I remain faithful to you, even when I send you sorrows; remember that I am with you . . . What more do you desire? . . . I am your God . . . And I think of you . . . From all eternity I have thought of you; I have written your name in the depths of My Heart in order that I might never forget you . . . I am your God . . . And I arrange all for your happiness . . . I am your God. . . and I truly love you . . . I know all that grieves you . . . I see every glance; I hear every word that pains you . . . Accept all with tranquility and peace, because I Myself have allowed and ordered all; you, be faithful to Me and persevere, and I shall reward you for all . . . I am your God . . . Are you alone? I shall be your friend . . . No one speaks kindly to you? . . . Come close to Me and I shall be your ALL in the Blessed Sacrament . . . I shall be to you a compensation for all that the world denies you . . . I am your God . . . What more do you desire? Be of good cheer . . . May nothing seem too hard for you, because he who possesses My Heart and My Love has all he needs . . . The world passes away . . . Time is fleeting . . . Men forsake one . . . Death shall carry off everything from you . . . One Thing alone shall always remain with you . . . YOUR GOD . . ." (From my scrapbook collection.)

Failure to keep the quiet five minutes alone with God during the week is to recite the Divine Praises three times, in reparation for our sloth that we have not governed time in such a way as to allow God His spiritual Communion.

SENSE MORTIFICATION

This week the sense of smell is to be mortified. We shall put a drop of good perfume on our sheets and pillowcases in honor of Christ within us. This beautiful mortification is conducive to relaxation and a feeling of peace which one receives in a flower garden.

To overcome set ways and in reparation for having wasted food in the past, every day this week let us tie, with string, a dry crust of bread to a bush in the garden for the birds to eat. If we should grumble at this practice, let us put honey on the bread for the bees.

SCRIPTURE READING

Let us open our Bibles at random and what we read—three lines—consider as a conversation with Jesus.

Psalm
Let us sing the first line we read as our gem for the day.

Devotedly,
Cora

Twenty-Sixth Letter Lesson

July 5, 1954

Dear Father,
Continuing with our thoughts in mind-extension as little children in the classroom where Mother Mary teaches, let us consider that we are at recess on the school playground. As we are all children of the royal household, we feel free to listen to any one of the informal group discussions. You and I are approaching a group that we have observed as giving the impressions of agitation, unrest, near-hysteria, and indecision through both voice and action.

We listen and find that we have joined a group discussing Communism. One little boy expressed his fears that Communism could spread over the entire world. Another child fearfully asked, "Would that bring about the end of the world?" A small boy made reply, "Why doesn't God stop this evil? He is all-powerful!"

A hush came over our group as we all looked toward the gate entrance. A man was entering. He was tall and walked with a calm, easy stride. His dress was that of the ancient past. His loose, flowing toga was of a striped material in purple, orange, and gray, and his head veil, which hung down over his broad shoulders, was snugly fitted across his forehead as if tied with a rope. As he came closer to us, we observed that his personal appearance was one of immaculate grooming. He spoke in greeting, and we recognized that though his voice was stern, it had a quality that compelled us to listen. He bowed to our group and answered our mental question. He was Saint Matthew. .

Without hesitation he picked up the thread of our discussion, "I have overheard your fears about Communism overrunning the earth. Why do you fear? Do you not trust in the greatest promise the Master has offered for your protection? Do you forget that you are a *royal member* of His sacred household, and that before His death, He made provision for your preservation until the end of time. You must believe—'the gates of hell shall not prevail' (Mt 16:18–19), but His other promise is even more direct and it is this: 'And he who *falls on this stone*' (Rock–Peter–Rome–Vatican) *'will be broken to pieces; but upon whomever it falls, it will grind him to powder.'*"

In mind-meditation Saint Matthew continued his instruction, "The Communism you know today *has fallen on the stone* (Rock–Peter), and it (Communism) *'will be broken to pieces.'* It will eventually become as nothing. Why do you not trust in the providence of God? He will act upon the power of your belief in the promise. Thank Him for the promise. Praise Him for the promise, and tell Him that you know He will act in His power when the greater interests of the people are in the majority of those who trust. Let us remember that God moves slowly. His ways are not the ways of man. His will is for the good of all people—even for those who fall upon the Rock."

In vision-intellectual knowledge of the mind, let us continue thinking that Saint Matthew is talking to us in this age in which we live. In regard to the complaint of the little boy who asked why God did not end all strife, for He had it within His power, Saint Matthew said, "We must cease blaming God for everything for He, too, must deal with human free will. Free will is a precious freedom which He allows us until death. With it as our war spear, we work out our salvation. Through prayer, we ask His divine providence to overtake us and watch over us until the end. True, God can do all things—He has all power—but it is a law that we must ask God's help through prayer, or why would there be any reason for prayer, which is a means of keeping us humble and submissive? Through our prayers, God's will will be done."

Saint Matthew continued, "Let us cease blaming God for everything that hurts. If in our human nature we must blame someone (see Wis 10:13–16), let us blame the fall of Adam. And let us remember that the devil has a will through which he and our enemies act. God has banished neither the devil nor our enemies from the world; therefore, they have a particular right to live or exist. Man has a right—even in his evil designs which cause enmities between men and even nations (wars)—to work on the laws of his salvation. If, in doing, he takes us into the grasp of war, we must bear with conditions patiently and look forward to the mass migrations of people that they may see the joys of God in seeking peace rather than war.

"In kind defense of God and so that we do not blame Him for everything, let us remember a quotation from the book entitled *Confidence in God*,[10] by the Rev. Daniel Considine, S.J.: 'We should cut down our estimate of what God sends us very considerably.' Let us know in the wisdom of knowledge that our sufferings and torments of injustice—war and its horrors—are all the will of man who is suffering because he seeks not 'first the kingdom of God,' His peace and way of love (see Mt 6:33). And we must not forget what is so clearly stated in Scripture, 'Blessed is the man (or woman) who endures temptation; for when he has been tried, he will receive the crown of life which God has promised to those who love him. Let no man say when he is tempted, that he is tempted by God; for God is no tempter to evil, and he himself tempts no one'" (Jas 1:12–15).

Saint Matthew left quietly as he came, and we were left alone with our thoughts. The bell rang and we hurried back to our classroom. Mother Mary instructed us saying, "Let us not forget in your sufferings from the inflictions of man that this life ends—this earth is not your Heaven. All, even the cruelty of man, will be taken from you. And remember this, even though the angels may chill your hearts with fear, I plead with you to remember the 'cornerstone' and the promises of my Son. This life is a valley of tears, and until the end of time it will roll in the mist of human tears—for there will always be war. War lifts the soul of man to God in prayer as no other known implement, and upon that conviction of God in one's life rise empires where peace dwells, until man in the majority forgets God again. Empires rise and fall; governments renew their standards, and civilization blossoms anew after each war. These are facts worth remembering, for my Jesus permits evil that good may come from distress, discouragement, and

10 ibid.

despair when hearts, broken and crushed, turn to the mender of the potter's clay.

"The valley of tears has two shepherds. One is my Son and the other, the devil. Both shepherds are fighting for you. Stay close to the Rock, and rest and sleep within its shadow. Watch the daily unfolding of Heaven's mystery as God takes the gold of your prayers and magnifies it as the silence of dawn and lifts man to the silencing peace where man talks alone with God. My Son has said that you cannot be saved in ignorance; therefore, let us study the Scriptures and the laws of Rome which tell us of tradition, history, nations, and cultures of people.

"Knowledge and education are the beginning gifts of prudence and wisdom and the broadness that everyone is a child of God, unless his free will allow him to seek the dark path to hell. Let not the thought escape you that you are of the *royal household*, and in dignity you must always act. You wear crowns and the purple. Keep yourself unspotted before the world and harm not the least of God's creatures. Follow law and order in all things and first things first, and life will offer a smile and a foretaste of Heaven while you live on earth."

Mother Mary arose and bid us good-bye with the promise that she would come to the classroom again.

As the people in the school of love left the classroom, a student touched another on the shoulder and said, "*Quo Vadis?* It is no small wonder some people are surprised at where they are; they didn't watch where they were going."

Quietly, the student who had been greeted with *Quo Vadis?* resolved to himself that he would never fall to the road of the weak who were satisfied in ignorance. Rather, he would rise on the wings of wisdom in the royal household and not fear the footstep of the "commonisms," which rise on foundations that know not brotherly love and faith in the Rock and the promise of Christ that "he who falls upon the Rock will be broken to pieces" and eventually become as nothing.

SCRIPTURE STUDY

Matthew 21:42–44; Ephesians 4:17–24; Psalm 56 [55]

SENSE MORTIFICATION AND APPLICATION

This week we are to make three examinations of conscience each day. If we should fail to do so, we must move three beads on the counter for each time missed. Then at the end of the week, and according to the number of beads moved, we shall take a bite of raw potato sprinkled with pepper and eat it without the natural scowl and complaint. When we are ignorant of the things that belong to God, we are as raw and bitter as the potato and as hot in temper as the pepper, a symbol of the animal nature in us. Let us curb him and put on the new Man— Christ. (The sense of taste is to be mortified.) Saint Luke on self-examination, 6:39–45, may serve as inspiration.

Devotedly,
Cora

Twenty-Seventh Letter Lesson

July 12, 1954

Dear Father,
As we walk through the great and imaginary castle-rooms of Rome which reach across the world, shall we stop to reflect upon the Beatitudes? Each is a good meditation in the pauses of the mind as we shift from one study to another or from one type of prayer to another. The Beatitudes (see Mt 5:3–12) are the little keys with which we open the dark, little rooms of our hearts. Then as value, appreciation, and gratitude allow the human mind to be flooded with greater light from the sentiments of the heart, we seek for the greater knowledges known in the light of man as the SEVEN SACRAMENTS.

Today, before the week begins, let us write the titles of the *seven sacraments* on small slips of paper and place them in a box into which we may reach and daily choose a paper with the chosen assignment for our practice of that day. If we choose the slip of paper which reads "confirmation," let us read a good book on the subject of confirmation and discuss the subject with the members of the family. This is a way of learning and keeping alive the will of wanting knowledge, as well as broadness in the belief that everyone has the right to express his or her opinions. Failure to keep these seven days as a study on the seven sacraments makes it necessary for us to move seven beads on the counter for each day's failure. The mortification for our failures will be written later in this letter lesson. We must keep count of the number of beads moved until the end of the week as an obedience.

The following little poem is a gem of good thoughts on the *seven sacraments*. It is my hope that it may prove a help to us all. It is taken from my scrapbook.

The Seven Sacraments

The Church has seven sacraments,
As we must all believe.
These means of grace we all must seek,
To know or to receive.

BAPTISM washes out the sin,
Which Adam did commit,
The sins which we ourselves have done,
True PENANCE will result.

The HOLY EUCHARIST is
The Body and Blood Divine
Of Jesus Christ, both God and man,
In form of bread and wine.

In CONFIRMATION, we believe
the Holy Ghost is given;
In EXTREME UNCTION we get grace
To die in hope of heaven.

In HOLY ORDERS, the bishops
And priests get power and grace,
And MATRIMONY blesses those
Who married life embrace.

All praise and thanks to Jesus be,
And to His Precious Blood,
By which we have the sacraments,
The source of every good.

Let us pause and reflect on prayer in regard to the seven sacraments. They are seven keys needing the touch of our prayers either for self and friends, or for those outside the fold of Christ. How far has our own charity flown on the wings of prayer today?

Let us imagine, since we have the knowledge of the Holy Spirit, that It, as a dove, is caged within our hearts. How often are we merciful and let It out to soar into the heights of meditation or contemplation? It is the Holy Spirit within us Who longs for the heights unknown to us, but with our will and constant trying, He will enlighten us and take us to the delights where only prayer can reach. A paragraph or two from a book entitled *The Devout Life*[11] by Saint Francis de Sales may give us a greater appreciation for prayer.

Prayer brings divine Light into our minds and inflames our wills with the love of God. *It is our great means of purifying our mind from inordinate affections.* From it, as from a fountain, good desires flow and by it are made fruitful. It washes away the soul's imperfection and calms our passions. This is especially true of mental prayer. Begin prayer by recalling the *presence* of God.

Begin prayer by recalling the presence of God. Let us consider Jesus the Second Person standing beside us. Shall we please Him by just talking to Him instead of just saying worded prayers at Him (see Is 29:13)?

You will soon feel the benefit of such a practice. God is everywhere. There is no place where He is not. Let birds fly where they will, they always encounter air; so we are always where God is. We all believe this but do not always act on it. A blind man cannot see his king, but, told of his presence, he *maintains an attitude of reverence;* yet, for want of seeing his king, that blind man is apt to forget his presence, and so lose his reverence. So it is with the presence of God. Although faith tells us "God is here," we are apt to act as if He were far off.

Keep your thoughts on the *meaning of what you say,* not striving as much for *long prayers* as for *fervor* in *shorter* ones. THE LORD'S

11 Saint Francis de Sales' *Introduction to the Devout Life* was first published in French in 1609. Considered a masterpiece, it is available from various publishers.

PRAYER SAID DEVOUTLY IS OF MORE VALUE THAN LENGTHY PRAYERS RUSHED THROUGH.

In contemplation let us imagine that we are standing beside an ivory tower—in height—beyond the heights of the clouds. And in our hands we carry golden cages wherein repose restless doves. Our own dove is our pathfinder for the great beyond. The great tower seems endless in its height—it is as smooth and perfect as ice. At the very top we can see a beam of golden light searching over the earth. Look! One little dove's eyes are on the light. Suddenly, his flutterings are wild with excitement. He wants his freedom. Quickly, upon his release, he flies around and 'round the tower's mighty base, and each time he makes the circle, he has flown to a greater height.

As our eyes hopefully scale the walls, we notice that there is not even a vestige of a ledge, nor a snag—not even a windowsill upon which the tiny claws might find security for rest. Around and around the dove continues to fly, and as his noiseless wings cut the air, we hear the music—words of his heart which sing, "Bless, bless, bless my friends." Now he has circled so high that he resembles a speck of dust—and in one of those mysteries of God, we know his thoughts. He is tired and he looks longingly at the golden light above—he cannot make it! Pity strikes our hearts. We could do anything in our power to help him, but we cannot. He circles more and more slowly and finally, he glides and swoops into the dark clouds at the tower base. Exhausted, defeated, alone, and sad, his limp wings dust the earth at our feet. It is a pitiful sight. We feel his loss. There are no words for the great little warrior who lost, but he is still alive—perhaps, in the providence of God, he will bravely try again (see Is 38:12–18). These are our natural avenues of thinking, but let us take another lane of thought, which may tell us the dove is the symbol of our own spirit at death, and we could not make the height, and we fell back into the cloud darkness known to us as Purgatory. If the dove symbol of each of us could speak, no doubt he could say, "If you, my body, had only prayed with much fervor and imitated Christ—through which you could have gained His strength and mind conviction—I could have reached the top."

This symbol of death has made us ask ourselves, "When death comes, how strong will we be on the flight of ascent? Will weakness overtake us? And in our exhaustion will the angels take us to the Divine Mercy Hospital, better known as Purgatory, for our convalescence? Let us resolve to have mercy on the spirit of self and save it that terrible embarrassment. Let us rid ourselves of the animal nature that clings to inordinate affections and silly possessions of earth. Let us each make of ourselves a flame of zeal for the love of Jesus (Lk 12:49) and His ambassadors, the priests, through whom we receive the *seven sacraments.*"

SCRIPTURE STUDY

Romans 8:26–27; Psalm 28 [27]

SENSE MORTIFICATION AND APPLICATION

If we find that we have failed three or more times during the week to live the days according to the choosing of the different sacraments and their study, meditation, and discussion, we must take a ride on the nearest bus to our homes and ride to the end of the line. While we ride and watch one side of the street, we shall count the liquor stores and cocktail bars. Then, on the return side, for each number of stores and bars counted, we must say an Our Father prayer in reparation for the harm of which these places of business have been the cause. Also, we shall say a Hail Mary prayer in thanksgiving for the good that has come through these same places of business.

Devotedly,
Cora

Twenty-Eighth Letter Lesson

(ECCLESIASTES 5:1)

July 19, 1954

Dear Father,
Another day, another week is upon us, and seemingly each brings along its multiplicity of the usual monotonies. Are we among the poor sick people known as escapists? How well it is to learn the rule that we cannot escape life and the unique trials that our chosen vocations bring upon us. Let us consider substituting the word "trials" with *trails* in this week's lesson. Certainly, every day is a new path extending through the valley of tears—this life. We encounter hills, tall peaks, hollow caves, deep crevices, and broad green meadows. Often, when we stop for rest, we think our progress is as slow as an old wagon wheel.

It is this form of dismay that brings about the thought of escaping through some make-believe complaint. If we succeed in escaping during this life, then our stay in Purgatory will fashion us as we should have been fashioned in life. Let us accept the truth that our *trails* have many laws and commands for work, rest, and play, and if we play the game well, all Heaven rejoices with us, for our merit is great. Let us pretend as we walk along the trails of life that our hearts are harps upon which we strum the music of our thoughts and deeds. What kind of music are we sending to God? Are we "off-key" because of harsh, coarse words? Are our harps telling of humdrum words, with the sound of a savage beating upon tom-toms of dried wild boars' skins stretched across hollow gourds? This sound of savage beating could be idle words. The Master has warned us against them—are we obedient?

As a recollection, let us know that we are never alone. If we are speaking with one or two friends, we still have our invisible congregation of angels and saints. Perhaps they number into the thousands. Would we blush from shame if God chose to draw aside the curtain that we might see? Let us keep watch over our actions and words for they dim the fire of us. It is this "fire" which the angels and saints see and by means of the visible dimming, they know that we have sinned and allowed grace to slip away from us.

As we rise from our rest in the green meadow, let us make resolutions to keep better guards on our tongues (see Sir 28:18, 24a–26). "Make a just bridle for thy mouth." Let us seek to love silence and the beautiful peace of good music, which should remind us of our interior harps and how they are mystically heard before the courts of Heaven. Suddenly, as we walk along the path which is not much different in turns and roughness than the trails we walked last year, we notice on the side of the path a one-man-sized elevator. It is best described in a colloquialism—it is "cute." The scroll patterns in gold high-relief are most unique. To our surprise, the door opens and an angel walks out to greet us with a smile. We eagerly press him with the query, "Please, Angel, tell us—is there a reason for the elevator's being here?"

He knowingly nods yes and replies, "This meadow, up to this point of meditation—or up to the elevator—is known by you as the land of meditation. Through its long and tiring lanes, bypasses, and detours, you have learned the arts of submission and the beginnings of appreciation, the justice of authority to Peter and the mystical keys which he holds. In this land, you have learned law and order and the just and right use of creatures and things according to your vocations. But it is here, *at* this golden elevator symbol, that souls become absorbed in the knowledge of monotony and, in their tiredness, they feel as though they are losing faith and appreciation for the traditional gifts of time.

"This is the place, if you will, for a contemplative flight. It is a rest and a vacation away from the regular routine of meditation. It is a flight that is good for the spirit. Why don't you try it? If you rise in this flight, you will experience the prayer of simplicity, or as some people understand it, the prayer of quiet. Simplicity means that you pray or speak with few words—everything is simplified without the trimmings of sentimentalism. Also, this way is known as the rapier of quiet, for you rise above the wants and petitions of earth. This way is a oneness with God. This nearness with Jesus, even though you do not see Him, is to have everything in life. This could be a moment of perfect love, and true love wanteth nothing. Seek to love Him, to praise Him, and to adore Him—all else He will bless."

The angel, stepping aside, beckons to a table where he asks us to deposit our earthly surplus of prayer-ties: our books, prayer cards, and pamphlets. He is saying, "This light is to experience the delights of spiritual poverty. TIME of two thousand years will seem as nothing and, for an instant, you will find yourselves to be each a citizen of Jerusalem. You will be as the first Christians—in poverty and simplicity. They did not have prayer books; nor were there any beads and pamphlets; nor did they have crucifixes except in memory. If this contemplative flight takes you to a scene of the Passion, what will you say? How will you address Him? Will you add weight to His cross by asking favors? Would it not be wise to console Him by saying, 'Jesus, I believe you are the Christ!' Is that not a prayer of simplicity? It is an act of faith, of trust, and of hope. The contemplative flight is to feel a moment of complete abandonment—a foundation upon which to cling for further growth in the spiritual life. In His reciprocating love of generosity, He will care for all of your desires and petitions which are mentioned in the meadows of meditation. If you choose the flight, you must enter the elevator alone—for contemplatives travel alone; it is a oneness with God."

Now, let us pretend that we (you—for each of us is alone) are in that golden flight elevator. After we have found our rest in a position of ease, let us think that we are quietly walking toward the fires of His Sacred Heart. We feel its warmth—His embrace—and we each tingle with delight that we are above the cares of the world. This minute is to be alone with the Master. The simplicity of this sublime love is knowing that we are loved. In our enlightened intellectual vision through knowledge, we wonder what we would say if we should see Him coming before us? We know that He is hidden, and He stays hidden unless He chooses to come down and lift a person through the portals into mysticism, which we must not want nor have the least desire to attain if it were possible.

All that mystery and choosing must be left to God and His designs. Our prayer should often be, "O Lord, give me only what I can stand."

Suppose He approached us; would we as children of the royal household know the right words to use and have the mannerisms and pose worthy of our station? That hour will come at our death. That is why it is so necessary to live good lives and traditionally to seek the refinement and cultures of our heritage, for these knowledges will go with us in death. We will be either very regretful or gratefully happy. Which banner are we choosing? Let us, in all things, be prepared to meet the Master. Contemplation is slow in our mind actions. We have suddenly become real star actresses and actors on the mystical stage. Let us act well in any scene of the Passion of Christ. Those moments with Him are ours for the least little willingness.

Already we have returned to the meadow of meditation. We are awed at the suddenness and how much we have thought that life is not long enough to master the perfections we desire. There is not a minute to lose. Let us start our climb to the smile of the King. We are filled from the flight with an interior peace—a peace that the world cannot give. It is something that we must have again and again. We are as a spider caught in a web after it has been swept from its stem-to-stem nesting. We are caught in our prayers—there is no turning back; we cannot undo the web—we must rest and not build sandcastles that a broom could sweep away. Let us bask in the quiet and allow the providence of God to whisk us where He will; this is a taste of Heaven.

A FEW QUOTATIONS THAT MAY HELP US

From a book entitled *Our Forgotten Guest.*[12] Imprimatur: Edward J. O'Dea, Bishop of Seattle. "Even when we do not consult the Holy Spirit, *a habit of listening to Him is an essential part of our spiritual life; without it, prayer can never be supernatural or more than a pious habit, not a real* familiarity with God, or *union with Him.*"

From the same book: "*It is Jesus' dearest desire that we pay to His Holy Spirit our highest homage,* and that we consecrate our heart to be

12   Publisher's note: Out of print.

an *everlasting sanctuary in which ceaseless worship, praise, and love shall be offered to Him* for all eternity. Our devotion to the Holy Spirit will be the golden *key* wherewith we shall *gain free access to His infinitely rich* treasure chamber."

Is our own life only a pious habit? How often do we use the golden key or elevator for contemplative flight—to be with Him ALONE—above the cares of the world?

A Thought from My Scrapbook

"Cry no more to Heaven
Each fondness that you lack,
Love that once was given
Cannot be whistled back;
But old loves, wept and despairing,
Because they proved untrue,
Shall, when you rise unerring,
Lend luster to the new!"

Father Garrigou-Lagrange says, "Purgatory was made for those who did not wisely use their period of probation here on earth."

Saint Francis de Sales states, "Whatever vocation we have, we can and *we must always strive after perfection.*"

Saint John of the Cross advises, "The whole of perfection consists in seeking in all to please God and only to please God."

Saint Therese of Lisieux wrote, "It is for us to console our Lord, and not for Him to be always consoling us."

SCRIPTURE READING

1 John 2:28–29; 1 John 3:1–6; Psalm 90 [89] in its entirety

SENSE MORTIFICATION AND APPLICATION

The sense of hearing is to be mortified this week. From now on, when we hear the clicking of women's high heels on tile, we shall close our eyes and thank God that we are in meditation allowed to hear the hammer as it strikes the nail which pierced Christ's hand.

We shall try making three contemplative flights each day this week. Our failures to do so obligate us to move three beads on a counter. At the end of the week according to the number of beads moved, we shall take the elevator rides in a building some distance from home or office, meditating all the while upon the loss to our spirits in golden flights missed.

We shall attempt to overcome the tenacious hold set ways have on us by drying our hands three times a day (no more and no less) on an old silk scarf.

Devotedly,
Cora

Twenty-Ninth Letter Lesson

(ECCLESIASTICS 1:17, 2:20)

July 26, 1954

Dear Father,
It is well to remember that in the eyes of God we are as little children. We could ask ourselves, are we willing to learn? Are we willing to accept correction? In these attitudes, let us pretend that we are again among the little children in the classroom with Mother Mary, our teacher. Already, she has chosen a paragraph to read from the book entitled *The Divine Crucible of Purgatory*[13] by Nicholas Ryan, S. J. (Imprimatur: Vicarius Generals).

She begins to read—but, as always, not until after first giving us her captivating smile which speaks to our hearts with the reassuring love of a mother, "All our masters in the spiritual life emphasize that when the soul is free and empty of all inordinate attachments, God can then work without all hindrance; He is free to accomplish His own divine designs."

Closing the book, she addresses us saying, "My children, consider carefully the paragraph that I have just read, and let us seek the deeper meaning of the words, 'inordinate attachments.' Anything inordinate means the unnecessary or trivial things in life. It is also understood as the gluttonous dispositions of the human body wanting delights beyond its need. It is dangerous to have anything beyond individual

---

13 Publisher's note: Out of print.

need—if one is not endowed with the gift of wisdom and its knowledge on how to govern charity.

"I will enumerate a few of the inordinate attachments from which most people suffer and the possession of which could hinder a 'perfect death' (see Jer 9:23). As I recall them to your minds, answer quietly to yourselves whether or not you could be disciplined into the housecleaning of self to remove the sand which is a weakness in your individual life:

- Do you seek for the knowledges of God above the deeds and ways of gaining wealth (see Sir 1:26)?
- Do you seek the security of this life ahead of the eternal (see Prv 23:4–5, 26)?
- Are you gluttonous? Do you eat too much? Do you sleep too many hours? Do you ever drink? Do you know the discipline of temperance in all things? Do you waste time (see Prv 23:19–21)?
- Are you slothful (see Eccl 10:17–20)? Are you an escapist? Do you feign illness (see Sir 3:27)? Are you fanatical and narrow (see Sir 6:37)?
- Do you *choose your friends with the care Jesus chose* the Apostles (Sir 6:1–17)?

Mother Mary continued, "Many people are burdened in life with their slaves of inordinate attachments. Remove them one by one, and know the freedom of self which allows Jesus to work out His divine designs. Since there is such a thing as inordinate attachments, then reason tells us there is a right use of God's gifts which He loaned to us until death. Do we each consider every gift with the joy of appreciation? Appreciation is the foundation of love. The greater the appreciation, the greater the depths of love one may attain in life and in the supernatural contemplative life. If an object or person brings us closer to God, then, we may consider their existence as a good 'possession.'

"Considering the subject of friends, it is wisdom to know that spiritual friendships are greater than blood relationships (see Ru 1:14–16). Few people in life have seen my Son, yet they love Him with a greater love than their love for their parents. It is the will of Jesus that a man love his wife more than he loves his parents; a wife's love is considered on the plane of spiritual friendships. Spiritual friendships know no distance, and there is not a severance of immediate communication either in life or in death, for love bridges that which the eye cannot see. Spiritual friendships are built upon the traditions of heritage which have come to us as a root system of two thousand years. The root system of blood relationships is not always conducive to the spiritual climb into contemplation, for the slaves of each other's inordinate attachments are often at war.

"The practice of loyalty in family relations is an *expression* of love, while spiritual friendships rise above loyalty and consider only love and giving as people love themselves and would give to self. 'True love wanteth nothing'; therefore, loyalty is not even wanting. Doubtless, you will find your true spiritual friendships among the citizens of Heaven, where you will no longer hear an unkind word nor see an unfriendly gesture. Truth, tradition, and heritage have given you the fond attachments in spiritual friendships, and on earth you may find a few of these friends of God. Have you found one?

"Carefully choose your friends, for remember you are of the royal household—you are sons and daughters of God. Do the friends you choose know the value of souls and the life of eternity as a set goal? Are your friends as wax before my Son Who is the Light of the world? Do they allow Him to melt His characteristic virtues into them? Do you see His mark upon them in the gifts of hospitality, kindness, love, and appreciation? Upon these characteristic virtues of God in your people, seek your spiritual friendships and you will have joy and not despair.

"Jesus had special attachments to both nature and friends. In His Humanity, He was deeply attached to the beauty and wonder of the sunrise. And He loved the twilight, especially at sundown when earth's ball of fire rose and fell as a playful ball on the darkening waves of the sea. And He smiled at the stars in their apparent littleness from this earth. He found especial delight in the copyings of man making drawings of the heavens which would form the bear, warrior, and snake in the lanterned sky.

"Jesus was also deeply attached to His friends. He found many who were disciplined in the love of appreciation. He loved them as He loves you. Is not love an attachment? And He had spiritual friends, too; He loved thinking about the prophets who had foretold His coming. He sought out the places where they had lived and often venerated the ground upon which they had walked. His love was appreciation and the knowledge of what they represented to the people on earth. Are you following Him? How often do you kneel before a saint's shrine and meditate upon his or her progression of knowledge in the love of God?

"As you kneel in the unfolding history of the past and see the dark days as well as the bright ones traced with pageantry as a thread in a tapestry, do you scoff at pageantry? Are you among those narrow souls who would blot it out from the earth? Do you realize that God Himself started the glad colorings of pageantry for our lives? Pageantry is the beginning of pomp, ceremony, ritual, and national pride."

Better to prove her story, Mother Mary opened the Scriptures and bid us follow her in the book of Sirach 45:6–13.

He (God) *exalted* Aaron . . . He made an *everlasting covenant* with him and gave him the priesthood of the nation and made him blessed in glory. And He girded him about with a *glorious girdle* and clothed him with a *robe of glory* and *crowned him with majestic attire.* He put upon him a garment to the feet, and breeches, and an ephod, and he compassed him with many little bells of gold all round about, that as he went there might be a sound, and a noise made that might be heard in the temple, for a memorial to the children of his people. He gave him a *holy robe of gold,* and blue, and purple, a woven work of a wise man, endued with judgment and truth: of twisted scarlet, a work of an artist, with precious stones cut and set in gold, and graven by the work of a lapidary, for a memorial, according to the number of the tribes of Israel. And a *crown of gold upon his miter, wherein was engraved holiness; an ornament of honor, a work of power, and delightful to the eyes for its beauty.* Before him there were none so beautiful, even from the beginning. No stranger was ever clothed with them, but only his children alone, and *his grandchildren forever.*

Mother Mary closed the Scriptures and said, "My children, even that which we know as pomp and pageantry is a good and holy attachment. Fear not using beautiful things for the service of God as well as in your homes when they lift your mind to God in thanksgiving. And allow yourself the beauty of thinking majestic thoughts, for it is like classical music rising to Heaven in contrast to the beat of calloused fingers on tom-toms. And in contemplation, allow yourselves the freedom of enjoying the pageantry of the ancient past. The birth of my Son was announced by the pageantry of angels in assumed human forms, dressed in colors pleasing to the human eye."

The mind's intellectual vision of Mother Mary and ourselves in the classroom faded away, and we were left alone with our thoughts before a shrine of a saint. Seemingly for the first time, we were seeing the color and majestic beauty known as pageantry before us. We each looked at the saint's face and then without realizing it, we were caught up into rapture before Saint Ignatius de Loyola. Time with us had lost its identity. We were very much alive with him in his age. We ventured to speak but we found no words. We had petitions, but they too, were now gone. Each of us thought—dare we take his time? No, he is still in a hurry. He turned and spoke to us as if he were singing to us in his language that we might follow him:

"Know you the journey that I take?
Know you the voyage that I make?
The joy of it one's heart could break.

No jot of time I have to spare,
Nor will to loiter anywhere.
So eager am I to be there.

For that, the way is hard and long,
For that, gray fears upon it throng,
I set my journey to a song.

And it grows wondrous so,
Singing, I hurry on for oh!
It is to God, to God, I go."
    (From my scrapbook)

SENSE MORTIFICATION AND APPLICATION

Lest we forget our weekly mortification, let us consider the sense of touch and daily—five times, no more and no less—make a touch-down prayer of thanksgiving for pageantry and the arts the Church has preserved for us even though it has been chided and warred upon for the cause of pomp and ritual, which must be fanned with pageantry. The touch-down prayer is to touch the forehead to the floor. Our neglect of this discipline necessitates a visit to a church and the finding there of a large statue of Christ and actually touching the open wounds, mindful of His real ones, for the number of times we neglected making the prayer.

Our general mortification for overcoming set ways is for us to sip a cup of coffee or tea in the presence of a friend and yet not drink of the beverage. We shall moisten the lip in memory of Christ's refusing the common wine, even though it was close to Him (sponge) when He was hung on the cross. We may trust that we are not noticed in the act of discipline, but if we are, we shall simply say that we are mortifying ourselves.

SCRIPTURE READING

Our Scripture reading has been given in the letter lesson. However, we may add Proverbs 23 in its entirety and Psalm 84 [83]:11. Have we stayed one day in the courts?— before the saint's shrine (where the relics of the saint are present).

Devotedly,
Cora

Thirtieth Letter Lesson

(PHILIPPIANS 4:4)

August 2, 1954

Dear Father,
For the hour, let us use the imaginative gifts and link the ancient past with view of the present. Suppose our present Holy Father gave us a command, as Moses gave to his people that they should leave their present occupations, home, relatives, and the luxury of shade and water and travel with him for forty years over a barren desert, with nothing more than his own word that he would lead them into the promised land (Heaven). Would we believe him? Would we question? Would we rather have life than the assurance of the promised land? Would we find it impossible to loose ourselves from the long fingers of materialism?

I believe the majority of us would say, "No" [it is not impossible]. The above question, in another light of meditation, could mean death and that we must spend forty years of wrong living—no one could say, "No," for it would be a must.

In the imaginative gifts, we exercise *will* when we link the ancient past with the present, and our *will* is an atomic, invisible power that we have not yet tapped to the fullest of its wisdom. Considering the desert, privations, trials, sorrow, and real Purgatory which most of us must venture into, let us not waste time and offer our life, monotony, and obedience as our Purgatorial purgation. Our *will* has the power of that accomplishment.

The people who followed Moses were singularly blessed with a miracle: a pillar of fire from Heaven charted the way. By day, it was a cloud protecting them from the heat of the earthly sun. The pillar of fire was a visible manifestation of God the Father, true Spirit, on earth, yet none of the people could approach close to the fire, for none could stand the effects of Its nature. But since the coming of Christ the Second Person, our human nature has been lifted up to a high point of perfection. Therefore, if we were to travel across earth's desert for forty years, we would suffer in greater intensity than the people of the ancient past because of our heritage which they began to form for us. In our makeup we have refinement, culture, wisdom, knowledge, and the arts of tradition which lift man's intellect to a quickness above the crudeness and force of the animal nature.

Today, our consolation would be in the *wills* of holy men who would sacrifice their lives to become priests that we might have Christ—another form of manna from Heaven, which was food for the Israelites to keep them alive. But the Flesh and Blood we eat *deifies us*, and we become One with Jesus as He and the Father are One. We are, as Israelites, crossing a desert, and our priests bring down from Heaven our veiled fire.

The *will* of man to do this or that is a powerful force which is often overlooked. If we could see the invisible accomplishments made possible through the power of *will*, we must freeze in a mystical death. It is well to reflect upon a few suggestions on the power of *will*. Man *wills* that he promote the human race, then God infuses the living soul. Man *wills* to love God or reject Him. The *will* of man creates charity, kindness, and love of neighbor, and it is in his power to create hate, revenge, and war. A mere word guided by *will* produces a mystical change even on substance; for example, a person in grief and tears over loss and in dismay over disappointment may say, "God, take all these tears and pangs of sorrow and accept them as expressions of love for Thee." That instant that *will* is granted, but *will* must act first. Also from that same quickness of *will*, evils are wrought upon the earth— man gives the devils the freedoms they want. It is of no wonder Jesus admonished us to guard against idle words and thoughts.

The Holy Father has asked us to follow Him during our life of pilgrimage, and to do so is to receive the "promised land." But how well are we following Him? After we have made resolutions to follow and heed not the materialism call, are we turning back? [That call] tells us of dance halls, bars with their din and noise, and the jungle music which induces men and women to imitate the ape. We are even taunted with their nakedness and loud laughter ridiculing the human body, which Christ has raised to a higher dignity and desires to become dignified. Temptations are many and, at times, the pleasures of the world are coaxing, but let us keep to the desert of this life and follow discipline of the five senses in order that we may escape the desert of Purgatory.

We must not consider the desert travel as a way of sadness. It is a journey of rejoicing—we are getting closer and closer to God. On that journey, let us become leaders and organizer of happiness. Let us repeat the Master's words when tiredness and discouragement come over our friends. He told them their mistakes and illogical thinking were the result of not having studied the Scriptures. The study, not reading, of the Bible can be a great source of joy. Christ knew the people of His day, as well as now, need the crystal waters of refreshment that the *Bible* can give. We must drink freely of philosophy, law and order, history, and the lifeline of civilization. Upon these knowledges of appreciation, the height of love is formed.

Father, let us pretend in the imaginative powers that we are watching a pilgrimage of people crossing a desert. They appear as tiny people, all dressed as miners with "cute" golden nuggets of knowledge from the depths of the Bible. Suddenly we are listening to a glad cry from one miner. What rejoicing! He is as a dwarf dancing among his friends and showing them the precious gold. As he gazes upon his wealth, his intellect is sharpened and he calls all his friends to listen, for he has unearthed a beautiful truth made brighter for this age of intellect.

"Look," he calls, "this nugget is a further explanation of *will*. It is astonishing to believe that man has hardly used his will. Truly man has been slothful—what reparation there is to be done! Friends, how have we glossed over this great mystery of will—did you know when the Israelites gathered the manna that it was like dew in color and size; at man's will, it tasted and satisfied as any food they desired at the moment? I will read from the book of Wisdom 16:20 and you can see for yourselves."

He opens the book for all to see, and he reads, "Thou didst feed Thy people with the food of angels, and gavest them bread from Heaven prepared without labor; having in it all that is delicious, and the sweetness of every taste. For Thy sustenance showed Thy sweetness to Thy children, and serving every man's *will*, it was turned to what every man liked."

Father, let us realize the power of will and learn more and more about its traditional history, which forms gratitude, carefulness, and delights within our own souls, for better do we know how to serve God. It is no wonder Saint Paul said "*Rejoice* in the Lord always, and again I say, *rejoice*" (Phil 4:4).

From a book entitled *Confidence in God*,[14]

If we want to serve God, joy should be not only an element, it should be the *staple* of our life. Our difficulties are so great, our enemies so many, that unless we are supported by *joy*, we *shan't* do what God wants us to do. It is a point of great consequence. There is a sort of impression that in the service of God there ought to be a certain sobriety, an earnestness—yes, SADNESS, which makes the distinction between servitude of the world, and the service of God; and that those who serve God must expect more tribulation and uneasiness of mind. ENTIRELY FALSE. Saint Paul, speaking under the dictation of the Holy Spirit, says, "REJOICE, again I say, REJOICE." If we think the ideal of a religious person is to be sad, it is quite wrong, it is the direct opposite of the truth. We are never so much fitted to cope with the difficulties of the spiritual life as when we are in joy.

Read carefully the Acts of the Apostles; no one can read them without being struck by the spirit of buoyancy and exaltation that fills and pervades them; one might almost call it high spirits. The Apostles carried their lives in their hands; they were scourged, and came forth from their severe flogging full of joy, rejoicing they were found worthy to suffer for their Lord. We certainly then can't be doing wrong in making our lives of joy (see Acts 5:41).

SENSE MORTIFICATION AND APPLICATION

This week the sense of taste is to be mortified on our journey across the desert of time. A good suggestion is for us not to take a second

14 ibid.

helping of anything when we are at table during the week. To do so is to move a bead across the counter, and at the end of day for the number of beads moved, we shall read the following poem applying its thoughts to self.

Promise For Tomorrow (Our Promised Land)

"The wind is never cruel to the leaves
Nor pulls unwilling beauty from a tree.
This is a clear design that surely weaves
The cycle of perfect destiny.

Rejected are the leaves, their task complete—
Rejected with a bright magnificence
That savors not of sadness nor defeat,
Nor backward looks to summer's eloquence.

Oh, foolish heart, can you not watch and learn
To cast away each dead and useless thing?
Let memories and sorrows briefly burn
And hold the knowledge of recurrent spring." (Eternity)
(Taken from my scrapbook)

SCRIPTURE READING FOR THE WEEK

We shall read as much as we can of the Acts of the Apostles.

Psalm 68 [67]:35

"Awesome is God from His holy place, the God of Israel; He gives power *and strength to* His people; *blessed be God."*

Our general mortification is for us to make a neat paper bookmark for our own Bibles with the above verse from Psalms written on it in our own handwriting.

Devotedly,
Cora

Thirty-First Letter Lesson

August 9, 1954

Dear Father,

How are we adorned and what is the condition of our souls as we approach the altar of God for an hour of adoration? This is a worthy subject of thought. Shall we choose it for our study this week?

Borrowing from the gifts of knowledge which we have gained through reason, history, and tradition, let us probe into the past. It will better serve us to highlight the present hour of our lives as well as to help us to learn the arts of application through questioning of our exterior and interior selves.

One of the first laws, as the principle of reasonable will approaches, is to feel the hidden promptings that we should worship God. In any state of life, and more especially in the contemplative atmospheres, have we considered how we look before God and His angels and saints as we enter a church? What have we done to perfect our deportment, actions, and the logical order of our prayers? If we were to approach and visit the President of the United States, we would put some thought into our preparations as to how we should greet him and how we should act. Then with greater preparation we should approach our God. We must never forget that we are members of the royal household. Come, let us make our holy hour of adoration with the above thoughts as considerations.

Are we clean in both body and soul and neatly dressed in an effort to be worthy of being in His presence? (Considerations are, of course, to be according to the different vocations in life, as well as according to means.) First, let us consider the importance. Are we as important as an ordinary ornament in the Church? Our answer must be "yes" because we have a living soul. Let us look at an ornament—a marble angel on the altar, and think about the care and workmanship that someone put into its creation. Since we possess a living soul, we are of greater worth; therefore, as members of the royal household, our preparation should be of even greater care—for we have our senses to perfect after they have died to self.

Let us suppose the marble angel could speak as we enter this church. It would shock us to no end if we heard him say, "It is more regrettable that a prince or princess of the royal household would appear adorned like that! Does he not know he should be dressed in the royal purple (mortification of the senses)? Why, he is of no more interest than an ordinary museum piece. I see no improvement over the last time he was here; in fact, he is more unkempt in both body and soul. What a pity he cannot see his procession of angels and how sad they appear because they are called to the 'Holy of Holies' with an unkempt master. This unkempt person would run for shame if he could see the invisible holy pageantry that comes over the church by angels and saints when a true prince of wisdom enters through the doors. All Heaven is brought to attention and the broad corridors are cleared that he or she may have direct ascent to God's throne."

Father, is it well for us to ask ourselves whether or not Heaven is glad or sad when we approach the altar of God? Our answer can be "yes," if hourly and daily we have striven for perfection for the love of God. It is of no value to seek perfection with fervency one week and the next fall into lukewarmness. God forbid that we should become museum pieces such as the marble statue, worthless, with the exception that as human beings we would have hope—hope that someone's prayers might be the means of final grace allowing us the terrible detour into Purgatory.

It is of great wisdom to consider ourselves as portable tabernacles (see 1 Cor 3:16–17 and Old Testament version Ex 29:41–46) in which God lives. This is better known as the indwelling, which allows Jesus to continue His life of the Resurrection in and through us. What a holy thought: to know that because we have received the King of Kings, we are magnificent, living sacramentals making everything we touch blessed. Our exterior, then, should always be clean, dignified, and groomed according to custom, means, and vocations in life. Our exterior is our individual tabernacle veil.

How well are we each keeping the laws of acceptance in our daily living of chiseling self—senses—as if we were working on a piece of marble, making something beautiful for God? Are we foolish in the expression "haste?" A sculptor does not make a masterpiece in a day. A scale of time has been given to us if we would but seek the symbol meaning of life. A steady life of rigid mortifications should show some results after a period of nine months. We each were hidden and formed in a dark quarry (our mother's womb) for nine months before we were unearthed and exposed to the sunlight and helping hands of masters of life who would lead us, teach us, and show us the way to Heaven. Our own first break as the savage self was to cry in rebellion because of hunger. We are slowly mellowed in the knowledge of a time and place for everything. Even though we reach to the age of ninety, we must continue to overcome ourselves and set ways of savages. We must do this in the knowledge that we were not made in a day and that Heaven is not going to be reached in a day. Life, from our beginnings, was a slow, steady growth under pressure, darkness, storm, water, frost, and pain.

If an artist such as Michelangelo could make himself visible as we chisel on ourselves by sporadically working diligently one day and forgetting well-formed resolutions the next, he no doubt would exclaim in disgust, "My, what blundering idiots!"

As sculptors, do we always have our tools readied for use and within a second's notice? Are they as first aids in emergencies when tempers might mar the delicate workmanship of a week's work? A drill and driver are symbols of courage, while a square and level are symbols of fortitude. A hammer is known as prayer and trust, and a sharp knife—the confessional. A buffer and polish are daily mortifications and the blueprints are the will of God. A sculptor always has a model, and ours should be none other than Jesus. We each must form ourselves into His likeness.

In a contemplative flight, let us take a walk through a quarry (Carrara) with Michelangelo. He is seeking a perfect piece of marble that he may sculpt the likeness of the Blessed Virgin. Later, in a great courtyard, he stops with disgust and gazes upon what had been a perfect piece when some person had had its great bulk removed from the quarry. It is still beautiful in its recognizably ruined state; it stands before us an eighteen-foot monument to the amateurish haste which characterized the insincere efforts of someone as he hacked into its perfection in a feeble effort to make something which would be considered as art. Stunned with the import of such incredible audacity, Michelangelo stands dejectedly at our sides, and we hear him disgustedly utter in protest, "What blundering idiot started this work and then cast everything aside?"

We can well understand Michelangelo's dejection and indignation. He is a good "brother's keeper" and cannot bear to see anything of worth lost. He has an evident appreciation of time and how God has planned the making of marble that man may work out his desires in creative objects. He is rapt in thought, and as animation of the heart wreathes his face in smiles, we thank God that through the eyes of an expert viewing ruination, we may see the hope of future beauty. When, at last, all the preparations are completed and our flight with him is resumed, Michelangelo picks up his mallet and tools and begins, with feverish chiseling, the release of beauty through love. One of his friends interrupts his work to ask, "Why didn't you continue in the search for the marble you sought? Surely, you don't mean to work on something someone else started? Not with your creative genius?" Michelangelo's pensive calm and smile gives credence to his simple reply, "Yes, there is an angel hidden in there, and I intend to let him out."

Are we as careful with our friends as Michelangelo was with marble? Do we try bringing out the good virtues instead of the bad in people? What kind of "brother's keeper" are we? From out of the seemingly ruined marble, Michelangelo sculpts the "Shepherd Boy"—his world-renowned *David* (see Psalm 78 [77]:69–72).

Shall we consider ourselves back in the expressions of our own times and walking down the center aisle of our own church thinking about our planned hour of adoration? Time is nothing. If God willed, we could be caught up into death this very instant—and what would we hear Him say? Would it be, "Well done, my faithful servant; you have given me something beautiful from your life." Or, would we hear His expression of disgust in our words, saying, "Some blundering idiot began this work of art and then cast it aside for the idle pleasures and wealth of the world?" Questions we should ask ourselves:

- Do we appreciate our worth? The infinite care God has taken in our sculpturing? Do we consider our friends at work in their own "studio" (self), chiseling on a masterpiece for Heaven?
- Are we not of more worth than the angel statue who day after day kneels beside the tabernacle? Should we not increase the number of our visits to the Blessed Sacrament?
- Is the perfection of our souls in better condition than since the last visit?
- Have we kept the interior of ourselves bright with the Light of the World by frequently receiving Jesus (see Jn: 1:10, 3:19–21)?
- Have we forgotten that we are not alone walking down the aisle? Are our angles embarrassed at our souls' slothful conditions, mannerisms, and dress?
- Have we forgotten that we are portable tabernacles continuing the life of Christ's Resurrection, and that we are "doers of the Word?"

To the slothful or to the one who has given up the race (see 1 Cor 9:24–27) for perfection, we could say, "A man does not give up medicine because there are quack doctors, and no man has a right to give up his mastering of Christianity because there are spurious or inconsistent Christians." (Taken from my scrapbook.)

Father, the following poem is food for thought in regard to ourselves as portable tabernacles.

Your Little Church

There is a little Church I know
Not very far away
You'll be surprised to hear of it
Yet you see it every day.
You need not walk to reach this Church
No riddle, this, but true
Nor wonder on that street it is
That little Church is you.
Is not your noble brow the tower?
Your eyes the windows bright,
Your heart the sanctuary lamp
That casts its crimson light?

Is not your voice the organ sweet
That sounds the hymn of love
Your holy thoughts the altar pure
Whence God comes from above?
Is not your soul, your precious soul,
The tabernacle white,
And your poor body not the veil
That hides Him from your sight?
Your tongue the table of the Lord
Your lips the open door,
Your prayers the tinkling of the bell
Your humble mien the floor?
Then place your hand upon your breast
A thousand times a day
And in your own dear little Church
Oft' loving visits pay.
(From my scrapbook collection)

SCRIPTURE READING

We shall continue reading the Acts of the Apostles.

Psalm 103 [102]:8

"The Lord is merciful and gracious, slow to anger and abounding in kindness."

SENSE MORTIFICATION AND APPLICATION

The sense of smell is to be mortified this week. We may forget the bead marker or counter this week and wear, or arrange in a bouquet, flowers whose fragrance we dislike. Our practice for the overcoming of set ways shall be to write a letter with pencil to a dear friend.

Devotedly,
Cora

PART TWO

Thoughts from the Heart

A.M.D.G.

IHS

September 28, 1955

Dear Father Frank,
As you already know through one of my letters, the Master appeared
to me on the 15th of September and gave to me the following message:
"With Father's permission and on the day Father sets as a beginning,
Saint Aloysius will appear to you every day for a year, and during that
time teach you the deeper tones of philosophy which will be the devot-
edness of and to little things."

Also, the Master further stated, "A great ship asail, especially
through the storms, mists, and sleet that you have encountered needs
a collier.[15] Refueling, polishing, and repairs are a necessity before further and greater travels are made, which I desire for you to make. Also,
the smiles and exchange of views from the collier crew (saints) will be
good for you. The lessons during the year will be a greater learning
which will bring to light stronger foundations."

Father, thank you as of today for the permission to venture into
such a mission of knowledge and grace. On the night of the 27th, I
was caught up into a rapture where blossomed the indescribable fired
arches which formed half-circles as a path to the interior of the Sacred
Heart. There in the arches, I saw my many friends and myself clothed
in the royal purple of the King's court. At times, we were approaching to the interior . . . and then retreated into the less dense light of an
exterior arch . . . many others backed away as though in fear, and the

---

15 In this context, a collier is one who stokes the fires of a ship's engine.

royal purple became clear again, instead of the crimson which seemed to clothe all who entered the fired hues of the arches. I understood the crimson-hued robes were symbols of martyrdom . . . a martyrdom over self such as this world knew and loved.

Then, visible before me sitting in the tall-backed chair, was Saint Aloysius. His graciousness was hospitality itself . . . he smiled and then said, as we both looked toward the vision of the Sacred Heart, "So much has been told you in this vision. However, there are a few points I would like to elaborate upon for your future good. The vision of the color change in the robes is a symbol of your clothing into the higher way of love for God. Become the crimsoned rose and bid your friends to follow, for did He not say that He had come to cast His fires out upon the world, and what would He that you become enkindled? Souls become enkindled one from another.

"All former lessons have formed a consciousness of the indwelling . . . the continuation of His life of the Resurrection in and through you. But there is a further step . . . it is the promise that to a few, He would give a foretaste of Heaven while they sojourned on earth. That foretaste is the basking in the fires of His Sacred Heart, which give peace such as the world and all its wealth could not buy. To win that peace, one must be undefiled. Nothing defiled can enter Heaven; therefore, it is necessary to battle against sin and to expiate whenever possible, better that spiritually you may bask in the Light of the Eternal Father made possible through the door of Christ's Heart. Thoughts or helps on the way of this possible perfection I will try teaching you during the coming year. Remember, to become a master of even one virtue is to have the degree of peace drawn to you on earth that you would have in Heaven. This is known as the peace reserved for the blessed.

"This way is a new horizon of spiritual health and wealth; it will call for many sacrifices of will and self-denial. Jesus has few friends who follow this way . . . in numbers they could be counted the world over as a small flotilla.

"Does not a small ship sway with the waves and have its sails trust to the trade winds? Does not this ship symbolize the spirit of flexibility and not fretfulness? Follow the pattern. These lessons will demand lightness of heart . . . Follow the guidance of the Holy Spirit . . . He gives you joy. This way is not for creatures who delight in their peeking-Tom curiosities, whose lives are of little worth and as lasting as an ephemera.

"And remember, the more you know the way of peace, the more you will fight the thoughts of intolerance. You must bend in charity for the poor who know not the way."

Saint Aloysius continued, "At times you too will experience the rise and fall of self in the fired arches. When you fall, remember the way of the cross . . . He rose and tried again. He is the way. Backsliders who care not and those who are easily defeated by the luxuries of life above Him grieve Him. Our fears and cowardliness disfigure Him as of two thousand years ago.

"In the past years, you have tried to become Christ [conscious] in the truths of the indwelling. Then you were clothed in the royal purple of the royal household . . . now you are being clothed in the crimson, which is a little above the purgative way. In those arches of His fire, you stand as a pilgrim on the very edge of Heaven. You stand peering as through lattices with all Heaven's citizens your guests. Be of great care in what you say, how you act, and how you pray, for they are peering at you through the window of His Heart. Dwellers in this nearness of Him have need of polish lest they become embarrassed . . . love and practice courtesies. In the august nearness to Him, your thoughts, words, deeds, and way of life reflect through Heaven as the tones of a great symphony, and when you retreat, your life resounds as the wildness of the tropics.

"Through the suggestions and helps in the way of peace, you will notice I do not suggest mortifications and penances. You are mature and should know through reasoning what to do. Every day it is wise to expiate for faults and neglects. Saint Francis de Sales, one of the collier crew, often said that souls in love with God should not be too harsh or severe with self. Follow moderation in all things."

MEDITATION THOUGHT

Hope to become a reflecting diadem, jeweled and ravished with His Light so that it may reflect and seek out the poor who need light and guidance. Become an example as Mary in modesty. Her life, her diadem, reflect upon you even today . . . your life will reflect perhaps for a thousand years; make your life beautiful . . . deeds are prayers for the generations to come. Unwillingness to follow the way is to cause Jesus to reflect upon the week of the Crucifixion."

I looked at Saint Aloysius in the chair, and his countenance took on the expressions of Jesus. Slowly, they were distorted in anguish because of the sins of immodesty, animalistic lusts, and sloth, the fertilizer of immodesty.

Again Saint Aloysius spoke, saying, "The subject matter for this day is MODESTY. Study well, for it has many root systems."

THE BEGINNING DAILY THOUGHTS
FOR THE YEAR BEGINNING SEPTEMBER 27, 1955

The following prayer is to be said and meditated upon for thirty days.

"I *vow* and consecrate to God all that is in me; my memory and my actions to God the Father, my understanding and my speech to God the Son, my will and my thoughts to God the Holy Spirit; my heart, my body, my tongue, my senses, and all my sufferings to the most Sacred Manhood of Christ." Saint Francis de Sales (1567–1622)

MODESTY

Modesty is Decency in All Things

Neatness and cleanliness . . .
Law and order in all things . . .
Properly groomed as children of God for every occasion.
Modesty in speech.
Modesty is not to exaggerate in one's greatness or littleness.
Modesty is of quiet voice.

Modesty Knows Gratitude

Greatness is proved by toning down personal opinions . . .
Our debt to our nation is to become an example of culture . . .

Question self upon leaving house: Will I be an imposition?
Modesty does not embarrass guests.

Modesty is Kind

Think of justice and culture when needs be you must admonish.
Modesty is polite . . .
Modesty is not gluttonous in food, drink, or medicine.
Modesty is reserved, not quick to speak nor angered.
Modesty is reserved in greetings, goodbyes, and in expressions of joy.

Modesty is Refinement

Strive for the manners of a King's daughter or son.
Know ye the art of poise?
HELPS: [When] sitting, do not cross knees. Cross ankles and have them drawn close to chair.
Do not fall into chair or on lounge . . . you are acting before the congregation of Heaven.
Hands should be reminders of peace . . . don't wave them about as something you would discard.
Cease being a picker at everything . . . [hands] should rest as wings of a folded dove when a person is reclining or resting.

PRAYER FOR DAILY NEGLECTS . . .
TO BE SAID ALSO FOR THIRTY DAYS

"Eternal Father, I offer Thee the Sacred Heart of Jesus, with all Its love, all Its sufferings, and all Its merits.

First: To expiate all the sins I have committed this day and during all my life. *Gloria Patri.*

Second: To purify the good I have done badly this day and during all my life. *Gloria Patri.*

Third: To minister for the good I ought to have done, and that I have neglected this day and during all my life. *Gloria Patri.*"

(Footnote attached to this prayer says, "A Poor Clare, who had just died, appeared to her abbess who was praying for her, and said to her, 'I went straight to Heaven, for, by means of this prayer, recited every evening, I paid all my debts.'")

Devotedly
Cora

A.M.D.G.

I H S

September 29, 1955

Dear Father Frank,
Today, let us think carefully on the subject, "QUIETNESS." Since the error of Quietism, it has been overlooked as a need in the world of activity and mental prayer. In regards to prayer, "QUIET" is the symbol of a peaceful soul. QUIET must not be confused with SILENCE.

The error of Quietism was like a thief trying to force the locks of Heaven's door in order to gain entrance to mysticism. That door cannot be forced or unlocked from the outside . . . God alone has the key, and He comes down to His creatures. The error of the Quietists [is to] believe they should make their minds as a vacuum . . . thinking about nothing . . . and then into that vacuum God would speak and give visions. This exhausted state of mind is as crippling to the human mind and body as the constant intake of liquor. God did not intend for us to become a silent criosphinx.[16]

The quiet soul is both filled with peace and active understanding. Christ was a quiet Man . . . He was not uncouth or rowdy. All His actions were done for the love of His Father. One of the virtues of quietness is the love of solitude and the will to seek loneness of self for at least five minutes a day, where soul and body speak alone with God.

1. Over a sink of dishes, we hear their clattering noise . . . in the laws of quietness, we can become a citizen of Jerusalem and pretend they

---

16 Editor's note: A sphinx with the head of a ram.

are the wild clatter of hoofs taking the soldiers to oversee the Crucifixion. A QUIET soul is an inventor.

2. In a state of loneness and when our lips are quiet, we may speak of gratitude from our hearts. And on the desert when our heart is awed with the vastness, our ears may feel the pain of desert noises.

In all quietness in the rise of God, there is and must be at least one of the senses in the state of activity. In quiet repose, the mind can be alert and working, following the Passion. We must shun QUIETISM, for it is mental sloth which brings forth dullards.

OFTEN GOD SPEAKS AND
ACTS THROUGH A QUIET SOUL

Reading Scripture alone is the veil of quietness. God may speak!
Admiration of the sheen on a still lake is quietness. God may speak!
Observing the calm of a forest, or the awesomeness of its wildness is
  quietness. God may speak!
Alone in a swing is quietness if we are thankful. God may speak!
Sleep is quietness. It is folding the blanket of TRUST over us . . . is it
  not the belief of God's trusting hand over us? Jesus slept in his boat
  as it tossed on a troubled sea.

MEDITATION

Sleep is the instrument of giving . . .
Giving God my quiet and gaining peace myself.
Fondly mother's watch their infants sleeping . . .
God in turn watches us . . . in quiet He finds no resistance.

Sleep a gift! I plead, Lord, take this body of mine . . .
In quietness of sleep place it on the altar in Your Heart.
Make the mirrored image of myself like Thine . . .
That my sleep of quiet may prove the joy of saints,
As they come in quietness through Heaven's floodlights and mists.

In their peace do they breathe across our earth, the body . . .
And do they say, "This earth is calm?
She breathes the quietness of the dawn!
She has given much to deserve this quiet . . .
No one comes this close to us,
Except they live QUIETNESS of selfless deed."

And in my active hours let me quietly sing . . .

"Be still, my heart, beneath the rod,
And murmur not;
He, too, was man—the Son of God—
And shared thy lot.

Shared all that we can suffer here,
The wrong, the loss,
The bloody sweat, the scourge, the sneer,
The crown, the cross.

The final terror of the tomb—
His guiltless head!
Self-consecrated to the doom
We merited.

Then languish not for Edens lost
Or vanished bliss;
The heart that suffers most
Resembles His."
　Sister M. Teresino

Devotedly,
Cora

I H S

September 30, 1955

Dear Father Frank,
How we must often appear in our uncouthness to Saint Aloysius. Ah, at times I think I must be akin to a mollusk, a cuttlefish, with an ink splash always ready to cover everything, even sloth. And tentacles to grab without first considering the rights of others in their way of peace. As these thoughts raced through my mind as I hastened to do my work, Saint Aloysius appeared and said, "Today we will choose the word, 'Haste,' and its usual implications to life, stress, or peace."

As near as I can remember, he said, "Haste is a flowering word with two tap roots. A flower can be ugly and a flower can be beautiful. One tap root leads to good and the other [to] evil. Haste for the good of doing good can be classed with zeal to accomplish learning, acts, and prayers for the love of God. Haste because of sloth and what might the neighbor think if this or that were not made right is placing God and His way second. Duties of a home should be kept in the path of law and order. There are few exceptions that should break the rule. If one is slothful, then the key of haste must come into use, and it usually brings evil. Haste is to give the impression to both people and angels that we are impatient, and haste leads to impatience, and impatience leads to anger and pride. Haste is a dance to the devil's flute . . . he laughs and makes merry the more you hasten outside the laws of order in all things.

"Haste hinders the sweet consolations that God would want to give. Haste is to exalt the devil; he loves disorder. Haste is the gown of the egoist. A person who does not live by rule and order for the love of

God, forgetting self, is habitually a selfish person with no regard for the 'brother's keeper' command our Jesus asked of us.

"The good tap root is spiritual impatience with self to hasten the time we may be alone with God in our thoughts. We must hasten through learning and acquiring devotions and respect of wisdom to make the hours alone with Him more golden and of such persuasions of joy that we hasten for the return. How beautiful to think that at the entrance of these golden hours with Him, an angel greets us with this song:

'May every blessing this life can hold
Be yours in the fullest measure,
May content, that is better
Than gems or gold,
Fill your future days with pleasure;
May clouds ne'er gather above your way,
Nor grief nor gloom oppress you,
And every hour and every day
May God befriend and bless you.'"

Saint Aloysius continued, "The fullest measure, the pleasure, and the nothing to oppress you are seldom felt when law and order are lived according to all and different vocations. Remember, haste is the key that allows evil to enter your heart, home, place of business, or play. Remember, Jesus was never seen to be in a state of haste."

Devotedly in the Sacred Heart of JESUS,
Cora

A.M.D.G.

IHS

October 1, 1955

Dear Father Frank,
Thought from *The Little Flower Prayer Book*:
"We should look for no support except JESUS. He alone is immutable. What *joy* to think that He can never change."
Life must be balanced well with joys and sorrows. The joys are the gems to the crown made from sorrows. In meditation and contemplation, there must be laughs and joys . . . all is not sorrow . . . Christ was a *happy* child. And even in the week of the Passion, there were moments of pantagruelism.[17]
When life ends, all things will be made right . . . then we shall understand why so much was hidden from our sight. If now we were to see God face to face, life would be without a crown, for all happenings contemplated in the joys of Heaven would be as a mere breath.
When trials are hard to take from friends and relations, let us pretend that we are smaller than a toddling child . . . let us contemplate the life of a papoose on his mother's back. He cares not this hour that he sees not his mother's face . . . she has work to do . . . his little life must be one of trust.
You do not see God face to face, yet He clothes and feeds you and more beautifully than all the flowers, for you are gilded with sanctifying grace. Like the papoose, He does not give you a mirror . . . you cannot see the beauty of your soul, nor would you, until after death, understand.
Does not the life of a papoose, so close to his mother, suffer fly and insect bites? Are not his eyes often tightly closed to the burning rays of

---

17 Editor's note: Broad humor or buffoonery.

the heat? And does not the early morning frost pinch his cheeks and mar the smile that warmth would bring? And does not he cry when a foot is cramped? All these are expressions of life . . . we are so close to His Face . . . yet we do not see, and all the time He cares for us in the way, the pattern, and scheme of life which is a battlefield. Life is not Heaven . . . we are soldiers fighting to either win or lose.

MEDITATION

Cease holding life a regret . . .
There have been many joys.
Count them and also those you have lent . . .
Yes, you have scattered Christ's toys,
Regrets are the clouds of midnight black . . .
It is the lowest ebb before the dawns.
How many nights? Cease . . . don't provoke . . .
Look up and ask, How many dawns?
God, the Baker, sifts His golden flour
You are the leaven in the wedding cake . . .
Begin your work, stir up your mind this hour . . .
Lest you die and see the Baker.
As you sow so shall you reap, this is part of life's recipe.

The Baker could say, "You have failed to raise the wedding cake . . .
Go your way, for I have yet many souls to stir . . .
And many golden dawns have I yet to sift,
Into the leaven of willing hearts.
Go back and become the leaven . . .
Tell your friends the Groom is not yet ready,
When the banquet is ready, I'll rise to meet you . . .
And I'll come in a day you least expect . . .
Begin your work, stir you your mind this hour . . .
I'm sending down graces to help you."

Devotedly,
Cora

A.M.D.G.

IHS

October 2, 1955

Dear Father Frank,
The atmosphere of a rapture is slowly moving away. Its quietness is the silence of a kitten's paw walking on silk in a fog. In rapture . . . what beautiful acquaintanceships with the saints! Would that we could always believe there is no distance to the beyond.

I am still marveling at the scene the saints and angels made possible for me, better than I may learn in symbols the meaning of "Dullard." In the intellectual vision, as clear as day, I spiritually heard the approach of a train. Saint Aloysius stood near me and said, "A dullard just died. A dullard, here en route to Purgatory, is known as a person who just made Heaven via this way because of a victim-soul's prayers. He loved the world so much that he has a trainload of luggage. Here he will learn detachment . . . that is the reason for Purgatory. Detachment, better that he may see God. Come, let us watch the items on the train and see what useless things and broken laws kept him from seeking God above the imitation gods. Often, he grumbled about life, but here he will spend a thousand times a life overcoming the mountains of earth's litter."

Slowly, the train approached us . . . it was a long, small train. Something like the children's trains that give such joy in city parks. In the engine sat the man's guardian angel . . . he was joyous, was not his mission in life over? Then car after car filled with just plain dirt. These cars represented scandal the man had given in life. At least one hundred other cars were filled with mannequins . . . all beautifully dressed

... they were the women he had enjoyed above rights of marriage laws ... for a while, he had made them his gods. The following cars of at least twelve were filled with waiters, all active in pouring water from glasses and then filling them with ink like water. These were emptied and filled with the water originally poured out of them ... the water could not be lost ... the servants were beside themselves trying to lose the water but somehow it managed to find its way back to the glass. These cards were labeled, "Duplicity." This man was always in a state of confusion ... never did he enjoy the joys of conviction.

Other cars moved slowly along, and they were filled with cook servants all making dumb-cakes. As they stirred the batters, they looked wise and heavenward and pretended knowing something from out of the air. The cars were labeled, "Fortune tellers and black magic." This man, delayed in Purgatory, taught his servants that on the eve of Saint Mark's Day, if they made a cake in silence, they would know who they were to marry.

Other cars too numerous to mention with all the gewgaws that life could bring to mind were portrayed in their uselessness. Then, trudging along came the decrepit sinner. He was pushing the long little train at a snail's pace. He appeared weary ... his fatigue made him tremble, but he said as he walked by as if he knew I was an earthly person on bilocation, "I am not worthy to seek nor beg prayers ... I alone must atone. I have just made Heaven because of a person's prayers ... someday in Heaven I will know that person who followed the way of Christ. Redeemers, redeemers all over the earth, so I am told, all saving souls for Heaven's joys. My heaven will be when I shake myself free from these useless things. I beg of you to plead with my friends not to make these useless objects their God. I must stay in purgation until all the friends, those whom I have led astray, sleep the sleep of death and they can no longer repeat nor discuss my actions ... one by one, as they die, the luggage you see will become less and less."

Other trains were slowly making the grade up Purgatorial Hill. On a signal sign I read, "This track for DULLARDS."

I turned and with Saint Aloysius walked toward home. He said,

"Life is to become a patient weaver . . .
A doer in all vocations.
A drone will never rise to conquer . . .
For him the devil is carnivorous.
Good people know their deeds, like weavers know their threads . . .
The finest are silver and gold, but there are black ones too,
Mixed with red and grey and white.
Notice, if you will, the blackest are the frailest . . .
Like cobwebs without a twist for strength.
Tread carefully when you weave with black . . .
Despair is trickery and iced.
But weave them slowly and with much thought for they will enhance
    the red.

And as you weave remember, the dawn is just ahead . . .
And soon the gold will leap like fireflies . . .
Believe, by thanking God.
To break your faith while weaving black is despair . . . loss of time and
    perhaps everlasting death.
And dullards too are born because of the grey and the black . . .
They care not to weave with other than gold . . .
They would make life without a crown . . .
And in devil's freedom they care not upon whom they tread.
Their friends, you ask . . . just a flask.
Weave carefully and you will not have time for the way of DULLARDS."

Devotedly,
Cora

I H S

October 3, 1955

Dear Father Frank,
Thought from *The Little Flower Prayer Book*:
"Behold, how good and how pleasant it is for brethren to dwell together in unity."

Friendship, not relationship is the thought for today. The graces of good friendship are the perfume of God's hidden gardens within us. His garden of souls is most unique . . . no two souls alike . . . and each will raise its thoughts and prayers to God in a different way. Ah, it is a wholesome gift . . . to know the soundings of philosophy, for there we find the patterns of souls and how best to help them grow for the love of God. And we learn the bouquets to choose and bring together for earth's greater peace.

An unlearned caretaker mixes all kinds . . . sunflowers and roses and thistle . . . true, they are a bouquet, but what disorder of culture . . . they bring a frown. Customs, culture . . . the way of love for God these bring confidence and oneness that all friends should have. Likeness to likeness is one little way of peace.

What kind of flower are we in His garden? If we see ourselves in the boldness of a sunflower, we may with God's grace change our style and culture . . . we are humans and not just the rooted flower. If we are content to stay the rough sunflower, don't expect to be picked and held in admiration with a rose. Are we a dahlia . . . huge in a boisterous manner? And it is usually showy in all its blustery color. And we could be a violet . . . it is beautiful but afraid . . . its coyness is to steal from man the little fragrance God gave. God does not want us to hide our spiritual gifts beneath a leaf or bushel. The rose is like a cup, a chalice, ever running over with its heavenly fragrance . . . And its velvet is not so frail that man cannot touch. It unfolds in such a plan of mystery that we long to follow it alone . . . to the eternal shores of God.

One rose has already captured Heaven's fragrance and it gives to friends . . . it has nothing to keep for itself. Two roses caught up together are more powerful in their giving and they lend beauty and dignity . . . a gift for God . . . they enhance the value of the other. As roses are alike in cares and love, so too should friendships have understanding and loyalty which means willingness to give one another in the fullest delight of integrity.

Catch the grace-like rains from heaven and with his mystical roses say . . .

"Dear Jesus, help me to spread Thy fragrance everywhere I go; flood my soul with Thy Spirit and life; penetrate and possess my whole being so utterly that all my life may only be a radiance of Thine; shine through me and be so in me that every soul I come in contact with may feel Thy Presence in my soul; let them look up, and see no longer me—but only Jesus!"

MEDITATION

Lord, let me never say . . . just a half an embrace . . .
Teach me in confidence that You are not a sword-like thorn.
In all life, there is a story of two sides . . .
The rose has both the fragrance and the thorn.
Are you not the kindly Father who would say, "Don't touch . . .
The thorn will prick you . . . touch the cup of Heaven's gold?"
Lord, let me never say . . . just half a friend . . .
Teach me the love and the lore of true friendships . . .
And then when life ends I'll not be afraid . . .
For I will have followed Your kind loving WAY.
Never did You give in just halves . . .
You gave the whole embrace of the cross to Your friends.

Devotedly,
Cora

IHS

October 4, 1955

Dear Father Frank,
PRAYERS TO BE MEDITATED (indulgence granted):
   "By the sign of the holy cross, deliver us from our enemies, O our God!"
   Jesus said, "If any man would come after Me, let him deny himself and take up his cross daily, and follow Me." Saint Luke 9:23
   Raise your arms sidewise . . . do you not resemble a cross? Since you well understand Saint Paul's teachings that it is no longer you but Christ within you . . . then your body is the suffering corpus. Daily we are to take up this body and move it along according to our vocations in life. It is a portable tabernacle taking Christ within it and allowing Him to bless, and through our senses, cheer the weak and give hope to the needy. He did not mean that we should find the easy path and fondle a metal and highly polished cross. We ARE THE CROSS!

Jesus is active . . . He smothers in the body of a drone.
He is ever creative . . . nothing in life is perfection.
He hopes in and through us to be lifted up . . . then through Him all
   things will be given Him.
(Life would have greater joys.)
He trusts that we will ever search first for the kingdom of God . . . know-
   ing that all we desire will be given us, for it is not possible for God the
   Father to refuse His Son, within us, anything.
Every day must be busy with our talents except the day of rest.

Temperance bars the injustice of sloth away from us.
His day of the Crucifixion was busy . . .
He was spat upon, jeered and laughed at . . .
He was mocked by termagants . . .
He was tired and thirsty . . .
He too suffered lonesomeness. His friends along the way hid behind
   stoic faces, pretending they did not know Him . . .
He too knew the monotony of being instant in prayer . . .
He was weary when calls came from the crowd asking for charity . . .
He was a teacher in the wheat field . . . a physician for the sick, the
   miracle man for the dead . . . and a cure-all for the lamb.
He was not lazy . . . He worked that others might have.

Regardless of our vocations . . . and there are many, we fit into the
pattern as we follow Him. Let us carry the cross as soldiers under the
banner of fearlessness. The cross is not a garment to be worn only for
today . . . it is a lifetime job. At death God will give us a change, until
then we cannot cast it aside.

THOUGHTS FROM THE HEART

O cross of me . . . don't break in faith . . .
O cross of me . . . don't have shattered nerves . . .
O cross of me . . . don't hide in a sheath . . .
O cross of me . . . follow Him . . . He serves.
On His way to Calvary, He did not say . . .
Could I be wrong?
On His way to Calvary, He did not say . . .
Quiet, people . . . My nerves!
On His way to Calvary, He did not say . . .
I'm sleepy . . . I'll raise My scepter another day . . .
Nor did he say when he saw me along the path . . .
You there, you do not need to serve.

Devotedly,
Cora

A.M.D.G.

I H S

October 5, 1955

Dear Father Frank,
The subject matter today is taken from the booklet titled *Confidence in God*[18] by Rev. Daniel Considine, S.J. Quote: "Do not dwell on the faults and sins of the past. Leave them alone; leave them to God. As soon as possible, make an Act of Contrition and never think of them again. Often the despondence cause by sin is more wrong and keeps one away from God more than the sin itself. Get up and go to God. Do not stand back hanging your head."

Dwelling on the past is to thrust joy aside. Joy may die if it is not watered with the trust that brings joy. We must not forget that joy is one of the [fruits] of the Holy Spirit. We must not neglect that gift. A joyous person is a peaceful soul even in the midst of adversity. Let us cast out morbidness and regrets as we would drive away pain with medicine and make light where there is darkness.

If, at least three times a day, we do not find our interior self exhilarated, then let us take meditation's shovel and dig out the joys of the past and of today. Unearth, as a grave-digger . . . the forgotten things in your soul for which you could be grateful. Dig up enough and soon you will be joyous and even laugh. Mystically we have a beautiful album within our hearts . . . open it often. Would not the first page tell us of the gift of faith? What joy to know we need not seek another God. Ah, and the grace of conviction is another joy that softens dejection and indecision.

18 ibid.

And count the deeds that you have done to give others joy! And have you not smiled the smile of joy when congratulations came your way? God is a God of consolations both for this earth and the next. We are caught up in His hand for a caress through consolation rather than fear. Joy is the belief that we will share in the Resurrection. Joy is the necklace of friends . . . we are not alone in this world. Joy is the symbol of self as a rose opening in the sun.

And if you are a gardener, you will feel disappointment as a bud fails to open. Why? A bud cannot sing nor speak at its opening. Its life is silence, yet living the laws it was ordained to do. The blossoming rose is the symbol of completion . . . giving all its perfection to man that he might have color and fragrance in life.

In this way, so too we please God when we continue to grow. How sad the unfolding music from our hearts when we dwell on the faults and sins of the past. Suppose we could hear a rose telling of its past history. It would not be interesting. No doubt it would bring a frown, and we would forget the fragrance it should give. A rose could say, *Really, I am not so beautiful . . . if you only knew what I thrived on, you would cringe. Often I am starved for water and in revolt I plan not another bud. And one day the sun parched the edges of my petals . . . I'm not so pretty because of that mar. And the hoe of the gardener came too close to my rootlets and I wept and I stormed, and in revenge I gave not a beautiful rose.*

To have heard a rose in its language we would have turned away in disgust, regardless of its beauty. Let us follow the life of growth and not dig into the soil around us. Let us just be self as God wants us and blossom for the day. He will bring good out of our imperfections if we adore, praise, and thank Him.

THOUGHTS FROM THE HEART

O joy of God's Heart clothe me . . .
I am such an imperfect rose.
O angels, fragrance me with your incense . . .
And scatter the pestling augurs.
At my roots they are as insect bites . . .

And their sting reminds me of the past . . .
A past of graceless art.
Now through joys of uplifted heart . . .
These fitish pasts I forfeit.
O glorious joy . . .
Your power is above the gorgon.
And hobbled minds run free . . .
Again, I am a child in Jerusalem.

Devotedly,
Cora

I H S

October 6, 1955

Dear Father Frank,
When Saint Aloysius appeared, he seemed to be holding two rosaries. They were of a glass texture; one was red and one was green. He said they represented two phases in everybody's life . . . namely, disappointment and hope. He said it would be a good practice, when disappointments pointed at us, to take up our rosary and, pretending we hold the red one, say on the cross, "Jesus, keep me cheerful through the power of Thy Holy Name." And on the large bead to say, "I am glad for this disappointment, for through it I have something to offer Thee." On the small beads: "Mary, you were meek . . . show me the way."

And now pretending we hold the green one, say on the cross, "Jesus, through You we have hope of everlasting life." On the large bead say, "Peace my troubled soul . . . I will not allow the enemy in to dim the Light of God." On the small beads say, "Hope is the song of the blessed."

Saint Aloysius continued, saying something to this effect, "Life is a battlefield of many wills. Through other wills, sometimes right and sometimes wrong, we are forced to take a detour in our original plans. This is a type of disappointment, but mind you, it is not defeat if you are of the right spirit, believing God will bring good out of evil and our disappointments too, which of themselves are not of evil but the will of friends.

"Meditate on the many facet ways of knowledge on the subject hope and you will wear the robe of a conqueror. Hope is not to condemn your [worst] enemy. Hope is to give peace in actions and deeds. Hope

is to forgive those who seem to torment us with paths of detours . . .
forgive them in your heart as Jesus forgave those who crucified Him.
Did he not say, 'Forgive them, Father, for they know not what they do.'
Remember too, blessed is the man or woman who can daily repeat the
words of our suffering Jesus. In our lives, we continue His life in and
through us, also we must continue repeating His words when disappointments flay us."

THOUGHTS FROM THE HEART

Take Thy scepter, Lord, and mark on me . . .
Your emblem of "right spirit."
I have wasted, Lord, the candle of light given me . . .
In dim dark halls I've been content,
To be the sconce of little worth in Your great house.
And in my light thieves have come and made plans . . .
That they might twist the minds of the royal household.
No longer though, in my light will they spoliate.
Take me, the rusty sconce, close to Thy Heart . . .
Close to the altar stairs . . .
In Thy reflecting Light I'll wear the gold and red . . .
I'll be another Sacred Heart.

Devotedly,
Cora

I H S

October 7, 1955

Dear Father Frank,
"By Thy help I can serve Thee." (Phrase taken from daily prayer book.) Help, when it is referred as coming from God, is another word for GRACE. Grace means that He has given us a crutch for our lame nature. Grace is the smile of God upon our frailties. Grace is His way of bringing contrition with tears for our sins and faults. Grace is His doctrine through which we aspire for the real, as well as spiritual education. Grace is the hope that we may make the goal to eternal life with Him. Grace is His HELP.

His personal help as Second Person is made possible to us because He suffered and died on the cross because He willed to help us. The cross on Calvary was the paddle that stirred our stilled waters and made us restless for the furtherings of truth which come through helps. The Holy Spirit is a HELP. He is time on wings, better to make us make haste, for the span of life is short. God's help makes us strong, and we stop cowering as a sparrow in the rain beneath a leaf.

Round about us and on every side, we are pinned or anchored by His HELPs (graces). God is the giver of helps, and in Him we trust. And God in His heavens looks down on us as through a window made possible through the Second Person, when He pulled aside the curtain and allowed Margaret Mary to see the Light of the First Person through His Heart. Through the eyes of faith, we too see the word-images she has drawn for us. God's ways are many and beyond our vision, and on faith, we love, trust, and seek His other guiding helps. Jesus said, "No one goes to the Father except through Me" (Jn 14:6). Let us seek the window opened for all, and listen carefully to the HELPS through the consolations of the promises.

And knowing we must follow Him all the way and He was the teacher; it is to believe that we too must become givers of knowledge, truths, and gifts to our fellow men. Our way of helps may come in many ways . . . feeding the hungry, alms, giving clothes and warmth of word and deed. Truth, too, because we have studied His laws and found them sweet . . . this honey cannot be shared unless it is given. How many helps have we given friends today? And also, how have we helped and added to our spiritual growth today? How many diamonds did we take from the banquet to give our friends? Grace is His HELP.

THOUGHTS FROM THE HEART

Lord, as I reach for Thy gifts known as graces . . .
Bid me remember to take a portion for another.
There are many friends, relations, and the sufferers of being over-cautious,
They ever taste of blight and never find the courage to try Thy way.
And there are friends who know of time through purgatorial's calendar.
Nothing then from Thy treasury must I take . . .
Unless I think of giving to another . . .
This is the culture of living Thy way.
Lord, help me that I may give Thy help . . .
Before the thread-like cusp of life,
Reminds me that life is ending . . .
And soon Thy holy face and helpful smile I'll see.

Devotedly,
Cora

I H S

October 8, 1955

Dear Father Frank,
True sorrows are not often shown by sadness nor great expressions of tears. There are sorrows so great no man can speak of their weight, and their depths reveal the face as wearing a stoic mask.

Many man-made crosses are caused by neglectfulness and unthoughtfulness on the part of relations and friends. They are the spear-points that cause slow martyrdom. In friends' hands, they are the little plows cutting across the fields of our hearts. The deeper the sorrows, the deeper the furrows, which in time will hold the most of Heaven's gifts, such as the rains of consolations which give greater life and gifts. Alone with the memories of such unfaithful and unkind friends, and even if our eyes are veiled with tears, we must not cease in the hope that good rains do come. God in His justice is kind to those who love and trust.

There are many kinds of tears, and it is well to analyze our tears as we would a conscience as to whether or not they toned with the hypocritical. Tears can be easily managed in a selfish person ... at will they appear to turn the faucet as with such grace as picking a flower. Little do they realize, in reality they are walking through God's flower garden of souls. And their self-pity, selfishness, and hate wallowing in tears mar the flowers of His Heart. They are the cause of ill health, insanity, breakdowns of courage and nerves. They cause the slowing of spiritual climbs and mar the budding perfection of a rose in His garden. Such selfish natures are thieves known as wolves, roaming through His gardens in sheep clothing. This type of ever-ready-fountain type person should be avoided as bad companions.

And there are tears of sorrow over loss. However, a person on the climb to God, who has practiced the crucifixion of the senses, will make short the days of mourning, for well they realize that time is short, and all must be given to adoration, praise, and thanksgiving. Loss of a loved one through death is a natural cause and should be regarded in the natural as with births . . . just a few days of rejoicing and mourning. An overindulgence of tears and mourning are the marks of a selfish person who uses every known means for the gaining of sympathy.

And there are tears known to us as the gift of tears, either through the wisdom of knowing our faults and how they have offended God or through the joys of His supernatural consolations. These tears are so precious they should be shed alone and spoken about to the closest friends who in wisdom know the depths of the interior life. These tears are the pearls that are not to be cast before swine.

And let us not forget the tears caused by pain to the body. Often endurances are far spent and allowed in life that we may know the littleness of self and how dependent we are on the acts of mercy through friends. Tears because of bodily pain are of great worth if one does not curse the pain and cause. Blessed is the man who in life knows the depths of engulfing pain . . . he has tasted of the greater life with Jesus on the cross.

Tears because of homesickness is but the knowledge that we are not yet mature. Nostalgia is of high regard when tears come, if the loneliness is for the eternal home. For such an illness there is one nostrum lest we become morbid, and that is the art of falling in love with Jesus.

THOUGHTS FROM THE HEART

I am just a reed standing in a pond . . .
My roots are in shallow silt . . .
My heritage has not been long,
I'm a convert.
In that pond I stand among husky types of sugar canes,

And of course the useless worldly nots.
I shrink from fear as [gnarled] hands with scythes
Cut the husky growths of good sugar canes.
Ah their tears of sweetness ooze into the pond . . .
They are the hidden strength for the little reed.
And they weep again, the husky canes when they are crushed . . .
And their tears caught up into vats . . .
The store-house of the Sacred Heart,
From where every man may draw the sustenance
For life and spiritual needs.
As I draw their nourishment, I beg . . .
God grant that I may not waste a tear.
May I know the weakness they cause . . .
Without the blush of shame.
For they could be the gifts of grace to tame an erring soul.
Help me to smile through veils of tears, for they could help the lame.
Let me thank God for the cutting ploughs that furrow my fields . . .
Never let me curse,
For these could be wealth for the poor in their purse.
And let me not forget, Jesus wept . . .
In union let me mingle mine with His.

Devotedly,
Cora

A.M.D.G.

I H S

October 9, 1955

Dear Father Frank,

The *ability* and courage to speak truth is the artistry of perfection. The Curé d'Ars once answered when he was questioned about his holiness, "I am not afraid of trouble; that is all." How well this great priest knew spiritual freedom because he had the ability to put desire into action. Spiritual freedoms are the doors of one's heart left open to the smile and wisdom of God, which knows no fear. In union with God, man had everything with which to plan his life. He has courage, endurance, will, vision of the future because he is a heritage builder for the young [and] not yet born.

The man of such freedoms knows that book learning is not enough. Tradition from tongue to tongue is not enough, and neither is the unbending Puritanism mood that no one else has a right to their opinions. In God's freedoms, man senses that he has many talents and that he is capable of skills . . . all must be put to work for the love of God and that His goodness may be manifest on earth. Jesus once said, "*Work* out your salvation; traffic until I come." [cf. Phil 2:12, Lk 19:13; author emphasis] Traffic means the ability to give, lend, and listen to the hearts of men and their cares and joys. Exchange delights and sympathize with the mourning. Exchange of philosophies are means of traffic until He comes . . . Good minds enhance each other, and wills are twined in tolerance and understanding, which lends to better living.

Any ability or will to do must have effort on man's part and true faith in God. Effort and ability walk hand in hand to perform acts of mercy, kindness, and teaching the way of God. Riches and wealth must be sought after with a prayer for good governing, for these lead to the means that furnish the power of ability. Great charities could not be given to institutions unless first someone had the faith, the ability, and the charity to work out his best in the knowledge of ability.

The sloth might try excusing himself, saying that he is ignorant and without any special talent. And man could lie at an aptitude test, better to prove that he was not able to work, or as the Master said, "Traffic until I come." Let the sloth in any walk of life question self as to who he is kidding? God knows everything and will exact from us what we have done with our talents when life is withdrawn from us. God will frown on man's neglected capabilities . . . it is a sin against justice.

Daily question self with thoughts like the following:

- Have I been sulky? Then I have misused the talents of smiles and forgiveness.
- Have I been cunning or proud of my shrewdness? Then I have misused the talent of truth and have been a glutton puffing myself into an unbalanced balloon.
- Have I feigned illness that I may have more rest? Then I have misused the talent of ability.
- Have I allowed my tongue to be the sword of snappy and unkind remarks? Then I have misused the talent of patience and kindness.

If we do not desist in wrecking talents, not only in self but others which smothers abilities, then we may class ourselves as one of the henchmen known in the devil's circles as knavish Abraham-man.

THOUGHTS FROM THE HEART

O Lord, if at times I lower the flag of ability . . .
With all its meaning and soul freedoms . . .
Prick my conscience with every sway of the trees,
And torment me with every whirred [buzz] of [gnats'] agilities.
Shackle my will and bid me study philosophy and history . . .
Better that my mind may have the capacity of simple welcome,

Understanding and wisdom for souls of different aptitudes.
Allow me in the ability of freedomed will . . .
Clothed in trust and charity to become a good Samaritan.
And with the ability of kindness to touch the slothful heart,
And hide-a-way into an awakening that they are not fooling God.

Devotedly,
Cora

A.M.D.G.

I H S

October 10, 1955

Dear Father Frank,
"For I am to preach the word of God fully—the mystery which has been hidden for ages and generations, but now is clearly shown to his saints. To them God willed to make known how rich in glory is this mystery among the Gentiles—Christ in you, your hope of Glory! Him we preach, admonishing every man and teaching every man in all wisdom, that we may present every man perfect in Christ Jesus" (Col 1:26–28).

Ah, the mystery of a saint . . . Saint Aloysius is truly a gift of consolations. I was disturbed in reason after having been drawn into conversation about Montfort[19] devotions . . . slave to the Blessed Mother. Knowing the converts-to-be and then stopped because of the knowledge of that devotion has made me question its depth and good for devotees to Jesus Himself.

Father, as you already know, I do love our Blessed Lady as much as is possible in a worldly love. I try remembering her feast days and try keeping recollected during that day as if I were visiting her. Before the Blessed Sacrament, I always remind our dear Lord to tell His Mother for me that I appreciate her kindness to the human race.

She was truly gifted . . . beyond compare. To her God gave the gift of the little Jesus. She loved and care for Him during His infancy and young manhood. What joys she had are beyond our imagination. This was the

---

19 Editor's note: Saint Louis de Montfort (1673–1716), author of *True Devotion to the Blessed Virgin* and promoter of total consecration to the Blessed Virgin Mary.

period of her holy motherhood. I do not think we have a right to pry into her life outside of what we know through private revelation and what is given in Scriptures. She herself told Saint Luke that she would be known through the generations to come as Blessed. Indeed she is His Blessed Mother! As He grew into manhood and was about to begin His life for us, He no longer came under her power. True, she asked Him, as any mother would even a married Son, to do some favor for her such as at the wedding at Cana. But we were in His Heart, the people outside the gate . . . we had not seen Him nor heard Him. To us, He gave His Humanity and the laws by which to live through the institution the Church.

These were my thoughts and reasonings, Father, when rapture caught me up and Saint Aloysius asked me to quote second Colossians 3:15. In His embrace, I quoted it as if I were reading it, saying

> And may the *peace* of Christ reign in your hearts; unto that peace, indeed, you were called in one body. Show yourselves thankful. Let the word of Christ dwell in your abundantly: in all wisdom teach and admonish one another by psalms, hymns and spiritual songs, singing in your hearts to God by his grace. Whatever you do in word or in work, do all in the name of the *Lord Jesus*, giving thanks to God the Father through *Him*." (Col 3:15–17; author emphases)

I was reminded to think carefully to the theme he once taught me on law and order . . . putting first things first in life as a means of interior peace. First, thank God the Father for the heritages and commandments of the ancient past through which we have gained our civilization of today. Second, worship the Holy Trinity and rejoice that the Second Person became Man and took upon Himself our nature, better that we would dare approach Him and know Him. Third, honoring and praising the holy priesthood, for indeed our priests are other Christs in so far as they extend His way of life to us through baptism, Communion, confirmation, sacrament of marriage, and the rules for a holy death and confession. Fourth . . . honoring and praising Christ's Mother . . . she was the Mother of the Second Person and symbolically the mother of priests. She is a queen above and beyond us . . . the fledglings of darkness. (To me, she is quite untouchable because she does not know our ways in our Original-Sin weaknesses.)

True, Jesus was not touched by Original Sin, but being God-Man for us He took it upon Himself to understand our greatest sins.

Fifth in line is our greatest saint, the foster father of Jesus, named Joseph. He was one of us in the truer sense . . . he knew sin and knew sorrows of regret, and he overcame sin. He knew denials beyond compare. (His life with Mary must have been quite difficult . . . he could have gossiped or become discouraged, but how did she listen? She knew not such littleness. I believe he must have been the leader type as a Trappist . . . he would love silence rather than offend her with tainted thought such as Original Sin brings into our hearts. And too, Mary was the most beautiful . . . the most perfect woman on earth . . . he was a man of temptations and overcame them for us. He too helped in our Redemption and should be given more credit.) How merciful and good God was to take Joseph before the Crucifixion in the sleep of death! Having Original Sin as a chain about him and living under the dictates of the old Law, eye for an eye and tooth for a tooth, Joseph might have killed Pilate and Herod. No doubt he would have pleaded with Mary to show her powers and save Jesus. Have we not thought of these protections when indignation rose as we meditated on the Passion? Mary, gifted to always be in a state of ecstasy and before the Beatific Vision, knew the greater good for our eternal gain through Jesus' suffering, but Joseph was not so gifted; he did not know every move of Jesus was going about doing His Father's business.

Then in the laws of order we may choose the saints to our liking and try formulating our lives after the pattern of theirs.

THOUGHTS FROM THE HEART

Often, coming out of rapture, Saint Aloysius asks, "What are the
thoughts of your heart?"
Jesus, my King . . .
In the garden, You threw open your heart . . .
And all my sins walked in.

Jesus, my King . . .
You know me better than my mother . . .
She knows not my ugly thoughts; she hears me sing.

Jesus, my King . . .
Your kindness to forgive—teaches me I did not alarm You . . .
You said, "Come to Me, you are burdened, and I will refresh you."

Jesus, my King . . .
You are trust, kindness, and new life . . .
I am lifted up . . . how can I help but sing?
Life is like the unfolding of a rose . . .
And Your refreshments!
Ah such desserts . . . revealing mystery after mystery.
And how I seek the mystery of the wisdom of Your Mother.
Her greatness was silence . . .
When the Church bid her wear the crown.
I believe she is the Queen of Heaven.

Jesus, my King . . .
Such mysteries, rare unfolding . . .
Roses everywhere . . . Your saints unfolding,
In the blossoming of Your garden.
And we, the visitors, at Your command . . .
Are asked to come and peer through lattices . . .
And what do I see?
Saint Joseph, our risen *worldly* King,
And at his side the Queen.

They were so much alike, and yet so different . . .
And across from them on other thrones were King Adam,
And Queen Eve . . . they too were so so different!
Adam was the true image and likeness of God . . .
All light and powerful;
Eve was a mere shadow, yet so beautifully intricate.
On these thrones, King Adam was the greatest . . .
And Eve was not a true image.
And on the other thrones King Joseph was the lesser light,
And Blessed Mary the greater.
In the scales of divine justice, Eve was now lifted to the True Image
In the new image of our Blessed Mother,

The holy Light between the two Kings and the two Queens
Arose as one . . . the original Adam!!!
And He in them in adoration worshiped the Eternal King.

Jesus, my King . . .
Returned have I from the garden of vision . . .
Take away from me the spirit that would evade.
Teach me the courtesies and how to bow before a Queen . . .
She who embodies as one all the righteous . . .
She who is so new in Heaven and new to us on earth.
Teach me, lest I appear stoic, for she is a creature alone . . .
I almost pity her . . .
Like a mind creature from another planet.

Jesus, my King . . .
I am yet cradled in the effects of Original Sin . . .
Send Joseph, her nearest, he will teach me the way.

    Devotedly,
    Cora

I H S

October 11, 1955

Dear Father Frank,
The interior self is a deep well of blackest mystery! In the laws of hospitality, charity, and love, we give to others of what we have, but our saddest and most angry thoughts with strife and cutting remarks we keep to ourselves . . . they are not fit to give away. And in that deep well we become hoarders of evil. Humility calls for the simple belief that where light is, darkness cannot last.

In that well, if it has become stagnant, may grow an octopus which in time could kill life. This octopus thrives on guilt feelings and tensions, and he eats the sugar of nervous breakdowns and laughs aloud that haste and broken rules have fed him well.

Putting first things first, we must put our own house (body) in order. We must turn the Light of God into that dark well through the confessional, and the conviction to live rightly must be accomplished. In convictions there are always adjustments to be talked over with the people with whom we associate. Without haste and displeasure and with God's grace working between two or more parties, a livable rule can be carried as the cross of peace. Avoid being crowded for time . . . Jesus never hurried. Live by rule and hours, and keep them day by day for the love of the Sacred Heart, and His grace will help you.

Rules, order, and cleanliness and putting first things first will not allow the octopus to find [in] your heart a birth. The light of the confessional is the Church's mind thinking for us and saying it is good to flood the deep well occasionally with His Light. His Light stirs the well . . . we must never allow it to become stagnant. Moving waters, (the soul) does not lose its freshness, and upon its surface moss cannot form.

Confession is not to be regarded as a plague. It is not something to make us overanxious and resulting in scrupulosity. Being overanxious is like a busy housewife without order in her cleaning . . . she is ever scouring and polishing and at a state of unrest if dust forms before the hour for dusting. Confession, too, is a business adventure with you and God. Does not every businessman know his bank account? Does he not know when he is in the red? These are businesses that have taken time and serious thought as to what can be done about it. So too with confession . . . it should be approached with that air of confidence and courage, as a man going before his banker for advice and perhaps a loan. (Loan of God's grace.)

Confidence at such a meeting in the confessional should be in a voice of clearness and with statements of exactness. Listings as to what is in the darkness of his well should be orderly and in his mind, for one by one they are going to be fished out by the Master Himself. The orderly mind is a gift of charity to both priest and people waiting in line. Composure too is charity . . . a priest is not a mind reader, and he does not like talking to a statue-human. Composure is not to weep . . . it could be seeking self-pity. The priest is merciful . . . he is an ambassador of Christ, and for that ambassadorship he must give exact account for his actions and kindness, though he is admonishing at times.

THOUGHTS FROM THE HEART

Ah, well so deep in me . . .
The stilled harbor of many sins.
Your depth and darkness are repugnant to freedom,
You are not a gift to eulogize.

The confessional light is coming close . . .
Storm your last if you must . . .
He will turn your blackness into sighs of eloquence,

He knows how to churn deep waters beneath your dust.
Cry, O darkness, for the ambassador will see . . .
Just how water-logged you are.
He misses not the slightest crevice . . .
And moss he destroys . . . you are in his care.

And, deep well, you will hear Him speak . . .
No doubt, he will say, "This musty mold is the effect,
Of bad companions . . . and they have etched a peak . . .
Like a mountain of pride . . . God's light will melt it down."

And, ah such rotted timber . . . from cankerous thoughts,
Like termites eating away at lasting strength.
And charred wood! Unusual in these depths . . .
Did you not know it was the burning of your conscience?

Ah, well so deep and dark . . .
Tomorrow you will be filled with a lightsome fog . . .
No longer will the Dove come and depart . . .
For nothing of darkness will mock.

Devotedly,
Cora

I H S

October 12, 1955

Dear Father Frank,
Putting into practice the virtues and their little rootlet systems is not easy. Neither was Calvary. Life without the virtues would be beastly. It is on their degrees of perfections that progress in civilization through people has grown. The practice of pleasing God is like practicing at a piano. The artist is not made in a day nor a year; therefore, we must not get discouraged. The hill to the spiritual Calvary is long and high. At times we find ourselves out of breath, and we pause for rest . . . And often in that rest period, we become slothful and the devil whispers, "It is not worth it." Or we could easily convince ourselves that we are so high that we are having a spiritual night of the soul or night of the senses, and upon these false convictions, we excuse ourselves from the constant walk.

And the worldly may ask, "What are you afraid of if you don't live the good life?" and then in disquietude we wonder whether it would not be easier to accept Purgatory after death rather than now according to our wills. These are thoughts from the devil and must be put out of our minds. He is a DEPRESSOR. He would like to crush every faint ray of light out of our being, but we must remember that even though grapes are put through a presser and lose their identity and become in substance like tears . . . they have not lost their color . . . neither must we become darkness instead of light.

The Depressor has many rootlets that are often overlooked in the way to progress. It is better to face them here than in Purgatory. Are we a

DEPRESSOR? How do we treat our loved ones in word and deed? Are we a depressor and kill their spirit because of our stinginess? To kill the spirit of culture or progress is to put out the eye of the soul . . . how beastly are we? Are we filled with contempt when charity begs our help? Do revengeful thoughts and actions show us as a depriver? When we deprive anyone their rightful needs, we also deprive ourselves the superhuman gifts of charity. How good are we to self? All these are parts of the ugly garb the devil wears as a cloak.

How often have we dressed ourselves in his puffed mask and acted on his stage as the perfect fool? How we would cringe if we could see all Hell watching and laughing at us and vying to welcome us when we die, if we do not amend. Christ is charity . . . He was not a depressor nor depriver . . . we must follow Him . . . this is part of the WAY.

THOUGHTS FROM THE HEART

Many times I have been a depriver . . .
The worst you ever knew.
At times I was a chief in my community,
A thief and coward too.
I laid down Christ's armor . . .
Deserted His crew,
I was ugly . . . I became a useless squid.

To be a depriver is to be a cursed with the devil's plague . . .
And any thought of prayer and grace seemed mythical.
Yes, I took joy and happiness from friends . . .
I cared not about their loyalty to their ancient heritage.
I scoffed at any thought of eternal judgement.
Any thought of a God did not fit into this modern age.

Ah the squid slime of me . . . a thief and squanderer of time . . .
Friends? I walked on them as if they were pebbles in my path.
I grew tired of this depriver life . . .
There was something deep within that liked smiles and not a groaner.
And I had peaceful sleep . . . I scoffed at crime and tongues of gossip . . .

I seethed when the young were deprived and suffered want . . .
And when our flag and customs were placed aside for another,
I then decided to become Christ's warrior.
And then I heard the latchet turn at my door . . .
Jesus with His lantern was there; He said, "I am in need . . .
A depriver, My worst enemy, just crushed the life from a soul,
Carry My lantern and be the Samaritan . . . a doer."

The light of our path grew lighter . . .
The Master just talked; He said,
"Retrace your steps . . . I'll walk with you,
A Samaritan never deprives his friends of his purse . . .
The joys and smiles you give to others is the interest I take . . .
And in My Heart I leave it there to burn,
Giving light to the wayfarer and the orphan and the widow . . .
These you must gift . . . be not a depressor of these . . .
Lest the fountains of Hell catch you alive.

His smile made my soul rich . . .
I vowed not the way of a depressor . . . rather I would be an eraser . . .
And remove all fears and ugliness from friendly lives.
The Master said as He turned His invisible way . . .
"In your heart, my earthly niche . . . I find delight. You have not re-
    fused Me love in any man . . .
All these expand your gifts . . . they are charity . . .
And I in you do not diminish.
We'll meet again on the cross-roads of life . . .
The cross-roads, are they not the cross on top the hill?"

Devotedly,
Cora

A.M.D.G.

I H S

October 13, 1955

Dear Father Frank,
It requires effort to live the interior life. How often have we prayed for the gift of effort and how to channel our gifts into the right river that will go the quickest into His Heart? Effort is one of the root systems to the growth of will. It takes effort when we have reason to live in the vocation we have chosen as a companion for life. To live that vocation is a must to make it happy with order and cleanliness and composure and quiet, a gift which does not tolerate hurry. Can you imagine a root of a redwood hurrying? Would you follow the life of a fly, scurrying every which way if you had wings? Are we guilty of trying to imitate the fly?

Neither the tree nor the fly have intellects . . . they are both doing what they should in the plan of God. Are we? The redwood does not look with envy to the flowering almond and wish its height had blossoms. And neither does the fly envy the buzz of an airplane nor try to become one. The redwood would say if it could talk, "I grow that man might be inspired at the majesty of God." And the busy fly could say, "I try the best I can to show God's people where filth is hidden, and I try to keep the cattle on the move lest through sloth they give not man his meat and drink."

And with man, it takes strong effort and voluntary exertion to stay and live in the vocation He has chosen. It would be easy to become a dreamer, and stay hidden, and take flights into an imaginary plane or travel the seas. Often these imaginary ills lead to frustrations that torture souls with the thought they have not reached their ambitions

... and they find solace in drink or drug which keeps alive the dreamer in his sloth within. And then this illness with sloth, unless they are brought under strict discipline and effort, brings destruction, despair, and loss of soul.

A redwood tree shows effort in its growth . . . God is its intellect. Since we are gifted with intellect and free will, we must cease with envy by effort; we must cease with sloth by effort. We must cease being a pedagogue and remember we are not here to try the patience of others. A man is not judged by his looks, his profession or degrees, or how much wealth he has accumulated . . . rather he is judged on what he has done with his talents and the efforts he has spent perfecting the way of life through discipline.

Effort is an attempt at doing something better in our vocations than we did yesterday . . . all for the love of God. It takes effort to wash dishes, but it takes greater effort to apply the washing of dishes to the interior life. While doing dishes, contemplate that you are back in Jerusalem with the Blessed Mother doing the dishes used at the Last Supper. Ask yourself, what were they thinking about? What were they saying? Could it be possible they were complaining about the Lord's work? Were they gossiping? Was the voice of ridicule as a clown in their midst, talking about a woman from the Orient? Did they not know the philosophy to bear with one another in custom and languages, and each creed of people has its way in life? All these actions and mind-contemplations, uniting two worlds together in our daily work, are the effort that brings the greater graces into our hearts. We must not allow the effortless life to saturate us . . . let us show forth the effort of wanting to do all things that are necessary in our walks of life, well, for God.

THOUGHTS FROM THE HEART

Heart of all wisdom . . . how little I have known . . .
I am blighted with effortless frost.
And yet I have known your indignation toward a drone . . .
Even a drone, if he makes amends, is not lost . . .
Heart of all wisdom . . . how little I have known.

O Sacred Heart . . . Thy Heart a garden . . .
On a withering bough I am green fruit.
I add neither beauty nor comfort to the tree . . . nor Your garden,
Send forth Thy warmth, lest I remain a green pericarp[20]
And my stone-heart a seedling that does not burst.
O Sacred Heart . . . I'm not worthy to be in Thy garden.

His sun-rays came, and made me wither more . . .
Until the rootless I had abandoned . . .
Went deep and with effort sought earth's moisture.
And the aridity of just pericarp warmed the stone entombed . . .
And I became a useful fruit inside His cloister . . .
Where His sunrays are life, effort, and will . . .
These three like sisters, with no wish to abandon . . .
Become like the work of a calendar . . . all in order . . .
knowing God would give more.

Devotedly,
Cora

---

20 Editor's note: The wall of a ripened fruit ovary.

IHS

October 14, 1955

Dear Father Frank,
Let us consider the words we often hear and read, "I would give, but first I must know if the person is deserving?" Did not Jesus say, "He who gives to the least of mine a drink of water in MY NAME, gives the drink to Me." Then in the relationship of self with life and its custom, do we ask whether Jesus is deserving to have this or that from us?

Let us now consider the modern word "FRUSTRATION." It is built upon a baffled soul . . . one who has not grown mature and acted upon conviction. Sad is the man who cannot think for himself and listen to others and obey the rules and laws he is born into without becoming bad-tempered and out of control like a car at high speed without a driver. Sad is the grown man or woman in body with a small child living within, who continues with his tantrums and knows not discipline.

Temper out of control is a spoiled, proud self. One who lives by the ugly rule of baffling, or defeating, balking, deceiving and tricking others, and to do this to others is also doing the same thing to ourselves in the light of grace and eternity. And as that ugly, undisciplined self grows older, he grows out of control and becomes a professional frustrated. Do we not have professional drunks? And do we not have professional dopes? Professional gluttons? Professional indecisions and anxieties? And we have as many others as listed. Frustration then, is to admit that we are drunk with self, and self cannot any longer stand self. Self is then on the road to despair.

And if this attitude and manner grows older with the person, he or she becomes known as a "frump." A frump is a frustrated person who cannot make up his mind that a life of discipline is his only way out of such an evil. He is now a mirrored reflection of what his interior self is, namely, he is unorderly, dowdyish in manners, a pig at the table. Yes, he has been hit by the returning boomerang, for what we sow, so shall we reap. And in an older age, these people are known as a sneering, gossiping, and joyless lot out of mannerism in national customs.

In order to save ourselves through His Grace, let us consider asking:

1. I will quiet my baffling mind . . . is He not deserving?
2. I will cease defeating self and others . . . is He not deserving?
3. I will cease balking . . . is He not deserving?
4. I will stop disappointing others . . . is He not deserving?
5. I will discipline myself away from the foolishness of being a child . . . is He not deserving?

He is deserving of all our goodness, and we are doers of the Word when we practice charity on His friends as proxy for Him.

THOUGHTS FROM THE HEART

Allow me, Lord, to know only one uncontrolled desire . . .
Uncontrolled love and hope for Thee.
In that freedom, You play upon my heart as a lyre . . .
Then no more can I offend Thee.

Thou hast said, "What we sow, so shall we reap,"
And in trust, Thy orchard gives fruits of love.
In Thy Way, there is no word *frustration* . . .
Guide me away from its shadow, Holy Dove.

Frost, thrust, lust, and too much must . . .
Blight the seeds of the Gardener.
And frost when engrafted to thrust . . .
Is the modern word, "Frustration."

And lust and too much must turn souls to mold . . .
Ah, this has brought tears to the eyes of the Gardener.
He cries, "Trust, that My Heart is like gold . . .
And so refined that you may take of Its garner."

And in His smile, He says, "Grow, grow for Me . . .
Equal well the child within and your body.
For the unity there is peace . . . both do not stampede . . .
They watch together and hope, if all is cloudy."

The seed of me in His garden prays,
"Let us follow the Master.
Let us build our heights with days . . .
And never hasten . . . it dims luster.

"That is the beginning of frustration . . .
Illness out of gear and frightful.
He has timed us to the Samaritan . . .
Walk in *calm* kindness . . . it is fruitful!"

  Devotedly,
  Cora

A.M.D.G.

I H S

October 15, 1955

Dear Father Frank,
Often, upon hearing the word "gleaner," we think of the woman Ruth
in the Scripture story. Let us symbolize her as the converts to the one
true Faith. To an adult convert, faith is a gleaning of tradition and
education in His wheat field . . . Ruth did not say, in complaint upon
seeing a few small grains, "I will not pick those . . . I'll wait until I find
larger ones." To glean in His wheat field is to take all, the small and
large, the blighted and the polished, and when they are all together
when day is spent . . . we have food for health, thought, and faith, and
the beginning growth of us, the mustard seed.

Let us pretend that we are with Ruth . . . daily she gleaned for her
eternal gain and with the hope of gaining the Bridegroom's love. She
was introduced to her future mother-in-law . . . are we not introduced
to our mother, the Church? Ruth accepted her mother-in-law in the
spirit of humility and obedience . . . how well have we followed Ruth?
And Ruth, like all converts, felt the longing to return to her kin, their
ways of worship and love. She even watched them from her mountain climb as they thrived in their valley below. She realized she was
weakening, and she ran to her mother-in-law and begged, "Entreat
me not to leave thee." Are we that instant in prayer to the arms (the
sacraments) of our mother the Church? And we too, like Ruth, can
approach the Bridegroom . . . did He not say, "Come to Me, all ye who
are burdened and I will refresh you" (Mt 11:28).

His refreshments are given in many ways . . . often through smiles

277

and words of encouragements from friends. Loyalty to a friend is a mystical embrace . . . kindness is the balm to an open wound . . . charity is the robe of warmth for the cold.

How have we gleaned today? Have we thought only of self without the thought of planting seeds for the unborn who will live one thousand years from now? Have we thwarted the life of the mustard seed, the symbol of us? Have we trod carelessly through His wheat field without a thought of thanksgiving and appreciation? Have we thought how blessed we are to make decisions? Without tradition and education, we would have no need for making decisions. Is not faith and obedience a decision? Let us follow Ruth in courage and not turn back when we watch the valley of semi-savages making decisions in the pleasures of mirth and sin.

THOUGHTS FROM THE HEART

We are told that we are like unto a mustard seed . . .
The smallest of seeds known.
And unless we grow . . . what can we give as wisdom bread,
For a Ruth soul who may turn back or go down.

For them have we gleaned an abundance of joy and kindness?
Have we a silo of love?
Are we a semi-savage, greedy without gleaners' mint?
And do we frown at the thought of exchange of pearls for tears?

In our greedy slowness, have we failed to say, "we need thee"?
Have we failed to compliment their humility?
Have we failed to remind them they are clothed in His dignity?
Then it is shame for us . . . we have failed in ability.

Such weakness in a soldier is not tolerable . . .
He knows not appreciation . . . the price of suffering humanity.
His mustard seed is like molded frost . . .
He is worse than non-conversion . . . he is without charity.

With joy, to the Ruths let us say . . .
As we stand before our storehouse gates.
"Come, share with me while I speak of His way . . .
And that way is to glean bit by bit of education,

"And mix it well with spice . . . philosophy and wisdom . . .
And once a day pour in tears of penitence with a gurgling of joy,
And then we'll grow, grow, grow for God's kingdom,
And all evil we'll destroy.

"And in our seedling branches we will catch the winging Ruths . . .
And give them hope through food.
And kindly teach them love for their mother-in-law . . .
And how she will care for the growth of their mustard seed."

Devotedly,
Cora

A.M.D.G.

I H S

Dear Father Frank,
The expression "REST" is usually associated with sleep, but in the contemplative life it is understood as "Rest in the Lord." This type of rest can be acquired through peace of soul, joy, love, kindness, and with the knowingness that we are loved by God. Our assurance that we are loved is in the measure of how much we have followed or perfected His laws in the Beatitudes.

Saint Peter says that we are partakers of the divine nature of Christ, therefore we have every right to live the life of Christ within us in all the ways of His life. We represent the Mystical Body the Church on earth, and in another way a great root system to the tree of life. Many roots seem quite useless, but God in His time will put them to use. One, for instance, represents the lifeline throughout the ages known as the mystics. As of today, they have been more or less a contradiction to both Church and people, but happily most of them have given examples of great piety and firmness to their convictions. The reason for their existence is not yet upon us, but perhaps soon we may know their cause in life when men contact the peoples of other planets.

After the fall of Adam, man had to construct a language . . . no doubt the people on other worlds constructed theirs, which would make it totally unlike ours. The mystic's role in the divine plan of life will be in that golden age when the majority are contemplatives, and mystics themselves submit to strict obedience to their priest directors . . . in this knowingness with God he, the priest, may understand the minds of two worlds.

Let us not forget that the indwelling of Christ is furthering the life of His Resurrection among us on earth. He in and through us [is] doing good to the world. Another step in our life, since we have the heritage of the divine nature, is to ascend . . . man is well on his way with mechanical wings. Did not Christ say for us to follow Him . . . He ascended above all the heavens that He might fill all things (Eph 4:7, 10). And we must not fear what we would say, for the Holy Spirit will teach us all things.

Christ said to teach all creatures . . . then we must teach on other planets. It is possible that when that time comes that man will have perfected the expression "Rest," which I will term as ecstasy or rapture to such an extent that one hour of that union would be equal to one thousand hours of sleep. Man will then have control of the atom or (Adam) within, his nature, and at periods live the life of hibernation, which could last ten or more years, or in that earthly expression [of] hibernation, it could be bilocation. He then would be grafted into the root system of Henoch,[21] who will not taste death until the last hour of time. Man will overcome death with the exceptions as to the last hour of time.[22]

THOUGHTS FROM THE HEART

Our heart (our nature) is our slave . . .
In this twentieth century, it neither knows the art of sleep nor rest.
Ah! it is sunk in darkness . . . yet it is brave.
Deep within, it knows of a higher life . . .
It longs for the garden where Adam (Atom) roamed . . .
It is our rebellious nature that enslaves.

Do we not know our hearts are blessed?
It is blessed because it hungers for the eons . . .

21 Publisher's note: Henoch. Cf Enoch, an antediluvian (belonging to the time before the biblical flood) patriarch mentioned in the Canaanite genealogy as the son of Cain. In the Hebrew text of BS 44:16, Enoch pleased God and was taken up from earth. NOTE: "He died," explicitly said of others, is omitted of Enoch. BS 49:14 assert that no one was ever created on earth like him, for he was taken up from the earth. Enoch is mentioned in the genealogy of Jesus (Lk 3:37).
22 Reference: Evans, Cora. *The Refugee from Heaven, Book Three, Chapter 5, The Last Hour and Chapter 6, The Last Mass*. Half Moon Bay: The Mystical Humanity of Christ Publishing. 2014.

And it thirsts for justice for all men,
And for this, His promise is, "They shall have their fill,"
And live like Adam (Atom) before he fathered man.

Our hearts, like little children looking up . . .
Weighted down with sensual chains,
Knows someday we will find our rest and flight.
That "REST" is now being nurtured by the chalice cup,
Each time we sip, the chains grow less,
And we hear the message, "It is the Way . . .
Have I not sped eons to come your way?
Then too you must speed the other way.
I long to unslave and embrace."

And in that someday, in that sublime flight unknown to sight . . .
Man will tread other lands without the touch of soil.
He will know the symphony of minds and other hearts most valiant!
And with these knowledges man will not have time to spoil.

Ah, to dwell in the facets of His Omniscience!!!
And through His wisdom teach us His joys,
All, if we but listen in our prayers' surveillance . . .
Instead of talking, talking, and just talking about us.

Devotedly,
Cora

The Remarkable Story of Cora Evans

Saints are known by their stories. Their lives were given freely to the Lord in response to the circumstances at the time, and for the good of the whole Church. They did not ask for or expect to be in the situations in which they found themselves. These men and women radiated the holiness of God dwelling within them. It is the story of their lives, how they responded to grace, their impact on others, combined with God's proof by miracles in their name that led the pope to declare, "We know for certain this person is with God in Heaven."

Only God can make a saint. At this stage there is no certainty that Cora Evans will become a canonized saint. Today, she is a Servant of God,[23] and her cause for Beatification and Sainthood is under way in the Diocese of Monterey, California.

Cora Evans was born July 9, 1904, and she passed away March 30, 1957. Her first mystical experience, an apparition of the Blessed Mother, took place when she was three years old. It was an event she could not fully comprehend and would never forget. Many years would pass before she understood the vision and the message.

Cora was raised a Mormon and was married to Maclellan Evans in the well-known Mormon Temple in Salt Lake City, Utah. That event was the turning point in her life. She left the secret ceremony disillusioned and disappointed with Mormonism, especially the doctrine

---

23 "A Catholic whose cause of beatification and canonization has been initiated is called Servant of God." *Sanctorum Mater*, Congregation for the Causes of Saints, Title II, Article 4, February 22, 2007.

that placed man-made gods above the God of Abraham. "I was without a God and religion but had gained a very wonderful husband. As I looked at him and learned to love him more and more, I resolved to help find a God for him. After ten years of searching, we found the One True God in the Roman Catholic Church."

During the ten years that followed the marriage ceremony, Cora and Mack had three children. They suffered the loss of a child, Bobby, when he was ten months old. Cora investigated many religions, but believed it would be a waste of time to even inquire about Catholicism. Although she no longer considered herself a Mormon, she held on to pervasive anti-Catholic warnings she learned growing up in Utah.

On December 9, 1934, Cora was quite ill. The family lived in Ogden, Utah, at the time. Cora was in bed and the radio was on the other side of the room. No one was home and she was too sick to get out of bed to change the station when the Catholic Hour began broadcasting. Despite her aversion to Catholicism, Cora was forced to listen to Monsignor Duane Hunt[24] talk about the Blessed Mother and the teachings of the Catholic faith. His message conflicted with the negative stories Cora had been told about Catholics. As soon as she recovered, Cora went to nearby St. Joseph Catholic Church to inquire about the faith and have her questions answered. This was a courageous move for a former Mormon. A series of meetings followed, including debates in her home between the parish priest, Father Edward Vaughn, and several Mormon bishops. Cora quickly became aware of the truth of Christianity and the obvious false stories told about Catholics. She appreciated Father Vaughn's demeanor and the clarity of his responses to questions about Catholic doctrine. Cora was baptized March 30, 1935, and received her first Holy Communion the next day. Mack and their daughters, LaVonne and Dorothy, followed her lead a few months later.

Cora influenced many Mormons to visit St. Joseph's, inviting them to open house gatherings. Years later, Father Vaughn wrote a letter

---

24   Most Reverend Duane G. Hunt (1884–1960), consecrated Bishop of the Diocese of Salt Lake City, October 28, 1937. Bishop Hunt visited Cora in her home in Boulder Creek, California, shortly before she passed away in 1957.

confirming that through Cora's evangelization efforts there were hundreds of conversions of Mormons to the Catholic faith.

Vow Day for a Mystic

In July 1938, she had a profound mystical experience. Cora wrote about this event in the autobiography of her mystical life, titled "Captain of the Ship." During this deep ecstasy Cora made the choice to serve God for the rest of her life. She described the state of her soul as being intimately united to God, and referred to this as her *vow day:* "It was necessary for me to live my chosen vocation with Him as my companion. By loaning Jesus my humanity for Him to govern as well as dwell within, would make my life a living prayer for He was life, living life within me, and my body now dead to me was His living cross, His cross to take to Calvary, Calvary, the door to eternal life."

The Move to Southern California and Spiritual Guidance

Due to religious and cultural prejudices, it was virtually impossible for Cora's husband, also a convert, to hold down a job. In 1941 the family moved to Southern California. In retrospect, I recognize this as God's plan. Cora began having mystical experiences with much greater frequency. In response to her search for spiritual guidance, on February 20, 1945, Father Frank Parrish, S.J.[25] was appointed her confessor and spiritual director by the Provincial[26] of the Society of Jesus (Jesuits). The meeting took place at Loyola High School in Los Angeles.

On December 24, 1946, Jesus revealed the mission entrusted to Cora. She learned that she was to promulgate the Mystical Humanity of Christ, a way of prayer that encourages people to live with a heightened awareness of the indwelling presence of Jesus in their daily lives. It is Eucharistic spirituality, and Jesus promised to foster the devotion.

Father Frank served as the spiritual guide of Cora's soul for the rest

---

25 Fr. Frank Parrish, S.J. (1911–2003) is best known in Catholic circles for his blessing of terminally ill Fr. John A. Houle, S.J. with the relic of Blessed Claude la Colombiere on February 23, 1990. This led to a miraculous cure—a first class miracle. Colombiere, who had been the spiritual director of Saint Margaret Mary, was declared a saint and canonized by Pope John Paul II, May 31, 1992.

26 Fr. Joseph J. King, S.J. (1900–1986) served as provincial from January 1943 to August 1948. The geographic area served in 1945 included California, Arizona, Nevada and Utah.

of her life. His written account of events is testimony to Cora's heroic virtues and her reputation of sanctity.

Cora is considered a hidden mystic, and although there were many friends, including priests and religious, she was not known publically. There are many examples of visionaries who where unknown at the time of their death, including Saints Margaret Mary (devotion to the Sacred Heart of Jesus), Catherine Laboure (Miraculous Medal), and Sister Faustina (Divine Mercy). Like these women, there was never any publicity about Cora's private revelation.

The life story of Cora Evans, wife and mother, is that of a remarkable woman who practiced Christian virtues and earned a reputation for holiness. She became a daily communicant and one of her favorite devotions was the Stations of the Cross. At times she would say the stations in reverse, mirroring the way the Blessed Mother saw them as she walked home from the crucifixion.

Cora's gifts of mysticism: suffering the wounds of Christ, known as the stigmata; the phenomena of bi-location associated with deep insight, a mystical gift not fully understood; the fragrance of roses associated with her presence, known as the odor of sanctity; visionary experiences, known as ecstasy; and profound writings far beyond her education level are not in and of themselves sufficient grounds for the declaration of sainthood. It is the story of her life with the proof of heroic virtues that places everything else in context.

The Vatican granted *nihil obstat*[27] for the cause for Beatification and Canonization of the Servant of God, Cora Evans. The Diocese of Monterey, California, is proceeding with the investigation of her life and writings.

Prayer for the Intercession
of Cora Evans

Cora prayed that she would be given the same gift as Saint Therese of Lisieux, the Little Flower, spending her heaven on earth doing good, and promised to pray for all who asked for her intercession after first

---

27 Nihil obstat (Latin "Nothing stand in the way") is a term used for the approval for a given process to proceed. Granted by Angelo Cardinal Amato, S.D.B., Prefect, *Congregation for the Causes of Saints*, Rome, Italy. Letter March 29, 2012.

visiting the Blessed Sacrament. The Archbishop of San Francisco granted the IMPRIMATUR[28] for the intercessory prayer, written by Father Frank Parrish, S.J.

Dear Jesus, You blessed Cora Evans with many supernatural mystical gifts as a means of drawing us to a deeper and more intimate union with your Sacred Heart through Your Divine Indwelling, Your Mystical Humanity. I ask You through her intercession to help me in my special request (name the favor) and my efforts to do Your will here on earth and be with You, Your Blessed Mother, Saint Joseph and the whole Court of Heaven forever.

Say three times: the Our Father, Hail Mary, Glory Be to the Father.

The Mystical Humanity of Christ

Cora prayed, "Please give me the grace to remember the vision and understanding in Thy wisdom to better relate to friends Thy hidden mystery of love for them . . . help me, Jesus, to write them as You would like them written for Thy glory to be better known among men." The purpose of her life, the suffering she endured, and her writings inspire us to live with awareness of the presence of Jesus. When you practice this way of prayer, known as the Mystical Humanity of Christ, you take Jesus with you wherever you go.

Compelled to Write

Cora Evans felt compelled by our Lord to write and at the same time felt wholly unqualified to take on such a task. Due to childhood illnesses, she never completed a full schedule of elementary school, and with less than two years of high school her education was rudimentary at best. Add to that, she was thirty years old before she had any exposure to the Catholic faith and she passed away at age fifty-two. It is what transpired during the years following her conversion that is truly remarkable.

---

28 Imprimatur (Latin "it may be printed") approval to publish given by diocesan bishop provides assurance that the published text conforms to Church teaching. Granted Most Reverend George Niederauer, Archbishop of San Francisco. Letter February 18, 2011.

A mystic and a visionary, Cora was called up into the deepest state of prayer known as ecstasy and rapture, but what our Lord preferred to have known as *Divine Slumber*. It is a pure gift from God and the source of all private revelation. Because the revelation is private there is no burden of belief on Catholics to accept it.

Cora's diary reveals that our Lord entrusted her with the responsibility to write. She suffered greatly for the privilege. After an experience of ecstasy, which might last for many hours, Cora would sit at the typewriter and attempt to capture the stories revealed to her.

The Refugee from Heaven is the greatest story ever known. Cora Evans recounts the life of Jesus Christ as an eyewitness, beginning with the first meeting between Jesus and Peter, on the shores of Mount Carmel Bay. With vivid detail and dialogue, this unique account breathes new life into well-known figures of the Gospels. Readers gain startling insights into Mary of Magdala's conversion, Herod's ferocious personality, and John the Baptist's courage. Experience the awe of the disciples in the Upper Room at the Last Supper, and stand in the holy sepulcher at the moment of the Resurrection. With a book that is sure to renew appreciation for the loving Heart of Jesus, the author has created an enduring masterpiece.

For more information about the cause for Cora Evans, the availability of her writings, or speaking engagements and parish retreats contact *Michael McDevitt, Custodian for the Writings of Cora Evans, Mike@ CoraEvans.com* and visit *CoraEvans.com* AND *ParishRetreat.org.*

"If you buy one book in your lifetime, this should be it. Life changing."

"An extraordinary book—powerful. A treasure."

"No one can read this book and not thank Him daily for all He did for us."

Introducing a Masterpiece

From the Private Revelations of Servant of God Cora Evans

What if you could come even closer to Jesus?
With a book that is sure to renew appreciation for the loving Heart of Jesus, Cora Evans has created and enduring masterpiece.

Order online at CoraEvans.com.
Save 25% use the promo code SAVE25.

Bookstore Exclusive
Sign-up at CoraEvans.com/bookstore.
Order books at wholesale discounts.

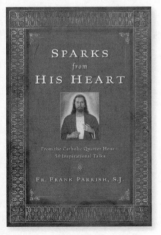

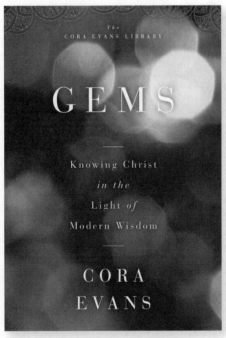